Addendum of Tidewater Ancestors
by Antonio Bilisoly Niemeyer, Jr.

prepared for publication by Nancy Neely

ISBN: 978-1-936288-90-8

Copyright © 2013
Sand Prince Publishing (USA)

ADDENDUM

TO

TIDEWATER ANCESTORS

BY

ANTONIO BILISOLY NIEMEYER, JR.

FOR

JOHN STUART NIEMEYER

INTRODUCTION

Tidewater Ancestors by Lewis Kirby was written using the information researched by Louise Niemeyer Fontaine. Mrs. Fontaine gave a hand written edition of our family history to Antonio Bilisoly Niemeyer, Jr. This genealogy of the Niemeyer family is one of my prized possessions. Being quite elderly at the time this copy was being made, she made certain minor errors. Other papers concerning my ancestors have come to my attention and changes, additions and/or deletions have been noted in the accompanying family histories.

Mrs. Fontaine was one of my high school teachers. As the epitome of the true meaning of teacher, she was one of those intellectuals who earned the respect of her students.

In Tidewater Ancestors the genealogical list ends with the author's family. In these revisions the list will trace the family of Antonio Bilisoly Niemeyer, Jr. It is suggested these notes be used as you read Tidewater Ancestors.

Antonio Bilisoly Niemeyer, Jr.

FAMILY INDEX

Under generation, the first column is the generation listed on page 3 of <u>Tidewater</u> <u>Ancestors</u> and the second column is for the Bradbury lineage. The persons from whom we are descended are in bold print.

Generation

1   **William Bradbury** m.

1   2   I-**Thomas Bodley** m. **Joan Leech** m. II-**Thomas Bradbury**

2   3 James   **Dionysea**   **Jane Bradbury** m.**Richard Leveson**
     Bodley   **Bodley**

                         m.

3   4 John   **Nicholas Leveson**(2nd son)
     Bodley

4   5

Dorothy	**Elizabeth**	Mary	John	Thomas	Nicholas	John
Leveson	**Leveson**	Leveson	Leveson	Leveson	Leveson	Leveson
m.	m.	m.		m.		
William	Sir	Edmund	No	Ursala		No
Streete	**William**	Calthrop	Issue	Gresham		Issue
	Hewet	Gent.				

Recap of Significant Data: Bradbury

Generation

    1   William Bradbury, father of Thomas Bradbury, was of Braughing in Hertfordshire.

    2   Sir Thomas Bradbury, Knight, was the Lord Mayor of London in 1509. He died on January 9, 1509/10. He married Joan Leech Bodley circa 1495. She was the widow of Thomas Bodley and died on May 11, 1530.

The present Niemeyers are direct descendents of this Bradbury line. In <u>Tidewater</u> <u>Ancestors</u>, the noted generation should be changed as follows.

15	16	Lt. Col. William Frederic Niemeyer, C. S. A.

m. Sarah Campbell Smith

16	17	John Frederic Niemeyer m. Lucrece Bilisoly
17	18	Antonio Bilisoly Niemeyer m. Lutie Stuart Spotts
18	19	Antonio Bilisoly Niemeyer, Jr. m. Alice Virginia Berry

19	20	William Frederic Niemeyer	Frank Berry Niemeyer	John Stuart Niemeyer
		m.	m.	m.
		Carolyn Louise Holtzhauer	Shannon Page Eadie	April Michelle Tripp
20	21	John Cameron Niemeyer	Jacob Douglas Niemeyer	John Stuart Niemeyer, Jr.
		Kyle Antonio Niemeyer		

Leech

Under generation, the first column is the generation listed on page 13 of <u>Tidewater</u> <u>Ancestors</u> and the second column is for the Leech lineage. The persons from whom we are descended are in bold print.

Generation

    1   **Dennis Leech**

1   2   I-**Thomas Bodley** m. **Joan Leech** m. II-**Thomas Bradbury**

2   3   James   **Dionysea**   Jane Bradbury m. Richard Leveson
          Bodley   **Bodley**

                               m.

3   4   John   **Nicholas Leveson** (2nd son)
          Bodley

4   5

Dorothy **Elizabeth** Mary   John   Thomas Nicholas John
Leveson **Leveson**   Leveson Leveson   Leveson Leveson Leveson
  m.   m.   m.   m.
William   Sir   Edmund   Ursala
Streete **William** Calthrop No   Gresham   No
       Hewet   Gent. Issue   Issue

Recap of Significant Data: Leech

Generation

    1   Dennis Leech was from Willingborough, Northampton-shire.

    The present Niemeyers are direct descendents of this

Leech line.   In <u>Tidewater</u> <u>Ancestors</u>, the noted generation should be changed as follows:

15	16	Lt. Col. William Frederic Niemeyer, C. S. A. m. Sarah Campbell Smith
16	17	John Frederic Niemeyer m. Lucrece Bilisoly
17	18	Antonio Bilisoly Niemeyer m. Lutie Stuart Spotts
18	19	Antonio Bilisoly Niemeyer, Jr. m. Alice Virginia Berry

19	20	William Frederic Niemeyer m. Carolyn Louise Holtzhauer	Frank Berry Niemeyer m. Shannon Page Eadie	John Stuart Niemeyer m. April Michelle Tripp
20	21	John Cameron Niemeyer Kyle Antonio Niemeyer	Jacob Douglas Niemeyer	John Stuart Niemeyer, Jr.

Bodley

Under generation, the first column is the generation listed on page 27 of <u>Tidewater</u> <u>Ancestors</u> and the second column is for the Bodley lineage. The persons from whom we are descended are in bold print.

Generation

1	1	**I-Thomas Bodley** m. **Joan Leech** m. II-**Thomas Bradbury**		
2	2	James Bodley	**Dionysea Bodley**	**Jane Bradbury** m.**Richard Leveson**
			m.	
3	3	John Bodley		**Nicholas Leveson**(2nd son)

Recap of Significant Data: Bodley

Generation

1   Thomas Bodley was of Dunscombe, in Crediton, Devonshire, England. The market town and parish of Crediton, in the hundred of Crediton, is eight miles northwest from Exeter. It is pleasantly situated in a vale near the Creedy, which unites with the river Exe, between Crediton and Exeter. Crediton was for many years the seat of a diocese of which a collegiate church founded there in the year 905, and dedicated to the Holy Cross, became a cathedral.

2   James Bodley, son of Joan Leech by her first husband, Thomas Bodley, died before his mother. His son, John, became Joan Leech Bodley Bradbury's heir. John did not live long and Dionysia Bodley became her nephew's heir.   3   Of this family and of a later generation, was Sir Thomas Bodley, founder of the Bodleian Library at Oxford. Lawrence Bodley, was Doctor of Divinity and Canon Resident of St. Peter's of Exeter. Another brother, Sir Josias, was "a skillful and

valiant leader in the Irish wars against Tyrone and Don John de Aquila."

The present Niemeyers are direct descendents of this Bodley line. In <u>Tidewater</u> <u>Ancestors</u>, the noted generation should be changed as follows.

15   15   Lt. Col. William Frederic Niemeyer, C. S. A.
          m. Sarah Campbell Smith

16   16   John Frederic Niemeyer m. Lucrece Bilisoly

17   17   Antonio Bilisoly Niemeyer m. Lutie Stuart Spotts

18   18   Antonio Bilisoly Niemeyer, Jr. m. Alice Virginia Berry

19 19	William Frederic Niemeyer m. Carolyn Louise Holtzhauer	Frank Berry Niemeyer m. Shannon Page Eadie	John Stuart Niemeyer m. April Michelle Tripp
20 20	John Cameron Niemeyer Kyle Antonio Niemeyer	Jacob Douglas Niemeyer	John Stuart Niemeyer, Jr.

Under generation, the first column is the generation listed on page 49 of <u>Tidewater</u> <u>Ancestors</u> and the second column is for the Leveson lineage. The persons from whom we are descended are in bold print.

Generation

	1	**Richard Leveson** m. **Agnes Clement**
	2	**John Leveson** m.
	3	**Richard Leveson** m. **Margery Clement(s)**
	4	**Richard Leveson** m.
	5	**John Leveson** m. **Agnes**
	6	**Richard Leveson** m. **Johanna de Rushall**
	7	**Nicholas Leveson** m. **Maud Prestwood**
	8	**Richard Leveson** m. **Joanna**
	9	**Nicholas Leveson** m. **Hillary**
2	10	**Jane Bradbury** m. **Richard Leveson**
3	11	**Dionysea Bodley** m. **Nicholas Leveson** (2nd son)
4	12	

Dorothy	**Elizabeth**	Mary	John	Thomas	Nicholas	John
Leveson	**Leveson**	Leveson	Leveson	Leveson	Leveson	Leveson
m.	m.	m.		m.		
William	Sir	Edmund		Ursala		
Streete	**William**	Calthrop	No	Gresham		No
	Hewet	Gent.	Issue			Issue

The children of Thomas and Ursala Gresham Leveson are listed on the next page.

```
13
Dionysia  Mary   Elizabeth Frances Ursala   Anne   Grefild
Leveson Leveson  Leveson  Leveson  Leveson Leveson Leveson


13  William  Thomas       John        Elizabeth Mary
    Leveson  Leveson      Leveson     Leveson   Leveson
       m.     No Issue       m.
    Rebotham         I-Christian II-Margaret
                       Mildman      Manwood


14   Thomas      Elizabeth Leveson   Elizabeth Leveson
                 Rachel Leveson      Margaret Leveson
                 Mary Leveson        Elizabeth Leveson
                 Christian Leveson
                 Frances Leveson
                 John Leveson
                 Richard Leveson
                 Thomas Leveson
                 Henry Leveson
                 Francis Leveson
```

Recap of Significant Data: Leveson (pronounced Lewson)
Generation

1   Richard Leveson was living at Willenhall in 1299.
Willenhall was written in the Domesday book as Winehale
signifying in Saxon, Victory, perhaps for the battle fought
in or near there in 911.   Richard married Agnes Clement,
daughter of William Clement.

2   John Leveson of Willenhall

3   Richard Leveson of Willenhall married Margery
(Margeria) Clement of Wolverhampton, Staffordshire.

4   Richard Leveson was living in 1305 and 1313. He

lived at Willenhall.

5   John Leveson of Willenhall, Staffordshire was living in 1357 and in 1370. He married Agnes.

6   Richard Leveson of Willenhall lived in the years 1361 and 1409. He married Johanna de Rushall, daughter of John de Rushall.

7   Nicholas Leveson of Prestwood and Wolverhampton was living in 1401 and 1460. He married Maud, or Matilda, daughter of John Prestwood, Esq.

8   Richard Leveson of Prestwood and Wolverhampton was living in 1460. He married Joanna.

9   Nicholas Leveson of Prestwood was living in 1482. He married Hillary (Hillaria).

2   10 Richard Leveson of Prestwood, Esq. was living in 1492 and 1503. He married Joan Bradbury in 1502. They had three sons, John, Nicholas and James. James was a merchant of the staple in Wolverhampton and Lillehall. By his first wife he had a daughter, Mary, wife of Sir George Curzon of Croxall who became his heir. From her descended the Duke of Dorset and the Earl of Thanet.

3   11 Nicholas Leveson, second son of Richard and Joan, of Halling and Whornes Place, succeeded to the estate of his brother, John, who died without issue. Nicholas was Sheriff of London in 1534. About 1558, he purchased his estate at Halling and "Whornes Place" and made the latter his seat. Whornes Place is in Cookstone Parish. William Whorne who had been Lord Mayor of London in 1487 erected it.

Nicholas Leveson married Dionysia Bodley, daughter of Thomas Bodley, Esq. of Black Notley in Essex. It appears that Nicholas married his mother's half sister. Dionysia Leveson died September 10, 1561. They had four sons and three daughters.

4   12   Elizabeth, from whom the present Niemeyers are descended, was the second daughter of Nicholas Leveson and Dionysia Bodley Leveson. She married Sir William Hewet, Lord Mayor of London.

The first son, John, married but died without issue before his father, Nicholas.

Thomas Leveson was twenty-eight when his mother died in 1561. He was of Halling in Kent and died April 21, 1576. He inherited his parents' estates. Thomas married Ursala, daughter of Sir John Gresham of Tillefley in Surry. They had nine daughters and three sons. The sons were John, Thomas who died without issue and William who had a son, Thomas, who was born in 1594 by a daughter of ? Robotham of the wardrobe to Queen Elizabeth.

13   John Leveson, the eldest son, was born in 1555 and succeeded his father. He married first Christian, daughter of Sir William Mildman, Chancellor of the Exchequer. John and Christian had five daughters and five sons. He married second Margaret Manwood, daughter of Sir Richard Manwood, chief Baron of the Exchequer. They had three daughters.

14   John Leveson, Knight, the eldest son of John and Christian Leveson, held court at his estate in 1615. Richard, the second son of John and Christian Leveson, was born in 1588 and created Knight of the Bath at the coronation of King Charles I. Richard held court at the family estate until he sold it circa 1634.

The present Niemeyers are direct descendents of this Leveson line. In Tidewater Ancestors, the noted generation should be changed as follows.

15   23   Lt. Col. William Frederic Niemeyer, C. S. A. m. Sarah Campbell Smith

16	24	John Frederic Niemeyer m. Lucrece Bilisoly		
17	25	Antonio Bilisoly Niemeyer m. Lutie Stuart Spotts		
18	26	Antonio Bilisoly Niemeyer, Jr. m. Alice Virginia Berry		
19	27	William Frederic Niemeyer m. Carolyn Louise Holtzhauer	Frank Berry Niemeyer m. Shannon Page Eadie	John Stuart Niemeyer m. April Michelle Tripp
20	28	John Cameron Niemeyer Kyle Antonio Niemeyer	Jacob Douglas Niemeyer	John Stuart Niemeyer, Jr.

Clement

Under generation, the first column is the generation listed on page 49 of <u>Tidewater</u> <u>Ancestors</u> and the second column is for the Clement descendency. The persons from whom we are descended are in bold print.

Generation

1	**William Clement**
2	**Agnes Clement** m **Richard Leveson**
3	**John Leveson** m.
4	**Richard Leveson** m. **Margery Clement(s)**
5	**Richard Leveson** m.
6	**John Leveson** m. **Agnes**
7	**Richard Leveson** m. **Johanna de Rushall**
8	**Nicholas Leveson** m. **Maud Prestwood**
9	**Richard Leveson** m. **Joanna**
10	**Nicholas Leveson** m. **Hillary**
2	11	**Richard Leveson** m. **Jane Bradbury**

The present Niemeyers are direct descendents of this Clement line. In <u>Tidewater</u> <u>Ancestors</u>, the noted generation should be changed as follows.

15   24   Lt. Col. William Frederic Niemeyer, C. S. A.
              m. Sarah Campbell Smith
16   25   John Frederic Niemeyer m. Lucrece Bilisoly
17   26   Antonio Bilisoly Niemeyer m. Lutie Stuart Spotts
18   27   Antonio Bilisoly Niemeyer, Jr. m. Alice Virginia
              Berry

19   28   William Frederic   Frank Berry   John Stuart
              Niemeyer   Niemeyer   Niemeyer
                 m.   m.   m.
           Carolyn Louise   Shannon Page   April Michelle
              Holtzhauer   Eadie   Tripp

20   29   John Cameron   Jacob Douglas   John Stuart
              Niemeyer   Niemeyer   Niemeyer, Jr.
           Kyle Antonio
              Niemeyer

de Rushall

Under generation, the first column is the generation listed on page 49 of <u>Tidewater</u> <u>Ancestors</u> and the second column is for the de Rushall descendency. The persons from whom we are descended are in bold print.

Generation

1	**Henry de Rushall**	
2	**Richard de Rushall**	
3	**John de Rushall**	
4	**John de Rushall**	
5	**Richard Leveson** m. **Johanna de Rushall**	
6	**Nicholas Leveson** m. **Maud or Matilda Prestwood**	
7	**Richard Leveson** m. **Joanna**	
8	**Nicholas Leveson** m. **Hillary**	

2	9	**Richard Leveson** m. **Jane Bradbury**		
3	10	John	**Nicholas**	James
			Leveson	m.
		died	m.	
		w/o	**Dionysia**	
		issue	**Bodley**	
	11		Mary m. Sir George Curzon	

Recap of Significant Data: de Rushall

Generation

1   Henry de Rushall, armiger, of Wolverhampton, in Staffordshire, England, was living about the year 1275. The family had been long seated near here, as King Henry II (1154-1189) gave Rowley in Stafford to Richard de Rushall, and King John (1199-1216) confirmed it to Richard de Rushall, his son.

10   Three sons were born to Richard and Jane Bradbury Leveson of Prestwood. John, the first son died without issue. Nicholas, the second son was Sheriff of London in 1534. He

was of Halling and Whornes Place. Whornes Place was usually called Horne's Place in Cookstone Parish situated close to the bank of the River Medway. William Whorne who was Lord Mayor of London in 1487 erected it. James was a merchant of the staple in Wolverhampton and Lillehall.

11 Mary, the daughter of James, married Sir George Curzon of Croxall. She was the ancestor of the Duke of Dorset and the Earl of Thanet.

The present Niemeyers are direct descendents of this de Rushall line. In <u>Tidewater</u> <u>Ancestor</u> the noted generation should be changed as follows.

15	22	Lt. Col. William Frederic Niemeyer, C. S. A. m. Sarah Campbell Smith		
16	23	John Frederic Niemeyer m. Lucrece Bilisoly		
17	24	Antonio Bilisoly Niemeyer m. Lutie Stuart Spotts		
18	25	Antonio Bilisoly Niemeyer, Jr. m. Alice Virginia Berry		
19	26	William Frederic Niemeyer m. Carolyn Louise Holtzhauer	Frank Berry Niemeyer m. Shannon Page Eadie	John Stuart Niemeyer m. April Michelle Tripp
20	27	John Cameron Niemeyer Kyle Antonio Niemeyer	Jacob Douglas Niemeyer	John Stuart Niemeyer, Jr.

William M. Mervine, a member of the Historical Society of Pennsylvania, made the research of the de Rushall family and its allied family prior to 1910.

Prestwood

Under generation, the first column is the generation listed on page 49 of <u>Tidewater</u> <u>Ancestors</u> and the second column is for the Prestwood lineage. The persons from whom we are descended are in bold print.

Generation

1 Henry Prestwood

2 John Prestwood

3 John Prestwood

4   **John Prestwood**

5   **Nicholas Leveson** m. **Maud or Matilda Prestwood**

6   **Richard Leveson** m. **Joanna**

7   **Nicholas Leveson** m. **Hillary**

2   8   **Richard Leveson** m. **Jane Bradbury**

Recap of Significant Data: Prestwood

Generation

4 John Prestwood, armiger, of Prestwood, in Staffordshire, England, son of John Prestwood, grandson of John Prestwood, and great grandson of Henry Prestwood, bore the following coat-of-arms: Azure, a chevron gules between three cinquefoils sable.

Prestwood stands upon the north side of Smestall Brook, about a mile below Swinford. "It should seem to be a member of Swinford Regis, and that both Morve, Pensenet Chase, Ashwood, and a great part of that country, are within the forest of Kinfare."

The present Niemeyers are direct descendents of this Prestwood line. In <u>Tidewater</u> <u>Ancestors</u> the noted generation should be changed as follows.

15	21	Lt. Col. William Frederic Niemeyer, C. S. A. m. Sarah Campbell Smith		
16	22	John Frederic Niemeyer m. Lucrece Bilisoly		
17	23	Antonio Bilisoly Niemeyer m. Lutie Stuart Spotts		
18	24	Antonio Bilisoly Niemeyer, Jr. m. Alice Virginia Berry		
19	25	William Frederic Niemeyer m. Carolyn Louise Holtzhauer	Frank Berry Niemeyer m. Shannon Page Eadie	John Stuart Niemeyer m. April Michelle Tripp
20	26	John Cameron Niemeyer	Jacob Douglas Niemeyer	John Stuart Niemeyer, Jr.

Kyle Antonio
        Niemeyer

Under generation, the first column is the generation listed on page 77 of <u>Tidewater</u> <u>Ancestors</u> and the second column is for the Hewitt lineage. The persons from whom we are descended are in bold print.

Generation

	1	**Nicholas Hewett**
	2	**Edmund Hewett**
1	3	**Elizabeth Leveson** m. **Sir William Hewett**
2	4	**Anne Hewett** m. **Sir Edward Osborne, Knight**

Recap of Significant Data: Hewitt

Generation

1   Nicholas Hewett of the county of York, England, living in the year 1490, was the first known ancestor of this family.

2   Edmund Huett was of Wales, a township of Yorkshire a few miles from Kinston.

3   In the 27th year of the reign of Henry VIII, Sir William Hewett (Hewitt, Hewet) of London bought the estate of Kingston Manor in Yorkshire. Sir William Hewett, citizen and cloth worker, was one of the most successful merchants of the time. He was Lord Mayor of London in 1559. He purchased lands in Essex and others near his native town in Yorkshire. From his relatives descended the Hewetts of Shireoaks and other families of the name in Yorkshire and Hartfordshire, but he, himself, had only one daughter, his heir, who was aged twenty-three at the time of his decease.

Sir William's house and shop were on London Bridge, which at that time was covered from end to end with mansions and with stores and dwellings of merchants. A careful apprentice named Edward Osborne assisted him in his business. This Osborne could judge the value and quality of cloth almost as accurately as his master, and on occasion, when it became necessary, he could perform other feats with equal success. He was the type of bold and shrewd London apprentice of the time.

"The Accident To Sir William Hewet's Daughter"

"The Mayor at this time was that eminent citizen and clothworker Sir William Hewet, the son of Edmund Hewet, of Wales in Yorkshire. This knight was possessed of an estate, value 6,000 l. per annum, at his death, and was blessed with an issue of three sons and one daughter; of which daughter we have the following tradition from the most noble family of the Duke of Leeds: Sir William, her father, living at that time on London Bridge, it happened that the maid-servant, as she was diverting the infant-miss on the edge of an open window, accidentally let her drop into the Thames, and, to all appearance, without hope of being saved: But a young gentleman, named Osborne, then apprentice to Sir William the father, and one of the ancestors of the Duke of Leeds in a direct line, seeing the accident, immediately leaped into the river after her boldly, and brought the child out safe, to the great joy of its parents, and admiration of the spectators. This brave and friendly action so engaged the affections of Sir William, the infant's father, that, when she was grown to Woman's Estate, and asked in marriage by several persons of quality, especially by the Earl of Shrewsbury, the Knight rejected all their advantageous proposals, and, with a deep sense of gratitude, betrothed his daughter, with a very great dowry, to her deliverer, and with this emphatical declaration, 'Osborne saved her and Osborne shall enjoy her.' Part of the estate given with her in marriage was the estate of Sir Thomas Fanshaw, late of Barkin in Essex, and several other lands now enjoyed by the most noble family of the Duke of Leeds, in the parishes of Harthill and Wales, in the county of York. This remarkable story is represented in a Painting, carefully preserved by that most noble family."

According to the manuscript record of the Mayors of London in the tyme of Queene Elizabeth, prepared in 1609, "he dwelled in Philpott Lane by Fanchurch Streete," in the year 1566.

Sir William Hewett died 21 January 1566/7 and was buried near his second wife, Alice, in the church of St. Martin Orgar, which he attended in Candlewick Street.

"He was the benefactor to divers of the hospitals in London, and to the poor of the several parishes. He bequeathed to the poor in the hospital of St. Thomas in Southwark, whereof he was president 20 l. and to every poor maiden's marriage, that shall be wedded in the parish of Wales, or Harthill, in county Ebor, within a year after his decease, vi s. viii d. each. He bequeathed to his nephews, Henry and William Huet, sons of his brother Thomas Huet, his mansion and dwelling in Philpott-Lane in London.

The children of Sir William Hewett and Elizabeth Leveson are:

1. John Hewett
2. Solomon Hewett
3. Thomas Hewett
4. William Hewett
5. Mary Hewett
6. Elizabeth Hewett
7. Anne Hewett

The present Niemeyers are direct descendents of this Hewitt line. In Tidewater Ancestor the noted generation should be changed as follows.

12	14	Lt. Col. William Frederic Niemeyer, C. S. A. m. Sarah Campbell Smith

12   14   Lt. Col. William Frederic Niemeyer, C. S. A. m.
               Sarah Campbell Smith
13   15   John Frederic Niemeyer m. Lucrece Bilisoly
14   16   Antonio Bilisoly Niemeyer m. Lutie Stuart Spotts
15   17   Antonio Bilisoly Niemeyer, Jr. m. Alice Virginia
               Berry

16   18   William Frederic   Frank Berry   John Stuart
               Niemeyer   Niemeyer   Niemeyer
                  m.   m.   m.
             Carolyn Louise   Shannon Page   April Michelle
               Holtzhauer   Eadie   Tripp
17   19   John Cameron   Jacob Douglas   John Stuart
               Niemeyer   Niemeyer   Niemeyer, Jr.
             Kyle Antonio
               Niemeyer

Source: Louise Fontaine's data

One of these houses on London Bridge was the residence of my ancestor, Sir William Hewett, Lord Mayor of London, 1559. This photocopy was made from "The Horizon Concise History of England" by R. J. White, University Lecturer in History and Fellow of Downing College, Cambridge, England. Published by American Heritage Publishing Co. Inc., 551 Fifth Avenue, New York, N.Y. 10017

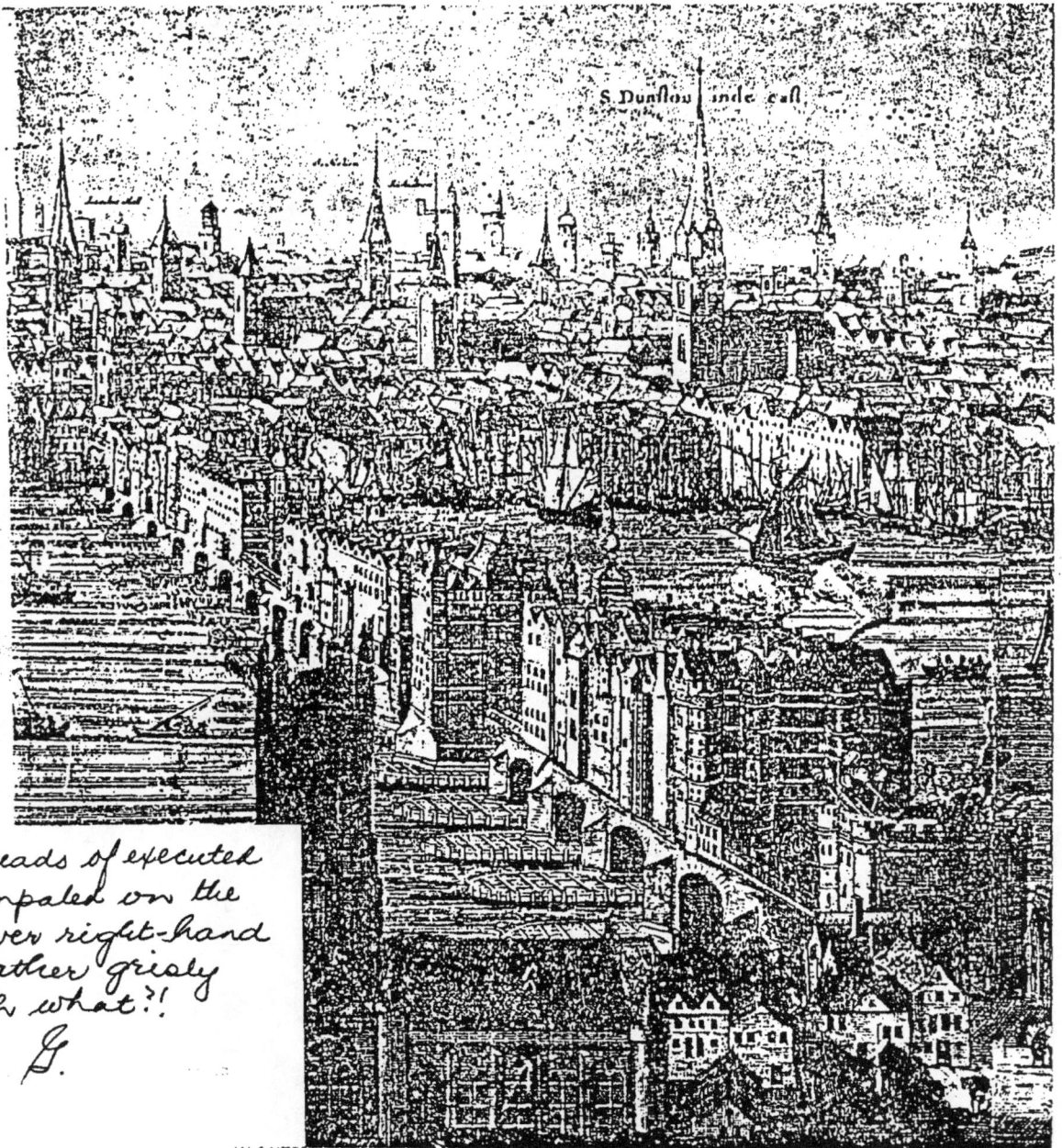

A version of Cornelis Visscher's famous view of Elizabethan London includes this detail of the bustle and congestion around London Bridge.

Note the heads of executed persons impaled on the tower - lower right-hand corner. Rather grisly picture, eh what?!
G.

This engraving was executed by Cornelis J. Visscher in 1616, the original of which is in the Guildhall Library, London, England. The church in the foreground is Southwark Cathedral, also called "St. Mary's of the Ferry."

The original photograph of this seal was quite dark and even with the copy control on the lightest reproduction number it turned out this dark. Bill said he will reproduce this on film one day and we will then send you a much better copy.

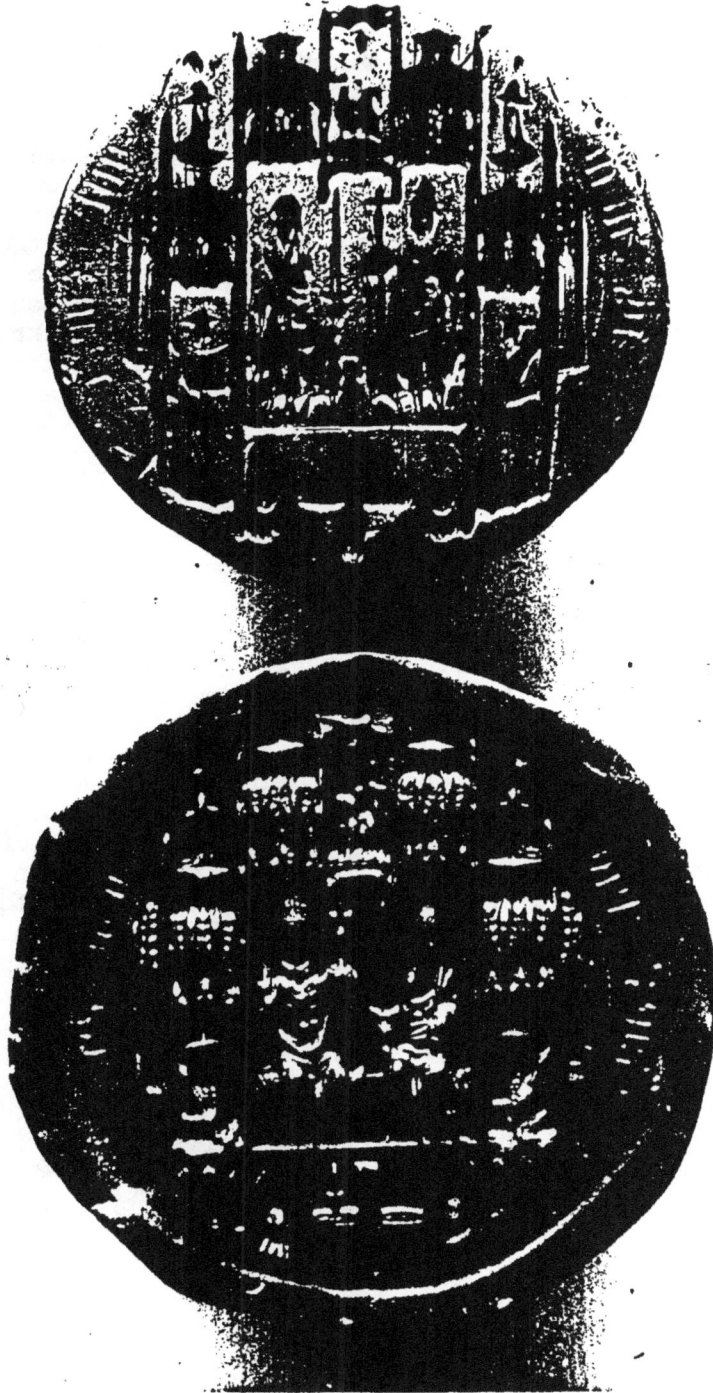

INCHES

Sir William Hewitt, Kt., 1559, and Sir Edward Osborne, Kt., 1583

The Mayoralty seal pictured overleaf was made in 1380, and apparently designed and executed by the goldsmith responsible for some of the great seals of Edward III and Richard II. The design conveys a rich Gothic architectural facade, comprising, in the first place, a wide groined niche of three arches supporting, between two heavy canopies, a smaller niche in the upper part; on either side of this niche is another, with a heavy canopy, supporting a pedestal and a balcony with pinnacled and crocketed tabernacle work, supported on a bracket beyond; and in the base is a flat-headed compartment. On the right side, in the central niche, is a representation of S. Paul, London's patron saint, holding a drawn sword erect in his right hand, in his left a book, seated and resting his feet upon a prostrate figure, and on the left, the figure of S. Thomas of Canterbury, lifting up his right hand and holding a long crosier in his left, also seated. In the little niche above is the Blessed Virgin, crowned and enthroned, and supporting with the left arm the Holy Child, who stands upon her knee; on each of the balconies of the two other niches is a man-at-arms drawn at half-length, with low cap, holding a mace or club aloft; on each of the pedestals above is a kneeling angel, with wings expanded and hands closed in prayer; and in the compartment at the base are the arms of the city supported by two demi-lions rampant guardant each under a round arch.

SIGILL'. MAIORATUS. CIUITATIS. LONDON.

The prostrate figure under the feet of S. Paul is designed for Elymas the sorcerer. The figure of the Blessed Virgin commemorates the great reverence and devotion in which she was held in medieval England. Possibly the two men-at-arms were intended for Gog and Magog, the last survivors of a mythological race of British giants, who are also patrons of the city. Unhappily, the impression of the seal available for illustration has been sadly rubbed but, notwithstanding, it is sufficiently clear to enable us to fairly gauge its magnificence and beauty, and to appreciate the superb skill brought to bear upon its execution. Designed with studied and elaborate ornateness, displayed with judgment and taste, it constitutes an exquisite piece of Gothic art, and one of the richest specimens of seal engraving extant. Compared with certain of the purer and more simple designs of an earlier period, it suffers through an excess of ornament and detail, but as an exponent of the art in its contemporary phase and character, it is one of the most telling and beautiful instances available.

The Latin inscription simply means 'the seal of the Mayoralty of the City of London'.

The above description of the Mayoralty Seal of London is to be found in the book "Borough Seals of the Gothic Period" by Gale Pedrick, Fellow of the Royal Historical Society, published in London by J. M. Dent and Co.

Osborne

Under generation, the first column is the generation listed on page 85 of <u>Tidewater</u> <u>Ancestors</u> and the second column is for the Osborne lineage.   The persons from whom we are descended are in bold print.

Generation

1   1   **Richard Osborne** m. **Elizabeth Fyldene**

2   2   **Richard Osborne** m. **Jane Broughton**

3   3   **Edward**   Thomas   Julian
                     m.
              I-**Anne** II-Margaret
              Hewit   Chapman
                         no issue

4   4   Sir Hewit   Edward   **Anne**   Alice
          Osborne   m.   m.
            m.   **Robert**   Sir John
          Joice   **Offley**   Peyton
          Fleetwood
                         unmarried

     5   Sir Edward   Alice
            m.   m.
          I-Margaret II-Anne   Christopher
          Fauconberg Midleton   Wandesford

     6   Edward   Sir Thomas   Charles
                       m.
          died   Lady Bridget
          young   Bertie   unmarried

7 Edward	Thomas	Peregrine	Elizabeth	Anne
m.	died	m.	unmarried	m.
Elizabeth	young	Bridget		I-Robert II-Horatio
Bennett		Hyde		Coke Walpole

two sons
died young

no issue

Sophia	Martha	Catherine	Bridget
m.	m.	m.	m.
I-Donatus	I-Edward	James	I-Charles
Lord O'Brien	Baynton	Herbert	Fitzcharles
II-William	II-Charles		II-Dr. Philip
Fermor	Granville		Biese
			no issue

8 William	Peregrine		Bridget	Mary
Henry	Hyde		m.	m.
unmarried	m.		Rev. Mr.	I-Henry
I-Elizabeth	II-Anne	III-Juliana	Williams	Somerset
Harley	Seymour	Hele		II-William
				Cochrane

no issue

9	Thomas	son
	m.	died young
	Mary Godolphin	

10 Osborne	Thomas	Francis Godolphin	Harriot
died	unmarried	m.	died
young		I-Lady Amelia II-Catherine	young
		Darcy Anguish	

11 George	Mary	Lord	Sydney	Catherine
William	Henrietta	Francis	Godolphin	Anne
Frederic	Juliana	Godolphin		Mary
m.	m.	m.		
Lady Charlotte	Thomas	Elizabeth		
Townshend	Pelham	Charlotte		
		Eden		

12 Francis
Godolphin Darcy
    Osborne

Recap of Significant Data: Osborne
Generation

1 Richard Osborne of Ashford, County Kent was born circa 1480. He married Elizabeth Fyldene, of the parish of St. Mary's, daughter of.... Fyldene of Kent.

2 Richard Osborne married Jane, daughter of John Broughton, Esq. of Broughton, Westmoreland. Richard was born circa 1510. Jane was the sister and heiress of Edward and Lancelyn Broughton.

3 Sir Edward Osborne was born about 1540. He was an apprentice to Sir William Hewet, Knight of London, of the clothworkers' company. While Sir Edward was an apprentice, the maid accidentally dropped the daughter of Sir William from the window of his house on London Bridge into the Thames. Edward immediately leaped into the river and brought the child out safely. Edward afterwards married Anne and with her got an estate in the parish of Barking in Essex together with lands in the parishes of Wales and Harthill in Yorkshire.

Sir Edward was sheriff of London in 1575 and Lord Mayor

in 1582. He was knighted at Westminster. He served in parliament for London in 1585 and died on February 2, 1591. He was buried in St. Dionis Backchurch near Fenchurch Street in London.

Sir Edward Osborne married a second time to Margaret Chapman who was buried near him in 1602. There was no issue from this marriage.

Charles Kingsley has immortalized our ancestor, Sir Edward Osborne with the following quote. The dinner was held on the abandoned ship, Pelican, in which Sir Frances Drake visited the New World.

"The Lord Mayor is giving a dinner to certain gentlemen of the Leicester House party, who are interested in foreign discoveries; and what place so fit for such a feast as the Pelican itself?

Look at the men all round; a nobler company you will seldom see. Especially too, if you be Americans, look at their faces, and reverence them; for to them and to their wisdom you owe the existence of your mighty fatherland.

At the head of the table sits the Lord Mayor; whom all readers will recognize at once, for he is none other than that famous Sir Edward Osborne, clothworker, and ancestor of the Duke of Leeds, whose romance is in every one's hands. He is aged, but not changed, since he leaped from the window of London Bridge into the roaring tide below, to rescue the infant who is now his wife. The chivalry and promptitude of the 'prentice boy' have grown and hardened into the thoughtful daring of the wealthy merchant adventurer. There he sits, a right kingly man, with my lord Earl of Cumberland on his right hand, and Walter Raleigh on his left the three talk together in a low voice on the chance of there being vast and rich countries still undiscovered between Florida and the River of Canada. Raleigh's half-scientific declamation, and his often quotations of Doctor Dee the conjuror, have less effect on Osborne than on Cumberland (who tried many an adventure to foreign parts, and failed in all of them; apparently for the simple reason that instead of going himself, he sent other people), and Raleigh is fain to call to his help the quiet student who sits on his left hand, Richard Hakluyt, of Oxford."

4 Sir Hewit Osborne was born in 1567. He was knighted at Menoth in Ireland in 1599 having valiantly behaved against the rebels. He married Joice Fleetwood, daughter of Thomas Fleetwood, Esq. She later married Sir Peter Frechevile, Knight.

Edward Osborne died unmarried in 1625.

Anne Osborne married Robert Offley of London. It is from Anne that the Niemeyers are descended.

Alice Osborne married Sir John Peyton of Iselham.

5 Sir Hewit had a son, Edward, and a daughter, Alice, who married Christopher Wandesford of Kirklington, Yorkshire. Edward Osborne was created a Baronet on July 13, 1620 having before received the honour of knighthood. Sir Edward first married Margaret Bellafyse Fauconberg and by her had a son, Edward, who was killed by the fall of some chimneys at York manor on October 31, 1638. He married secondly Anne, widow of William Midleton and daughter of Thomas Walmsley. They had two children, Thomas and Charles. These two boys were on their way to their brother's apartments when the chimneys fell but they were not hurt.

6 Sir Thomas, First Duke of Leeds, was made treasurer of the navy in 1671 by Charles II; on May 3, 1672, one of the privy council; on June 19, 1673, he was constituted lord high treasurer of England; and on August 15, 25 Car II was made a

baron by the title of Baron of Kiveton. On the 27 June, the year following was advanced to Earl of Danby; on April 21, 1677 he was elected Knight of the Order of the Garter.

In 1678, he was impeached of high treason; in 1679 a new parliament was summoned, the Commons prosecuted him and a bill of attainder was brought in, but before it had passed, he delivered himself up and was sent to the Tower where he lay five years. In 1689 he was created Marquis of Carmanthln.

In 1690 an attempt was made to revive the impeachment and in 1695 an impeachment against him was again voted for receiving presents from the East India Company but was let drop. On May 1694 he was created the Duke of Leeds. He died in the eighty-first year of his age on July 26, 1712 at Easton in the county of Northampton.

He married Lady Bridget Bertie and they had three sons, Edward, Thomas and Peregrine, and six daughters. Lady Elizabeth died unmarried; Anne married Robert Coke and secondly Horatio Walpole; Bridget married Charles Fitzcharles and secondly Dr. Philip Biese; Catherine married James Herbert; Martha to Edward Baynton, Esq. and secondly to Charles Granville and Lady Sophia married first Donatus Lord O'Brien and afterwards William Fermor.

7   Lady Anne died on August 5, 1722 at age 64 without issue. Bridget had no issue by Charles Fitzcharles. She died May 9, 1718. Edward Lord Latimer married Elizabeth Bennet and had two sons who died young. Edward died in 1688 without any other issue. Thomas died in infancy. Peregrine succeeded his father in his honours. He married Bridget Hyde and they had two sons and two daughters. Bridget died March 8, 1733-4.

8   Lady Bridget married to the Rev. Mr. Williams. Lady Mary married first Henry Somerset and secondly on Oct. 15, 1715 to William Cochrane. She died February 4, 1722. William

Henry was born in July 1691 and died of smallpox at Utretcht on August 16, 1711 at twenty-one. Peregrine Hyde, the youngest, became the third Duke of Leeds. He married first Lady Elizabeth Harley who died in childbed on November 20, 1713 at age twenty-eight. They had a son, Thomas. Peregrine married secondly Lady Anne Seymour who died November 27, 1722. They had a son who died young. In April 1725 he married thirdly Juliana Hele. They had no children. She later married Charles, Earl of Portmore, and died on November 20, 1794 at age eighty-nine leaving one son. Peregrine died on May 9, 1731.

9 Thomas, Fourth Duke of Leeds, was born on November 6, 1713. He married on June 26, 1740 to Lady Mary Godolphin. Lady Mary died on August 3, 1764 at the age of forty-one years. They had a son who was born in May 1741; Lady Harriot who was born in November, 1744 and died a few days later; Thomas, who was born on October 5, 1747 and died of small pox on August 15, 1761 and Francis Godolphin who became the Duke of Leeds. Francis Godolphin died March 23, 1789.

10 Francis Godolphin Osborne, fifth Duke of Leeds, was born on January 29, 1751. He married on November 29, 1773 Lady Amelia Darcy. They divorced in May 1779. They had issue: George William Frederic, Mary Henrietta Juliana who was born September 6, 1776 and Lord Francis Godolphin Osborne who was born October 11, 1777. He married secondly on October 11, 1788 Catherine Anguish. Their children were Sydney Godolphin who was born December 16, 1789 and Catherine Anne Mary. Francis died January 31, 1799.

11 Mary Henrietta Juliana married in August, 1801 Thomas Pelham. Lord Francis Godolphin Osborn married on March 31, 1800 Elizabeth Charlotte Eden. They had a son who was born in July 1802. George William Frederic, sixth Lord of Leeds, was born July 21, 1775. He married on August 17, 1797 Lady

Charlotte Townshend.

 12 They had a child, Francis Godolphin Darcy Osborne, born on May 21, 1798.

 The present Niemeyers are direct descendents of **Anne Osborne** and **Robert Offley** of the first four generation of this Osborne line. In <u>Tidewater</u> <u>Ancestors</u>, the noted generation should be changed as follows.

13   13   Lt. Col. William Frederic Niemeyer, C. S. A.
                  m. Sarah Campbell Smith

14   14   John Frederic Niemeyer m. Lucrece Bilisoly

15   15   Antonio Bilisoly Niemeyer m. Lutie Stuart Spotts

16   16   Antonio Bilisoly Niemeyer, Jr. m. Alice Virginia
                  Berry

17	17	William Frederic Niemeyer	Frank Berry Niemeyer	John Stuart Niemeyer
		m.	m.	m.
		Carolyn Louise Holtzhauer	Shannon Page Eadie	April Michelle Tripp
18	18	John Cameron Niemeyer	Jacob Douglas Niemeyer	John Stuart Niemeyer, Jr.
		Kyle Antonio Niemeyer		

Under generation, the first column is the generation listed on page 85 of Tidewater Ancestors and the second column is for the Broughton lineage. The persons from whom we are descended are in bold print.

Generation

    1 **Everard Broughton**

    2 **John Broughton**

2   3 **Richard Osborne** m. **Jane Broughton**

Recap of Significant Data: Broughton
Generation

    1 Everard Broughton, Esq. of Broughton, Westmoreland.

    2 John Broughton, Esq. of Broughton, Westmoreland.

    3 There were three children of John Broughton; Edward, Jane and Lancelyn.

    The present Niemeyers are direct descendents of this Broughton line. In Tidewater Ancestors the noted generation should be changed as follows.

13	14	Lt. Col. William Frederic Niemeyer, C. S. A. m. Sarah Campbell Smith
14	15	John Frederic Niemeyer m. Lucrece Bilisoly
15	16	Antonio Bilisoly Niemeyer m. Lutie Stuart Spotts
16	17	Antonio Bilisoly Niemeyer, Jr. m. Alice Virginia Berry

| 17 | 18 | William Frederic Niemeyer m. Carolyn Louise Holtzhauer | Frank Berry Niemeyer m. Shannon Page Eadie | John Stuart Niemeyer m. April Michelle Tripp |

18   19   John Cameron   Jacob Douglas   John Stuart
          Niemeyer   Niemeyer   Niemeyer, Jr.
          Kyle Antonio
          Niemeyer

Fyldene

Under generation, the first column is the generation listed on page 85 of Tidewater Ancestors and the second column is for the Fyldene lineage. The persons from whom we are descended are in bold print.

Generation

1   1   **Richard Osborne** m **Elizabeth Fyldene**

Recap of Significant Data: Fyldene

Generation

1   Elizabeth Fyldene was of the Parish of St. Mary's. She was born about 1480. Her husband, Richard Osborne, was of Ashford, County Kent, England.

The present Niemeyers are direct descendents of this Fyldene line. In Tidewater Ancestors the noted generation should be changed as follows.

13   13   Lt. Col. William Frederic Niemeyer, C. S. A.
              m. Sarah Campbell Smith

14   14   John Frederic Niemeyer m. Lucrece Bilisoly

15   15   Antonio Bilisoly Niemeyer m. Lutie Stuart Spotts

16   16   Antonio Bilisoly Niemeyer, Jr. m. Alice Virginia
              Berry

17   17   William Frederic   Frank Berry   John Stuart
              Niemeyer   Niemeyer   Niemeyer
                 m.   m.   m.
              Carolyn Louise   Shannon Page   April Michelle
              Holtzhauer   Eadie   Tripp   18

18   John Cameron   Jacob Douglas   John Stuart
          Niemeyer   Niemeyer   Niemeyer, Jr.
          Kyle Antonio
          Niemeyer

Flowerdew

Under generation, the first column is the generation listed on page 107 of <u>Tidewater</u> <u>Ancestors</u> and the second column is for the Flowerdew lineage. The persons from whom we are descended are in bold print.

Generation

1   **William Flowerdew** m. **Katherine Payne** alias **Hall**

2   **John Flowerdew** m. **Catheran Sheers**

3

William	Thomas	Martin	Edward	Edmund	Frances	Margaret
m.	m.	or Mark	m.	Gent.	m.	m.
Frances	Jane	m.	Elizabeth		Thomas	I-William
Appleyard	Fane	Margaret	Foster		Amyas	Southals
		Hawes			(Amias)	II-Harman

	Christopher	John	Alice	Elizabeth	Amy
	m.	Gent.	m.	m.	m.
	Cecilia	m.	John	William	Michael
	Billingford	Elizabeth	Kemp	Hollis	Heath
		Slegg			

4

I-**Anthony**	Marie	Elizabeth		Edward	William	Edmund	Thomasine
Gent.	m.	m.		m.	unmarried	Gent.	unmarried
m.	I-Lilmore	Bradshaw		Bridget		m.	
Martha	(Lulman)			Stewart		Anne	
Stanley						Scott	
m.							
II-Capt. Godfrey							
Garrett				Humphrey	John	Thomasine	
						m.	
continued						Richard	
next page						Frere	

36

10	5	Stanley	Mary	**Temperance**	Elizabeth
			m.	m.	m.
			Dennis	I- Sir	Thomas
			Rossingham	**George**	Shilton
				Yeardley	
				II- Colonel	
				Francis	
				West	

6   Edmund Rossingham

Recap of Significant Data: Flowerdew
Generation

    The Flowerdew name has been used over the years as Flourday, Flowerdieu, Flourdew, Flowerdewe, and Flowerdew.

    1 William Flowerdew was of Wymondham, Norfolk County, England. Wymondham lies about nine miles southwest of Norwich. William married Katherine Payne, a daughter of William Payne of Wymondham. William Flowerdew died in 1536. <u>Tidewater Ancestors</u> gives William's wife as Katherine Hall alias Paine. Souil Garner gives her as Katherine Payne alias Hall. <u>Tidewater Ancestors</u> says she is the daughter of William Hall.

    2 John Flowerdew purchased Cromwell's Manor and settled at Hethersett, Norfolk County, England. Hethersett is only about six miles southwest of Norwich. John married Catheran Sheers, a daughter of William Sheers of Ashwell Thorp, Norfolk. John Flowerdew, a prominent landowner, died sometime in 1565 since his will was proved in September 1565. He, his wife and his son, Thomas, were buried at Hethersett Church. <u>Tidewater Ancestors</u> spells Sheers as Sheres.

    3 William Flowerdew was of Norfolk. He married Frances Appleyard, daughter of Roger Appleyard of Stanfield Hall and

his wife, Elizabeth Scott. William predeceased his father, John. William died before 1565.

Thomas Flowerdew died in 1564. He married Jane Fane of Cambridge.

Martin (Mark) Flowerdew married Margaret Hawes of Ipswich.

Edward Flowerdew became the 4th Baron of the Exchequer and Lord of Stanfield Hall. He wrote his will on 15 June 1583 and it was proved May 5, 1586. He was educated at Cambridge but took no degree. He was a judge.

In the winter of 1585-86 he went circuit in South Wales, and in March held the assizes at Exeter. Here goal fever broke out and he died between March 14 and April 4. He was buried at Hethersett Church.

He was a man of grasping temper but apparently not of fine feelings. In 1564 he purchased Stanfield Hall and its furniture of John Appleyard in order to live there, and he married Elizabeth, daughter of William Foster of Wymondham, who had been Appleyard's mistress. His lands were dispersed at his death and he left no heirs.

He left a lengthy will. One of his bequests said, "I give unto my nephew Anthony's daughters at their marriage day ten pounds a piece."

At an inquisition post mortem taken at Harlston, Norfolk County 12 October 1586, it was stated Edward Flowerdew died on the 31st March last past. Elizabeth, his wife, survives him. Anthony Flowerdew is his next heir being the son and heir of William Flowerdew, brother and heir of the aforesaid Edward. Anthony is aged twenty-nine.

The will of Edmund Flowerdew Gent. of Hethersett was proved in 1606.

Margaret Flowerdew married William Southals of Suffolk. She may have married a second time to a Harman.

Amy Flowerdew married Michael Heath of Little Massingham, 1586.

Elizabeth Flowerdew married William Hollis (Hillys), son and heir of Sir Thomas Hollis (Hillys), of Flitcham, Norfolk County.

John Flowerdew married Elizabeth Slegg of Comberton, Lincolnshire. He died in 1588.

Christopher Flowerdew who married Cecilia Billingford of Blackford Hall was still living in 1606.

4 Anthony Flowerdew was born circa 1557 and died before 1606. He married Martha Stanley, daughter of John Stanley of Scottow, Norfolk County, and his wife, Mary Marsham. Mary Marsham was the daughter of John Marsham of Norwich, Norfolk County and the widow of John Balle of Scottow. Anthony was heir and cousin of Baron Edward.

After the death of Anthony Flowerdew, his widow, Martha, married Captain Godfrey Garrett. In the will of Martha Garrett of Scottow, Norfolk County, dated 3 February 1625/26, proved 4 December 1626, she bequeaths"...unto my daughter, Temperance Yardie alias Flowerdew, my seal ring of gold..." She named her grandson, Edmund Rossingham as executor.

Thomasine Flowerdew married Richard Frere in 1577. Edward Flowerdew became the Flowerdew of Hethersett. His grandson became a London merchant and sold the manor. Edward's wife, Bridget Stewart, was the daughter of John Stewart of Marham.

William Flowerdew was a lawyer. He did not marry.

Edmund Flowerdew was a lawyer who lived at Thriplow in Cambridgeshire.

Thomasine Flowerdew, the daughter of John and Elizabeth Slegg Flowerdew, did not marry. She died before 1587.

5 Mary (or Marie), daughter of Anthony Flowerdew and Martha Stanley, was christened in Deopham, Norfolk County,

20 July 1579. She married Dyonis Rossingham, Gent. who was usher to James I. He was buried at Westminster Abbey in 1617.

Temperance had been thought to be the youngest daughter but Ruth Flowerdew advises of the discovery of a baptism on 9 May 1591 of an Elizabeth, daughter of Anthony Flowerdew. Temperance may have been born in the period 1579-1583. It follows then, that Mary (or Marie) and Temperance must have been the older daughters, and the daughters of Anthony that Edward Flowerdew had in mind when he wrote his will 15 June 1583.

Stanley Flowerdew, Gent.'s will was written 10 May 1620 and proved 16 August 1620. He was in Virginia for a time but appears to have returned to England in poor health about 1619.

Elizabeth Flowerdew was baptized 9 May 1591 at St. Ann's Church, Blackfriars, London. She probably married Thomas, son of Sir Robert Shilton.

6   Edmund Rossingham was in Virginia at one time.

The present Niemeyers are direct descendents of this Flowerdew line. In <u>Tidewater</u> <u>Ancestors</u> the noted generation should be changed as follows.

19	14	Lt. Col. William Frederic Niemeyer, C. S. A. m. Sarah Campbell Smith.
20	15	John Frederic Niemeyer m. Lucrece Bilisoly.
21	16	Antonio Bilisoly Niemeyer m. Lutie Stuart Spotts.
22	17	Antonio Bilisoly Niemeyer, Jr. m. Alice Virginia Berry.

| 23 | 18 | William Frederic Niemeyer m. Carolyn Louise Holtzhauer | Frank Berry Niemeyer m. Shannon Page Eadie | John Stuart Niemeyer m. April Michelle Tripp |

24   19   John Cameron   Jacob Douglas   John Stuart
                       Niemeyer   Niemeyer   Niemeyer, Jr.
                       Kyle Antonio
                       Niemeyer

Payne

Refer to Flowerdew family, generation 1

Under generation, the first column is the generation listed on page 107 of <u>Tidewater</u> <u>Ancestors</u> and the second column is for the Payne lineage. The persons from whom we are descended are in bold print.

Generation

0   1   **William Payne**

     2   **Katherine Payne** alias Hall m. **William Flowerdew**

     3   **John Flowerdew** m **Catheran Sheers**

     4   **William Flowerdew** m **Frances Appleyard**

     5   **Anthony Flowerdew** m **Martha Stanley**

10   6   **Temperance Flowerdew** m **George Yeardley**

Recap of Significant Data: Payne
Generation

     1   William Payne of Wymondham, Norfolk County, England had a daughter, Katherine, who first married a Hall and, secondly, William Flowerdew. Wymondham lies about nine miles southwest of Norwich.

The present Niemeyers are direct descendents of this Payne line. In <u>Tidewater</u> <u>Ancestors</u> the noted generation should be changed as follows.

19   15   Lt. Col. William Frederic Niemeyer, C. S. A.
                 m. Sarah Campbell Smith
20   16   John Frederic Niemeyer m. Lucrece Bilisoly
21   17   Antonio Bilisoly Niemeyer m. Lutie Stuart Spotts
22   18   Antonio Bilisoly Niemeyer, Jr. m. Alice Virginia

Berry

23	19	William Frederic Niemeyer	Frank Berry Niemeyer	John Stuart Niemeyer
		m.	m.	m.
		Carolyn Louise Holtzhauer Eadie	Shannon Page Tripp	April Michelle
24	20	John Cameron Niemeyer	Jacob Douglas Niemeyer	John Stuart Niemeyer, Jr.
		Kyle Antonio Niemeyer		

Sheres or Sheers

Refer to Flowerdew family

Under generation, the first column is the generation listed on page 107 of <u>Tidewater Ancestors</u> and the second column is for the Sheres lineage. The persons from whom we are descended are in bold print.

Generation

0	1		**William Sheres**	
	2		**Catheran (Catherine) Sheres** m. **John Flowerdew**	
	3		**William Flowerdew** m **Frances Appleyard**	
	4	Elizabeth	Mary	**Anthony Flowerdew**
		m.	m.	m.
		Bradshaw	Lulman	**Martha Stanley**
10	5	Marie	**Temperance**	Stanley
		m.	**Flowerdew**	Flowerdew
		Dennis	m.	
		Rossingham	**George**	
		Gent.	**Yeardley**	

Recap of Significant Data: Sheres
Generation

1   William Sheres was of Ashwellthorp, Norfolk.

2   John Flowerdew bought Cromwell Manor. He was buried in 1665.

3 William is the first of eleven children. He predeceased his father. He sold the manor to his brother, John, who married Frances Appleyard of Stanfield Hall.

The present Niemeyers are direct descendents of this Sheres line. In <u>Tidewater Ancestors</u> the noted generation should be changed as follows.

19	14	Lt. Col. William Frederic Niemeyer, C. S. A.

m. Sarah Campbell Smith

20	15	John Frederic Niemeyer m. Lucrece Bilisoly
21	16	Antonio Bilisoly Niemeyer m. Lutie Stuart Spotts
22	17	Antonio Bilisoly Niemeyer, Jr. m. Alice Virginia Berry

23	18	William Frederic Niemeyer	Frank Berry Niemeyer	John Stuart Niemeyer
		m.	m.	m.
		Carolyn Louise Holtzhauer	Shannon Page Eadie	April Michelle Tripp
24	19	John Cameron Niemeyer	Jacob Douglas Niemeyer	John Stuart Niemeyer, Jr.
		Kyle Antonio Niemeyer		

Appleyard

Prepared by:

Mrs. Wilbur C. Garner

Randallstown, Maryland

Refer to the Flowerdew family, generation 3

Under generation, the first column is the generation listed on page 107 of <u>Tidewater</u> <u>Ancestors</u> and the second column is for the Appleyard lineage. The persons from whom we are descended are in bold print.

Generation

1   **Bartholomew Appleyard m. Emma**

2 Sir William —m. I-**Margaret de Salle** m. II- **William**
    Curzon   **Appleyard**

3 **Margaret** m.   **Nicholas**   Edmund   m. Anne
   Thornbury   **Appleyard**   Appleyard

4 William **John**   Bartholomew   William Geoffrey Edmund
        Appleyard

5 **Sir Nicholas** m. **Agnes**   Sir Terry m. Lady Elizabeth
    Appleyard   Robsart   of Kerdistone

6

Alice Philip Mary **Roger** m.I- **Elizabeth** m.II-Sir William Lucy
  m.   **Appleyard**   **Scott**   John   m.
Robert   Robsart   Sir
  Kett   Edward
                                     Walpole

Children of Roger Appleyard and Elizabeth Scott					Children of Elizabeth Scott and Sir John Robsart		Child of Lucy and Sir Edward Walpole
7 John Appleyard m. Elizabeth	Philip Appleyard	Anne m. I-Alxr. Chapman	Bridget II-James Bigot	**Frances Appleyard** m. **William Flowerdew**	Amy Robsart m. Robert Dudley	Arthur Robsart	John Walpole
8		Dudley Robsart Chapman		**Anthony Flowerdew** m. **Martha Stanley**			
10	9			Marye m. Dyonis Rossingham	**Temperance** m. Sir **George Yeardley**	Elizabeth m. Thomas Shilton	Stanley
11	10			Edmund Rossingham	Elizabeth	**Argoll** m. I-**Frances Knight** II-Ann Custis	Francis

47

Recap of Significant Data: Appleyard

Generation

1   Bartholomew Appleyard was Bailiff of Norwich in 1372 and a member of Burgess in 1374. He died in 1386.

2   William Appleyard was the second husband of Margaret de Salle. Margaret was a ward of Bartholomew Appleyard. They married in 1401. William was the first mayor of Norwich in 1403. He was, also, mayor in 1404, 1405, 1411, 1412, and 1418. He was nine times burgess in Parliament and was Bailiff of the city in 1386 and 1395. He died in 1419.

Margaret de Salle married first Sir William Curzon who died in 1399.

3   Nicholas Appleyard was born in 1396. He died before 1466. Edmund Appleyard died in 1448. Mrs. Garner gives the birth of Nicholas Appleyard as 1396. This is before William Appleyard married Margaret de Salle. Therefore, if the dates are correct, Nicholas is probably not the son of Margaret.

4   John Appleyard was a son and heir of Nicholas. He died in 1473. William Appleyard died in 1481.

5   Sir Nicholas Appleyard of Brakene was the son and heir to John. He was born in 1444 and died on July 11, 1511. This figure may be 1517.

6   Roger Appleyard was the first husband of Elizabeth Scott. He died in 1528. In 1529 she married Sir John Robsart who was the Magistrate and High Sheriff of Norfolk and Suffolk in 1547. He died in 1553. She died in 1549.

7   Frances Appleyard married William Flowerdew who died before 1565. John Appleyard was born in 1526 and married Elizabeth. He was High Sheriff of Norfolk and Suffolk in 1558. He died in 1568. Philip Appleyard was born in 1529. Anne Appleyard married twice. Her first husband was Alexander Chapman whom she married in 1550. He died in 1554. She then

married James Bigot in 1554. He died in 1560. Anne, also, died in 1560.

8   Anthony Flowerdew was born in September 1557 and died before 1620. He married Martha Stanley of Scottow, Norfolk, England. Her will was probated in 1625/26. Dudley Robsart Chapman was born in 1551.

9   Temperance Flowerdew married Sir George Yardley in November 1617. He was baptized on 28 July 1588 in Southwark, London. He died in Virginia and was buried in Jamestown on 13 November 1627. Temperance married secondly Colonel Francis West. She died in 1629 in Virginia.

The present Niemeyers are direct descendents of this Appleyard line. In <u>Tidewater</u> <u>Descendents</u> the noted generation should be changed as follows.

19	18	Lt. Col. William Frederic Niemeyer, C. S. A. m. Sarah Campbell Smith		
20	19	John Frederic Niemeyer m. Lucrece Bilisoly		
21	20	Antonio Bilisoly Niemeyer m. Lutie Stuart Spotts		
22	21	Antonio Bilisoly Niemeyer, Jr. m. Alice Virginia Berry		
23	22	William Frederic Niemeyer m. Carolyn Louise Holtzhauer	Frank Berry Niemeyer m. Shannon Page Eadie	John Stuart Niemeyer m. April Michelle Tripp
24	23	John Cameron Niemeyer Kyle Antonio Niemeyer	Jacob Douglas Niemeyer, Jr.	John Stuart Niemeyer, Jr.

de Salle

Refer to Appleyard Family, generation 2

Under generation, the first column is the generation listed on page 107 of <u>Tidewater</u> <u>Ancestors</u> and the second column is for the de Salle lineage. The persons from whom we are descended are in bold print.

Generation

| 0 | 1 | **Rob de Salle** | |

| 2 | **Adam Humphrie de Salle** | Bartholomew de Salle |

| 3 | **Margaret de Salle** | Richard de Salle |

m.

I-Sir William Curzon   II- **William Appleyard**

Recap of Significant Data: de Salle

Generation

2 Adam Humphrie de Salle died in 1383.   .   3 Margaret de Salle was a ward of Bartholomew Appleyard. She first married Sir William Curzon. He died in 1399. She, secondly, married William Appleyard who was the son of Bartholomew. Mrs. Garner reported that they married in 1401 and he died in 1419. Mrs. Garner shows they had two sons, Edmund and Nicholas. However, if Nicholas was born in 1396 and Margaret and William were not married until 1401 then Nicholas may not be their child.

The present Niemeyers are direct descendents of this de Salle line. In <u>Tidewater</u> <u>Ancestors</u> the noted generation should be changed as follows.

19	19	Lt. Col. William Frederic Niemeyer, C. S. A. m. Sarah Campbell Smith		
20	20	John Frederic Niemeyer m. Lucrece Bilisoly		
21	21	Antonio Bilisoly Niemeyer m. Lutie Stuart Spotts		
22	22	Antonio Bilisoly Niemeyer, Jr. m. Alice Virginia Berry		
23	23	William Frederic Niemeyer m. Carolyn Louise Holtzhauer	Frank Berry Niemeyer m. Shannon Page Eadie	John Stuart Niemeyer m. April Michelle Tripp
24	24	John Cameron Niemeyer Kyle Antonio Niemeyer	Jacob Douglas Niemeyer	John Stuart Niemeyer, Jr.

Thornbury

Refer to Appleyard Family, generation 3

Under generation, the first column is the generation listed on page 107 of <u>Tidewater</u> <u>Ancestors</u> and the second column is for the Thornbury lineage. The persons from whom we are descended are in bold print.

Generation

0　1　　**Margaret Thornbury** m. **Nicholas Appleyard**

The present Niemeyers are direct descendents of this Thornbury line. In <u>Tidewater</u> <u>Ancestors</u> the noted generation should be changed as follows.

19　16　Lt. Col. William Frederic Niemeyer, C. S. A.
　　　　　　m. Sarah Campbell Smith
20　17　John Frederic Niemeyer m. Lucrece Bilisoly
21　18　Antonio Bilisoly Niemeyer m. Lutie Stuart Spotts
22　19　Antonio Bilisoly Niemeyer, Jr. m. Alice Virginia
　　　　　Berry

23	20	William Frederic Niemeyer	Frank Berry Niemeyer	John Stuart Niemeyer
		m.	m.	m.
		Carolyn Louise Holtzhauer	Shannon Page Eadie	April Michelle Tripp
24	21	John Cameron Niemeyer	Jacob Douglas Niemeyer	John Stuart Niemeyer, Jr.
		Kyle Antonio Niemeyer		

Scott

Refer to Appleyard Family, generation 6.

Under generation, the first column is the generation listed on page 107 of <u>Tidewater Ancestors</u> and the second column is for the Scott lineage. The persons from whom we are descended are in bold print.

Generation

0	1		John Scott m Elisabeth Skinner		
	2	Roger Appleyard	m.I	Elizabeth Scott	m.II	Sir John Robsart

3 John Philip Bridget Anne Frances Amy Arthur

Recap of Significant Data: Scott

Generation

1 John Scott was of Camberwell, Surrey.

2 Elisabeth Scott married ca. 1520 Roger Appleyard who was born of Stanfield Hall, Bracon Ash and Rainthorpe, Norfolk. He was the son of Sir Nicholas Appleyard. Roger died in 1528.

She secondly married Sir John Robsart (Robessart), Lord of the Manor of Siderster, Norfolk. Sir John died in 1553. Sir John and Elisabeth had one daughter, Lady Amy Robsart, who was half sister to Frances Appleyard, and one son, Arthur.

3 Amy Robsart was born in 1532 at Stanfield Hall. She died in 1562 in Cumnor, Oxford. Lady Amy married Robert Dudley in June 1550 at the Royal Palace of Sheen, Surrey. Robert Dudley was created Earl of Leicester by Queen Elizabeth I. Dudley died in Cornbury, Oxford, September 4, 1588.

The present Niemeyers are direct descendents of this Scott line. In Tidewater Ancestors the noted generation should be changed as follows.

19　14　Lt. Col. William Frederic Niemeyer, C. S. A.
　　　　　m. Sarah Campbell Smith

20　15　John Frederic Niemeyer m. Lucrece Bilisoly

21　16　Antonio Bilisoly Niemeyer m. Lutie Stuart Spotts

22　17　Antonio Bilisoly Niemeyer, Jr. m. Alice Virginia
　　　　　Berry

| 23 | 18 | William Frederic Niemeyer m. Carolyn Louise Holtzhauer | Frank Berry Niemeyer m. Shannon Page Eadie | John Stuart Niemeyer m. April Michelle Tripp |
| 24 | 19 | John Cameron Niemeyer Antonio Niemeyer | Jacob Douglas Niemeyer | John Stuart Niemeyer, Jr. Kyle |

Skinner

Refer to Scott Family, generation 1

Under generation, the first column is the generation listed on page 107 of <u>Tidewater Ancestors</u> and the second column is for the Skinner lineage. The persons from whom we are descended are in bold print.

Generation

0   1   **John Scott** m. **Elizabeth Skinner**

      2   **Roger**   m.I **Elizabeth**   m.II   Sir John
        Appleyard   **Scott**   Robsart

      3 John Phillip Bridget Anne **Frances** Amy Arthur

Recap of Significant Data: Skinner

Generation

    1 John Scott of Camberwell, Surrey married Elizabeth Skinner.

    The present Niemeyers are direct descendents of this Skinner line. In <u>Tidewater Ancestors</u> the noted generation should be changed as follows.

19   14   Lt. Col. William Frederic Niemeyer, C. S. A.
              m.   Sarah Campbell Smith

20   15   John Frederic Niemeyer m. Lucrece Bilisoly

21   16   Antonio Bilisoly Niemeyer m. Lutie Stuart Spotts

22   17   Antonio Bilisoly Niemeyer, Jr. m. Alice Virginia
              Berry

23   18   William Frederic   Frank Berry   John Stuart
              Niemeyer   Niemeyer   Niemeyer
                  m.   m.   m.
             Carolyn Louise   Shannon Page   April Michelle
              Holtzhauer   Eadie   Tripp

24   19   John Cameron   Jacob Douglas   John Stuart
                Niemeyer   Niemeyer   Niemeyer, Jr.
                Kyle Antonio
                Niemeyer

Refer to Flowerdew Family, generation 4.

Refer to Appleyard Family, generation 8.

Under generation, the first column is the generation listed on page 107 of <u>Tidewater</u> <u>Ancestors</u> and the second column is for the Stanley lineage. The persons from whom we are descended are in bold print.

Generation

0	1	**John Stanley** m. **Mary Marsham**
	2	**Martha Stanley** m. **Anthony Flowerdew**
10	3	**Temperance Flowerdew** m **George Yeardley**

Recap of Significant Data: Stanley

Generation

    1 John Stanley of Scottow, Norfolk County married Mary Marsham, the daughter of John Marsham of Norwich, Norfolk County. She was the widow of John Balle of Scottow. Martha Stanley is their daughter.

    2 Martha Stanley married twice. She married Anthony Flowerdew. Her second husband was Captain Godfrey Garrett.

    The present Niemeyers are direct descendents of this Stanley line. In <u>Tidewater</u> <u>Ancestors</u> the noted generation should be changed as follows.

19	12	Lt. Col. William Frederic Niemeyer, C. S. A. m. Sarah Campbell Smith
20	13	John Frederic Niemeyer m. Lucrece Bilisoly
21	14	Antonio Bilisoly Niemeyer m. Lutie Stuart Spotts
22	15	Antonio Bilisoly Niemeyer, Jr. m. Alice Virginia Berry

| 23 | 16 | William Frederic Niemeyer m. Carolyn Louise Holtzhauer | Frank Berry Niemeyer m. Shannon Page Eadie | John Stuart Niemeyer m. April Michelle Tripp |
| 24 | 17 | John Cameron Niemeyer Kyle Antonio Niemeyer | Jacob Douglas Niemeyer | John Stuart Niemeyer, Jr. |

Marsham

Refer to Appleyard Family, generation 8

Under generation, the first column is the generation listed on page 107 of <u>Tidewater Ancestors</u> and the second column is for the Marsham lineage. The persons from whom we are descended are in bold print.

Generation

	1	**John Marsham**
0	2	**John Stanley** m. **Mary Marsham**
	3	**Martha Stanley** m. **Anthony Flowerdew**
10	4	**Temperance Flowerdew** m. **George Yeardley**

Recap of Significant Data: Marsham

Generation

1 John Marsham was of Norwick, Norfolk County, England. He had a daughter.

2 Mary Marsham was married twice. She, firstly, married John Balle of Scottow and after his death she married, secondly, John Stanley of Scottow. Their daughter was Martha.

The present Niemeyers are direct descendents of this Marsham line. In <u>Tidewater Ancestors</u> the noted generation should be changed as follows.

19	13	Lt. Col. William Frederic Niemeyer, C. S. A.		
		m. Sarah Campbell Smith		
20	14	John Frederic Niemeyer m. Lucrece Bilisoly		
21	15	Antonio Bilisoly Niemeyer m. Lutie Stuart Spotts		
22	16	Antonio Bilisoly Niemeyer, Jr. m. Alice Virginia Berry		
23	17	William Frederic Niemeyer	Frank Berry Niemeyer	John Stuart Niemeyer
		m.	m.	m.

		Carolyn Louise Holtzhauer	Shannon Page Eadie	April Michelle Tripp
24	18	John Cameron Niemeyer	Jacob Douglas Niemeyer	John Stuart Niemeyer, Jr.
		Kyle Antonio Niemeyer		

THE ENIGMA OF TEMPERANCE FLOWERDEW

Mrs. Alan (Ruth) Flowerdew of Basingstoke, Hampshire, England has been engaged for a number of years in research of the Flowerdew name in general. Some time ago, when she learned that Temperance was an ancestress of mine, she volunteered much information concerning her ancestry, and since then has passed along to me several other important references to Temperance which she had later discovered. Ruth has now asked me to write an article on my ancestress for use in her quarterly publication titled, 'Flowerdew News-Ancient and Modern' and I have agreed to do so. I must admit, however, to some misgivings about the project, for over the years controversy has enveloped Temperance like a fog, and still does to this day. There have been so few pieces of factual and documented information discovered about her (and the accuracy of some of that has been questioned), that all who have attempted research of her have, of necessity, been compelled to ponder over the few known facts in conjunction with other pieces of circumstantial evidence, in order to make his or her own deductive conclusions about this lady. I will be no exception in this regard. Over the years, the various researchers have not always arrived at the same conclusions, and thus controversy surrounds her.

TEMPERANCE FLOWERDEW AND GEORGE YEARDLEY

"Approximately four hundred years ago, in England, there was born to Anthony Flowerdew and his wife, Martha Stanley, a daughter whom they named Temperance. She may have been born in county Norfolk, for her Flowerdew ancestors, so far as is known, lived and died in Wymondham and Hethersett of that county. Her father may have been an exception. It is known that he was in county Norfolk in his early years, but at this writing it is not known where or when he died.

At about the same time period, in Southwark, London, the second son of Raphe Yardley and his second wife, Rhoda Marston, was born, and was given the name of George. He was christened in St. Saviour's Parish, 28 July 1588, but he may have been born a few years earlier than that date. At an early age, the lad embarked on a career as a soldier, and saw active service in the battle of Oudewater.

The destinies of these two children, Temperance Flowerdew and George Yeardley, would eventually become intertwined, each with the other, and both with the Colony of Virginia. Where and how they met, and when and where they married are parts of the enigma of Temperance Flowerdew."

THE ANCESTRY OF TEMPERANCE

"The Flowerdew ancestors of Temperance can be traced back to her great, great grandparents, who were William Flowerdew of Wymondham, county Norfolk, England (died 1536), and his wife, Katharine Payne, alias Hall, daughter of William Payne of Wymondham.

Her great grandparents were John Flowerdew of Hethersett, county Norfolk, (died 1565), and his wife, Catharine Sheers, daughter of William Sheers of Ashwellthorpe, county Norfolk. They were parents of a large family. Both John Flowerdew and his wife, Catharine, are buried in Hethersett Church.

Her grandparents were William Flowerdew of county Norfolk (who predeceased his father, John Flowerdew), and his wife, Frances Appleyard, daughter of Roger Appleyard of Stanfield Hall, and his wife, Elizabeth Scott.

Her parents were Anthony Flowerdew (born circa 1557, died before 1606), and his wife, Martha Stanley, daughter of John Stanley of Scottow, county Norfolk, and his wife, Mary, widow of John Balle of Scottow, and a daughter of John Marsham of Norwich, county Norfolk. After the death of Anthony Flowerdew, his widow, Martha, married Captain Godfrey Garrett, and she died as Martha Garrett in Scottow. Her will was written 3 February 1625/26, and was proved 4 December 1626. The known children of Anthony and Martha Flowerdew were:

Marye (or Marie) Flowerdew, who was christened in the Parish of Deopham, county Norfolk, 20 July 1579. She married Dyonis Rossingham, Gent. who was usher to James I. He died in 1617 and was buried in Westminster Abbey. They had a son, Edmund Rossingham, who was in Virginia at one time, and whom his grandmother, Martha Garrett, named as Executor of her will in 1625/26.

Temperance Flowerdew, who is the subject of this article, and who probably had at least three marriages, the most notable of which was to Sir George Yeardley.

Elizabeth Flowerdew, who was baptized, 9 May 1591, at St. Ann's Church, Blackfriars, London. She appears to have been the daughter reported to have married Thomas, a son of Sir Robert Shilton, Knt.

Stanley Flowerdew, only son and heir. He may have been the youngest child. He was in Virginia for a while, but appears to have returned to England in poor health, about 1619. The will of Stanley Flowerdew, Gent. of Scottow, county Norfolk, was written 10 May 1620, and was proved 16 August 1620."

WHEN AND WHERE WAS TEMPERANCE BORN?

"The enigma of Temperance begins at the very first moment

that she entered this world. No record has been found of her birth, christening or baptism, so there is no certain answer to the above captioned question. It stands as the first of many questions concerning Temperance to which there are no answers.

There may be a clue as to when she was born, in the will of Anthony's uncle, Baron Edward Flowerdew, who wrote his will 15 June 1583, and it was proved 5 May 1586. It was a lengthy will, but one of his bequests said 'I give unto my Nephew Anthony's daughters at their marriage day ten pounds a piece.' At an Inquest post mortem taken at Harlston, county Norfolk, 12 October 1586, it was stated, '---Edward Flowerdew died on the 31st March last past, and Elizabeth, his wife, survives him. Anthony Flowerdew is his next heir, being the son and heir of William Flowerdew, brother and heir of the aforesaid Edward. The said Anthony is aged twenty nine---.' The information given at the Inquest places Anthony's year of birth circa 1557, which in turn tells us that Anthony was about 22 years old when his daughter, Marye, was christened. This suggests that Marye probably was his first child. When Edward, in 1583, made a bequest to 'Anthony's daughters,' it seemed to indicate that at least two daughters were then living. If so, one of them may have been Temperance, and in this case she was born in the period 1579-1583. On the other hand, it is also possible that two daughters were then living, but one of them may have died young, and Temperance may have been born later. In any event, she was probably born before 1590.

As to where she was born, there are two likely areas. If she was the next child born after Marye, it is likely that she was born in county Norfolk; however, if she was a later child, born closer to the time of the daughter, Elizabeth, she may have been born in London. Elizabeth was baptized in London, which suggests that Anthony and his family were living there at that time."

GEORGE YEARDLEY AND THE THIRD SUPPLY

"George Yeardley, upon returning from the campaign in the Low Countries, joined up with his old commander, Lieut. Gen. Sir Thomas Gates, and was appointed Commandant of his bodyguard. Sir Thomas had recently been commissioned as Governor of Virginia, and was soon to sail for Jamestown, carrying with him a new charter, and taking men and provisions for the relief of the Colony. He was authorized a fleet of 'eight good shippes and one pinnace, and 600 land men to be transplanted under your command.' Admiral Sir George Somers was in command of the fleet, which was known as the 'Third Supply.' The Admiral's ship was the 'Sea Venture,' (also referred to as the 'Sea Adventure'), and some of the other ships of the fleet were 'Falcon,' 'Blessing,' 'Unity,' and 'Diamond.' Among others sailing aboard the Admiral's ship were Sir Thomas Gates, William Strachey, Secretary of the Colony, George Yeardley, Parson Bucke and John Rolf and his first wife and their child.

At last, all being ready, the little fleet set sail on 15 May 1609, for the long voyage to Jamestown. The voyage appears to have gone well until, St. James his day, July 24th, being Monday, 'as William Strachey later wrote, the fleet encountered a storm of dreadful violence which continued for two days, scattering the fleet and blowing the 'Sea Venture' far off her course. Battered and badly leaking, the 'Sea Venture' was on the point of sinking when the island which we know today as Bermuda was sighted and they were able to run the ship aground on its coast. All of the ship's company were saved. Working for months, using tools and timber salvaged from the wrecked vessel, plus timber cut on the island, they managed to build two small boats, which they named 'Patience' and 'Deliverance,' and embarking in these they were able to make their way to Jamestown, arriving there nearly a year after they had left England.

The other ships of the fleet, also badly damaged by the storm, had somehow managed to stay afloat and survive, and had eventually made their way to their destination, arriving there during the month of August 1609. A member of the expedition who arrived at that time was quoted as saying, 'some of the ships had lost their masts, some their sayles blown from their Yards; the seas so overraking our ships, much of our provision was spoiled,---our men sicke, and many died; and in this miserable estate we arrived in Virginia.'

Captain George Yeardley, after arriving in May 1610, remained in Virginia and served with credit in a military capacity for several years thereafter. From the time of the departure of Sir Thomas Dale in April 1616, he was acting governor until 15 May 1617. In the autumn of 1617, he went to England and remained there throughout the following year. He was commissioned Governor of Virginia and knighted at Newmarket, 24 November 1618. Sir George departed England, 10 January 1618/19, on the ship 'Gift' bound for Virginia, and arrived there in April 1619. At his request, he retired as governor when his commission expired in November 1621. On 18 September 1625, he was appointed Deputy Governor in the absence of Sir Frances Wyatt. Later, he went to England carrying important petitions from the 'convention' assembly of that spring presenting the needs of the colonists and requesting the continuation of their general assembly. On 19

April 1626, he was again commissioned Governor of Virginia, and he held that office until his death in November 1627. He was survived by his wife, Temperance, and three children, Elizabeth, Argall and Francis."

WHEN DID TEMPERANCE GO TO VIRGINIA?

"In early 1624/25 (between 20 January and 7 February), a Muster of the inhabitants of Virginia was taken, and the particular muster of the household of Sir George Yeardley gave the following information:

Sir George Yardley, Knt., came in Deliverance in 1609.
Temperance Lady Yeardley, came in the Falcon in 1608.

Elizabeth Yeardley	aged 6 yeares)	Children
Argall Yeardley	aged 4 yeares)	born
Francis Yeardley	aged 1 yeare)	heare

The information given in this muster of the household of Sir George has become quite suspect as to its accuracy. We know that in 1609, Sir George was shipwrecked in Bermuda, and that the 'Deliverance' was in the process of being built. The 'Deliverance' and Sir George did not arrive in Virginia until May 1610. Also, there is no record of the 'Falcon' having been to Virginia in 1608, but, as noted above, it was one of the ships of the Gates-Somers fleet which arrived at Jamestown in August 1609. It is likely that Temperance arrived in Virginia on the 'Falcon' at that time."

WHY AND WITH WHOM DID TEMPERANCE GO TO VIRGINIA?

"In 1609, the Virginia Colony was only two years old and the plight of the colonists was desperate. It was a place of physical miseries and starvation, with death always close by, either from disease or by Indians. I asked myself many times, what possible circumstances could have brought this young lady to leave a life in England, where I feel sure she enjoyed a reasonable amount of the comforts which those years afforded, and go to this wilderness outpost where comfort of any kind was unknown? I could never arrive at a satisfactory answer. However, Ruth Flowerdew recently discovered an item which sent my speculative propensities on a rampage. It was the record of a marriage which she had found in the Computer Index for London:

'Temperance Flowerdew to Richard Barrow, 29 April 1609, at St. Gregory by St. Paul."

Assuming that this Temperance Flowerdew was one and the same as the Temperance who later married George Yeardley (and I have no proof that she was), the discovery of this marriage record was important for two reasons. First, it appeared to lend support to the theory that Temperance may have been born in London, or if not actually born there, had spent most of her early years there. Second, it seemed to be the missing part of this particular puzzle.

Knowing that this Temperance arrived in Virginia on the 'Falcon,' and also knowing that the 'Falcon' was one of the ships of the Gates-Somers fleet which left England, 15 May 1609, bound for Jamestown, it seems logical to believe that Richard Barrow had either volunteered or had been recruited as part of the '600 land men' which Sir Thomas Gates had been authorized to 'transplant' to Virginia, and so had pursuaded Temperance to marry him and go to Virginia as his wife. Temperance and her new husband Barrow, were probably aboard the 'Falcon' when it sailed for Virginia, 16 days after their marriage.

No record of Richard Barrow or of Temperance Barrow has

been found in Virginia. It is my belief that Richard Barrow lived only a short while after his marriage to Temperance. It is possible that he was one of those who perished during the violent storm of 24 June 1609, and that Temperance arrived in Virginia already a widow. If Barrow did reach Virginia, it is quite possible that he died shortly thereafter, either of starvation or disease, or at the hands of the Indians.

The arrival of the ships of the Third Supply only served to add to the woes of the colony, for they brought many people, but very little food supplies to sustain them, most of the provisions having been spoiled by sea water during the disastrous storm they encountered. I have no idea how Temperance survived the next several years, for she again disappears until she is later found as the wife of Sir George Yeardley. There are several important questions at this point for which we have no answers. Did Temperance, seeing the desperate state of affairs in Virginia, return to England at the first opportunity, and later married Sir George in England? Or, did she stay on in Virginia, bear with the miseries of life there, and at some later point in time, marry George Yeardley in Virginia? In either event, did she marry George as the widow Barrow, or had she ventured another marriage after Barrow and before Yeardley?"

TEMPERANCE AND HER CHILDREN

"Since no record of the marriage of Temperance to George Yeardley has been found, no one can say with certainty when or where it occurred. It is widely assumed that they were married in England in 1618. This date, for the most part, seems based on a letter dated 28 November 1618, written to Sir Dudley Carlton by her cousin, John Pory, in which Pory said,

'This Sir George Yeardley hath married my cousin German, and infinitely desires my company.' Apparently, Sir George had asked Pory to accept the position of Secretary of the Colony under his administration as Governor, which Pory did. However, I see nothing in Pory's statement that specifically implies that Temperance and George Yeardley were married in 1618. His statement would still be valid if they married in 1616 or 1614.

There is no question that Temperance was in England in the latter part of 1618, or that she then was the wife of Sir George Yeardley. Later, in 1619, John Pory then being in Virginia, wrote 'The Governor here, who at his first coming, besides a great deal of value in his person, brought only his sword with him; was at his last being in London, together with his lady, out of his mere gettings here able to disburse very near three thousand pounds to furnish him with the voyage.'

The marriage date of 1618 also appears to be supported by the ages of the Yeardley children as given in the muster of 1624/25- Elizabeth, 6 yeares (circa 1618/19); Argall, 4 yeares (circa 1620/21; Francis 1 yeare (circa 1623/24). However, once again the accuracy of this information source has been questioned. In May 1630, William Claiborne and Susanna Hall (they appear to have been two of the witnesses to the will of Sir George) answered a query in the case of Yeardley vs. Rossingham, regarding the ages of the Yeardley children at that time. Claiborne said that he did not know the age of the daughter, Elizabeth, but that the eldest son, Argall, was of the age of thirteen or thereabouts, and the second son, Francis, of the age of some twelve years or thereabouts. Susanna Hall replied that the daughter is some sixteen years of age or thereabouts, the eldest son is some fourteen years old, and the youngest son is some twelve years old. This testimony would place the children's years of birth circa 1614, 1616/17, and 1618/19, respectively. These conflicting records of the ages of the Yeardley children have led some to speculate that Elizabeth and Argall may not have been children of Temperance, but possibly children by an earlier wife, but I do not agree with this. In the absence of any proof as to when and where Sir George and Temperance were married, I am of the opinion that, whenever the children were born, their mother was Temperance (Flowerdew) Yeardley. That this is so, seems to have been confirmed when Ralph Yeardley of London, the elder brother of Sir George, was granted Letters of Administration upon the estates of Sir George and Temperance, on behalf of Elizabeth, Argall and Francis Yeardley, 'lawful and legitimate children of Dame Temperance Yardley (alias West).'"

THE LAST MARRIAGE OF TEMPERANCE

"Sir George died in Virginia in November 1627, and in March of the following year, his widow, Temperance, married Col. Francis West, at the time Deputy Governor of Virginia, and a brother of Lord De La Ware. This marriage was of short duration, for Temperance died intestate within the year following her marriage to West. I have not been able to determine the exact date of her death, the circumstances of her death, or where she was buried. After the death of his wife, Francis West hastened to England to lay claim against the estates of Sir George and Temperance, and much litigation ensued between West and Ralph Yeardley, the administrator.

The Yeardley children (all minors at the time) appear to have been sent to England, and likely were placed in the care and custody of their uncle, Ralph Yeardley. Later, Argall

71

and Francis returned to Virginia, and both became well known men who were prominent in the affairs of Virginia's Eastern Shore.   I know nothing further of the daughter, Elizabeth Yeardley."

FOR NOW, TEMPERANCE, AU REVOIR

"So, Temperance, dear ancestress of mine, given the few facts available about you, and considering the fragile trail that you left for me to follow, I have tried to tell your story as best I could, and as I think it happened. There are some who will disagree with my conclusions, as I have disagreed with theirs, but only you will know for certain which conclusions are correct and which are not. Granted, there are many gaps and breaks in the continuity of your story, but this fault is not really mine; you left not the slightest clue as to where you were or what you were doing at those particular times.

Possibly sometime, Temperance, in the not distant future, you and I will meet in that land beyond the stars, and if we do, we must have a very long talk together, for I have many, many questions to ask, and I know you have all of the answers. After you have answered all of my questions, and have told me the full story of your life, I will give a sigh of heavenly contentment; but also a touch of sadness will come to me as I recall the researchers I left on Earth, poor things.   I will see them sitting at their desks, with their notes and papers and reference books lying in front of them, frowning grimly and pondering over such questions concerning you as:- How many marriages did she have? When and where did she marry George Yeardley?   What was her name when she married him? Was that confounded Muster Roll correct or incorrect?   Was she really the mother of all three of Sir George's children?

And not finding the answer to those and many other questions, they will mumble a few choice words to themselves, and, in absolute frustration, they will kick the whole bit into a corner, to stay there until they have time to cool down again. I will certainly be able to sympathize with them, for I will have been one of them and know how they feel; but, like you, I will not be able to help them one little bit.

It appears, therefore, that on Earth the enigma of Temperance Flowerdew will continue far, far into the future. For now, Temperance, au revoir."

August 19, 1985   Souil William Garner

Conflicting Ideas

Conflicting ideas are given in the book, <u>George</u> <u>Yeardley</u> <u>Governor</u> <u>of</u> <u>Virginia</u>, written by Nora Miller Turman. Dates in this book have been changed to correspond to today's calendar.

George Yeardley was christened presumably on August 6, 1587. During the years 1609 to 1617, he was in Virginia. On June 9, 1617, Yardley left Virginia to return to England.

"The Sunday after landing in England, he saw a beautiful young lady who appeared to be with her sister and her family. He knew she was a maiden because her dress was not fastened high at the throat like the one worn by Elizabeth and older women."

"The second Sunday he was introduced to Miss Temperance Flowerdew... Her oval face, framed by a lace cap over dark brown hair, was beautiful. Her dress was a deep rose color and her farthingale reminded him of Elizabeth I."

"Temperance was living with her sister, Mary Rossingham, since their parents death... After a few formal calls the courtship began."

Yeardly sent a letter my messenger on October 1, 1617 asking her to marry him. He received an answer two days later. The announcement was read in the parish church on the second Sunday in October and the marriage took place one month later.

Yeardley was to return to Virginia but since Temperance was in no condition to go to Virginia, Yeardley asked to remain in England until late in the summer. On the last day of August 1618 Captain Yeardley's son was born. On the following Sunday he was christened Argoll Yeardley. Ralph Yeardley and Sir Edwin Sandys were the godfathers and Temperance's sister was godmother.

George Yeardley was knighted by James I on November 22, 1618. In the last week of February 1619 ships left England for Virginia with the Yardleys and George Rossingham, who was one of the owners of the Flowerdew Hundred Corporation. This was the son of Temperance's sister. John Pory who was secretary of the Colony later tried to discredit Yeardley.

In December 1620 Elizabeth Yeardley was born and a few days before Christmas in 1622 Francis Yeardley was born. Argoll was now five years old. One of Francis' godfathers was Sir Francis Wyatt.

Sir George left for England on June 15, 1625 and returned to Virginia on the Anne in June of 1626. He died and was buried on November 13, 1627. Witnesses to the will of Sir George Yeardley were Susanna Lyall and William Clayborne.

Yardley

Under generation, the first column is the generation listed on page 123 of <u>Tidewater Ancestors</u> and the second column is for the Yardley lineage. The persons from whom we are descended are in bold print.

Generation

1	1	**John Yeardley**
2	2	**Richard Yeardley**
3	3	**Thomas Yeardley**
4	4	**John Yeardley**
	5	**Oliver Yeardley** m. **Margaret de Eardley**
7	6	**John Yeardley** m. **Margaret Yeardley**
8	7	**John Yeardley** m. **Elizabeth Byrkes**
9	8	I-Agness Abbott m. **Ralph Yeardley** m. II-**Rhoda Marston**

10	9	Ralph **George** Anne John Thomas

Yeardley

m.

Temperance Flowerdew

11	10	Elizabeth **Argall** Francis

Yeardley

m.

I-**Frances Knight**   II-Ann Custis

12	11	Argoll Rose **Frances** Henry Edmund

Yeardley

m.

Colonel Adam Thoroughgood

Recap of Significant Data: Yardley

The information given here is from the Yeardley Family Tree Chart prepared by Robert Blake Yeardley from material in "Kenilworth Seals and Tokens" published by W. and T. Radclyffe and by Merridew & Sons, Coventry.

Generation

1   1 John Yeardley was of Eardley in Staffordshire. He was living in 1300 and during the reign of Edward II, 1307-1327.

2   2 Richard Yeardley of Eardley lived in the fourth year of the reign of Richard II (1381).

3   3 Thomas Yeardley of Eardley lived in the twenty first year of the reign of Richard II (1398).

4   4 John Yeardley of Eardley was living between 1461 and 1483.

     5 Oliver Yeardley was of Kenilworth and Yardley in County Stafford. He married Margaret de Eardley who lived during the reign of Edward IV, 1461-1483.

7   6 John Yeardley married Margaret Yeardley, daughter and heiress of John Yeardley of Kenilworth in County Warwickshire. She was the granddaughter of William Yeardley of Eardley, granted arms in 1491.

     In Tidewater Ancestors, John Yeardley of the fourth generation has a son, William, who has a son, John, and this son has a daughter, Margaret. This Margaret in The Yeardley Family Tree Chart is listed in the sixth generation as the wife of John Yeardley. We find one more generation listed in Tidewater Ancestors than we find in The Yeardley Family Tree Chart.

8   7 John Yeardley, eldest son, married Elizabeth Byrkes, (Burkes) daughter of William Byrkes of Stafford County.

9   8 Ralph Yeardley was born in 1551. He was a citizen and merchant tailor of Bionshaw Lane, London. He married twice. His first wife was Agness Abbott whom he married on May 15,

1575 at St. Mary's Woolwich. Agness died in 1575 (Tidewater Ancestors reports December 18, 1576). He married, secondly, in 1575 to Rhoda Marston, the daughter of James Marston and his wife, Catherine Chevall, daughter of Henry Chevell. Rhoda was buried on January 3, 1603/4. Ralph (Raphe) Yeardley wrote his will on August 25, 1603. He died while residing in the Parish of St. Saviours, Southwark. He was buried on January 15, 1603/4 and his will was probated on February 27, 1603/4. (See condensation of the will of Ralph Yeardley at the end of Recap of Significant Data: Yeardley.)

10   9   Ralph or Raphe Yeardley was a citizen and apothecary of London, dwelling in the Parish of St. Alban, Wood Street. He probably died in December 1655/56. His will was dated 5 June 1654 and was proved 4 January 1655/56 by John Yeardley, his son and executor.

George Yeardley/Yardley was the second son of Ralph and Rhoda. He was baptized on July 28, 1588 at St. Saviour's Parish in Southwark, London. His siblings were christened in the same parish. Raphe was christened on October 17, 1585, Anne on September 13, 1590, John on March 24, 1593 and Thomas was christened on October 11, 1595.

We do not know exactly when George Yeardley was born but it may have been earlier than 1588. When his father wrote his will in August 1603 he indicated that George was under twenty-one years of age.

George appears to have embarked upon a military career and spent some years of service in the Loew Countries before coming to Virginia. George sailed with an expedition to Virginia on May 15, 1609. The flotilla ran into a terrible storm. All, eventually, reached their haven except Captain Yeardley's ship, "Sea Venture". It was sinking when they landed on Bermuda. All survived and managed to build two small boats and in these succeeded in making their way to Jamestown. We assume that one of these small boats was called the "Deliverance" and that they landed in May 1610.

Later, he returned to England with a considerable estate acquired during his residence in Virginia. He returned to Virginia and was Deputy Governor from April 1616 to May 1617 in the absence of Governor Dale. He returned to London in 1617. On November 24, 1618, he was appointed Governor of Virginia and knighted by James I at Newmarket. He returned to Virginia on the ship, Gift, on April 19, 1619 and was Governor until November 18, 1621. In the massacre of 1622, twenty-two of his people were killed at Weyanoke, his plantation on the James River. In 1625 he was appointed deputy governor in the absence of Sir Francis Wyatt. On 19 April 1626 he was appointed Governor for a second time by Charles I and remained until his death in November 1627.

He was frequently engaged in conflict with the Indians. In 1616 he defeated the Chickahominies and in 1622 with 300 men devastated the country of the Nansemonds.

During his residence in Virginia, Sir George possessed large tracts of land. After his return in 1619 he visited Virginia's Eastern Shore and made friends with Debedeavon, "The Laughing King", the Emperor of the Eastern Shore. About 1620 Sir George was granted a large tract of land by Debedeavon. Sir George was granted patents on this 3700 acres at Hungars by order of the Court in 1625. Sir George never lived on this land.

Sir George's plantation was "Weyanoke" which contained 2200 acres. "When the settlers arrived at Jamestown in 1607, the Weyanoke Indians held the country on the north side of James River, between the Chickahominy River and Queen's Creek in Charles City County, which they called Little Weyanoke, and on the south side of the James River, from Upper Chippokes Creek to Powell's Creek, which they called Greater Weyanoke. A land grant issued in 1650 located Weyanoke Old Town at the head of Powell's Creek on the southside of the river".

In 1617 he received from the Indian King of the Weyanokes 2200 acres of land on Queen's Creek which was confirmed to him by the London Company. This land lay upon the Weyanoke bend of the river, between Queen's Creek and Mapsico Creek back to the headwaters.

Sir George owned 1000 acres on the south side of the river. He called this Flowerdew Hundred and in 1621 he erected a windmill, the first mill of any kind in this country. He later sold this land to Abraham Peirsey.

Sir George Yeardley died in November 1627 and was buried at Jamestown on the 13th day of that month. He is believed to be buried in the chancel of the church at Jamestown in the "Knight's Tomb" although the brass inscription plate was destroyed when the church burned in 1676. His will was probated on February 14, 1628 in London. He was the Governor of the Virginia colony from 1618 to 1621 and from 1626 to 1627.

From the book, George Yeardley Governor of Virginia and Organizer of the General Assembly in 1619 by Nora Turman, it can be determined that the marriage of Sir George and Temperance Flowerdew took place in November 1617 and that their first child, Argall was born 31 August 1618 in London, England. Argall was six years old when the Muster of the Inhabitants of Virginia was taken. Mrs. Turman says that Sir George, Lady Yeardley and Argall sailed for Virginia in February 1619.

Temperance Flowerdew, daughter of Anthony Flowerdew of Hethersett, County Norfolk was born ca. 1594 and died in

Virginia in 1629. Sir George and Temperance had three children. The eldest was Elizabeth, Argall the second was born in 1618 and Francis, the youngest, was born ca. 1623/4. In the Muster of persons living in Virginia in 1624/25, we find:

Sir George Yeardley, Knt. came in "Deliverance" in 1609

Temperance Lady Yeardley came in "Falcon" in 1608

Elizabeth Yeardley age 6 years

Argall Yeardley age 4 years

Francis Yeardley age 1 year   "Children born heare"

The information in this Muster does not agree with other information.   There is no proof that Temperance came to Virginia in 1608; no proof that Elizabeth is older than Argall and that he was born in Virginia except for the Muster.   On the other hand there is no proof that the information in the Muster is not correct.

Sir George wrote his will 12 October 1627 and it was proved 14 February 1628 by Temperance Yeardley, relict and executrix.   (See condensation of George Yardley's Will at the end of the Recap of Significant Data: Yeardley and following Ralph Yeardley's Will).

George left 3700 acres of land to his eldest son, Argall, who was nine years old.

Secondly, Temperance Yeardley, about 31 March 1628, married Colonel Francis West, brother of Lord Delaware, and at the time deputy governor of Virginia.   The marriage was of short duration as Temperance died intestate within the year following this second marriage.   After her death, the brother of Sir George, Ralph Yeardley, was granted administration of the estate of Sir George and much litigation ensued.   All of the children would have been underage at the time of their mother's death and Mrs. Turman says that Ralph Yeardley became guardian of the children. Soon after Temperance's death, her husband, Francis West, returned to England and entered suit against the estate of Sir George. He sued for a third of the estate. The outcome of this suit is unknown. Francis West later married Jane, daughter of Sir Henry Davis.

11   10   Argall (sometimes this name is given as Argoll) Yeardley, our ancestor, was a colonel. He was born on August 31, 1618 in England. He married twice. His first wife was Frances Knight whom he married on March 9, 1635/6 in the church of St. Stephen Coleman, London. She was of the parish of St. Giles in the Field, London. Argall and Frances returned to Virginia in 1639. Frances died prior to 1649.

An Elizabeth Yeardley married a Richard Alexander, 7 Nov. 1637, in Saint Andrew by the Wardrobe, London. This could have been Sir George's daughter who would have been age 17 at the time of her marriage. This is the only clue to what may have happened to Elizabeth.

The third child Francis about 1645 married Sarah Offley as her third husband. Sarah had previously been the widow of Captain Adam Thoroughgood and Captain John Gookin. Francis Yeardley died without heirs in Norfolk County, Virginia in 1655.

Records of Argall and Francis are found on the Eastern Shore. Argall Yeardley was granted a patent in 1638 for 3700 acres of land. This is the same land King Debedeavon gave to Sir George in 1620 and was confirmed by order of the Court in 1625. Argall lived on this land and became a man of prominence in the affairs of the Eastern Shore.

J. C. Wise in his history of Virginia's Eastern Shore describes the smallness of the houses. The residence of Argall Yeardley of Northampton (Mattawoman Creek) was equally small, containing a hall, a hall chamber, a parlor, two small chambers next to the parlor, a kitchen and a dairy, both of the latter probably detached.

It is probable that for a time Francis lived with his brother. In 1642, Francis Yeardley received his Commission as the first appointed Captain of the militia on the Eastern Shore. We are told that musters of the militia were regularly held at Argall Yeardley's plantation.

Argall was a justice of Northampton County and imported the first horse to the Eastern Shore.

He died in 1655. The appraisal of his estate was returned on October 29, 1655. Argall and Frances Knight had three children, Argoll, Rose and Frances.

Argall secondly, married Ann Custis, daughter of John and Joane Custis. Argall raised tobacco and shipped much of it to Rotterdam, Holland in his own ships. After the death of Frances, Argall, on a trip to Rotterdam married Ann Custis and brought her back to Virginia with him. Ann and Argall had two sons. Ann Custis' father had a tavern in Rotterdam where the English made their headquarters.

Colonel Argall Yeardley died intestate in Northampton County before 29 October 1655. Ann later married John Wilcox and, after he died in 1662, she probably married John Luke.

Tidewater Ancestors has the Niemeyers descending from Argall Yeardley and Ann Custis. Information from Gwen Garner shows that they descend from Frances Knight, the first wife of Colonel Argall Yeardley via Frances Yeardley, one of their daughters.

12   11 Argoll was baptized ca. 1644 in Virginia. Rose, the second child, was baptized ca. 1643 and the eldest, Frances, was baptized ca. 1641.

Tidewater Ancestors states that Frances is the daughter of Ann Custis. Later research by Mrs. Wilbur C. Garner finds that Frances, Argoll and Rose are children of Frances and

Argall while Henry and Edmund are the children of Argall and Ann Custis.

Argoll Yeardley was one of the five children of Argall Yeardley. Argoll was born in 1644 and married Sarah Mitchell, daughter of John Michael and his wife, Elizabeth Thoroughgood, daughter of Captain Adam Thoroughgood and his wife, Sarah Offley. Argoll wrote his will on January 3, 1681/2 and the will was probated on March 2, 1682. His wife died as Sarah Michael Yeardley Watt Maddux. Her will was written on March 20, 1694/5 and probated on March 29, 1697.

Rose Yeardley married, first, Thomas Ryding (January 4, 1662 in Hungars Parish) and, second, Robert Peale.

Frances Yeardley married Lt. Col. Adam Thoroughgood of Lynnhaven.

Ralph Yeardley's Will (condensed) is as follows.

After my debts paid and my funeral discharged I will that all and singular my goods, chattels and debts shall be parted and divided into three equal portions according to the laudable use and custom of the City of London. One full third part thereof I give and bequeath to Rhoda my well beloved wife, to her own use, in full satisfaction of such part or portion of my goods, chattels and debts as she may claim to have by the custom of the same city. One other full third part thereof I give and bequeath amongst my children, Raphe, George, John, Thomas, and Anne Yardley and to such other child or children as yet unborn as I shall happen to have at the time of my decease, to be equally parted, shared and divided between them, and to be satisfied and paid to my said sons at the accomplishment of their several ages of one and twenty years, and to my said daughter at the accomplishment of her age of one and twenty years or marriage, which shall happen first, etc., etc. And the other third part thereof I reserve to myself therewith to perform and pay these my legacies hereafter mentioned, that is to say, I give and bequeath to the poor of the Parish of St. Saviours in Southwark where I now dwell, twenty shillings to be divided amongst them by the discretion of the overseers of the poor there for the time being, and to such of the batchelors and sixteen men of the company of merchant tailors, London, as shall accompany my body to burial, twenty shillings for a recreation to be made unto them, and to the Vestrymen of the said parish, twenty shillings more for a recreation to be made unto them.

I give and bequeath unto my sister Palmer a ring of gold to the value of six shillings eight pence, and to my cousin, John Palmer, her husband, a like ring of like value and to my daughter, Earbye, my first wife's wedding ring, and to my son Earbye, her husband, my best cloak, and to my cousin Richard Yearwood, my black cloth gown of Turkish fashion. The rest and residue of all and singular of my goods, etc., etc. I wholly give unto my said children, etc., etc. Item I give and bequeath to my brother, Yardley, a ring of gold of the value of six shillings eight pence. And I ordain and make the said Raph Yardley, my son, to be the executor, etc., etc. and the said Richard Yearwood and my son, Edward Earby, overseers. As to my freehold lands and hereditiments, I will, devise, give and bequeath my messuage, lands, etc. in Southwark or elsewhere with my said children.

Ralphs' son in law, Edward Earbye died in 1616/17 and the wife, Catherine, who survived him, was probably "my daughter, Earbye" to whom he refers in his will. This is probably a child by his first wife. Edward Earbye's will was written 27 February 1616/17 and was proved 24 March 1616/17 by Catherine Irbie.

Condensation of George Yeardley's Will

To wife Temperance all and every part and parcell of all such household stuff, plate, linen, woollen or any other goods, moveable or immoveable, of what nature or quality soever, as to me are belonging, and which now at the time of the date hereof are being and remaining within this house in James City wherein I now dwell. Item, as touching and concerning all the rest of my whole estate consisting of goods, debts, servants, negars, cattle, or any other thing or things, commodities or profits whatsoever to me belonging or appertaining, either here in this country of Virginia, in England or elsewhere, together with my plantation of 1000 acres of land at Stanley in Warwicke River, my will and desire is that the same be, all and every part and parcell thereof, sold to the best advantage for tobacco, and the same to be transported as soon as may be either this year or the next, as my wife shall find occasion, into England, and there to be sold and turned into money, etc., etc. The money resulting from this (with sundry additions) to be divided into three parts, of which one part to go to said wife, one part to eldest son Argoll Yeardley, and the other part to son Francis and to Elizabeth Yeardley equally.

Signed Sir George Yeardley

Witnesses:

    Abraham Peirsey
    Susanna Hall
    William Clayborne

Extracts from "The Complete Book of Emigrants 1607-1660"

1619 Jul 30   Report of Proceedings of the General Assembly at James City, Virginia, under Governor Sir George Yeardley. (CSPC)

1620 Mar 6   Grant by Sir George Yeardley to George Harrison of Charles City, gent. of 200 acres for having transported three servants: Jeremy Whiniard, James Taylor and William Broomeman.

1624 Feb 28   George Yeardley (among many named who) signed a report from the Governor and Council of Virginia at James City to the king rebutting the accusations against the plantation made by Captain Nathaniel Butler. Six thousand, not ten thousand persons have been transported to Virginia who, for the most part, were wasted by the cruelty of Sir Thomas Smyth's government (PRO:CO 1/3/5)

1624 Sep 15   Licence to Governor Sir Francis Wyatt to return from Virginia to England on the decease of his father and for Sir George Yeardley to replace him, and if he should die, John Harvey. (CSPC)

1625 Feb 4   Musters of the inhabitants of Virginia. (Ages are shown after the name followed by ship and date of arrival where these are given). Sir George Yeardley's men: Maximillian Stone 36 by Temperance 1620; Elizabeth his wife by the same ship; Maximillian his son 9 months; Robert Guy 22 by Swan 1619; Edward Yates 18 by Duty 1691; Cesar Puggett 20 by Diana 1619: Allexander Sanders 24 by Truelove 1623; William Strachey 17 by Temperance 1620; George Whitehand 24 by Temperance 1620; Henery King 22 by Jonathan 1620; John Day 24 by London Merchant 1620; John Day's wife by same ship. Dwellers: John Root by Gift; Walter Blake by Swan; Thomas Watts by Treasurer. Dead: David Dutton; Richard Blake. The rest of his servants are reckoned at James City.

1625 Feb 4   Report of proceedings in Virginia of the complaint of Captain Martin against Sir George Yeardley and Captain (John) Bargrave, including the examinations of witnesses Henry Coltman, John Fludd, Matha (sic) Symonce, Nicholas Hoskins, Luke Boyce and Ensign Isacke Chaplen. (PRO:CO1)

1626 Mar 4   Commission appointing Sir George Yeardley as Governor of Virginia and Francis West, John Harvey, George Sandys, John Pott, Roger Smith, Ralph Hamor, Samuel Mathews, Abraham Piersey, William Claybourne, William Tucker, Job Whitaker, Edward Blaney and William Ferrar as members of council.

1626 Apr 19   To Governor Yeardley of Virginia. You are to send by the first ship a list of the several plantations, the number of people in each distinguished by sex, age, profession and condition, and the place of everyone's birth and the name of their parents here in England, as well as what property belonged to the late Virginia Company. (APC&CSPC)

1626   Lands granted by patent in Virginia (number of acres shown in parentheses after each name: Corporation of Elizabeth City. The Eastern Shore over the Bay. (Includes Sir George Yeardley (3700 at Hangers). (PRO:CO1/ pp. 4-27)

1627 Apr   Sir George Yeardley trusts that Sir Thomas Merry will be satisfied with what has been done in respect of John Puntis estate in Virginia. (CSPC)

1627 Dec 20   Governor Francis West certifies the death of Governor Sir George Yeardley of Virginia. (CSPC)

1629 Jul   Petition of Edmund Rossingham that his uncle Sir George Yeardley died before making satisfactiopn to him for having raised the value of his estate and that his brother Ralph Yeardley had taken out letters of administration. (CSPC)

1630 Jan   Petition of Edmund Rossingham. The King having taken the government of Virginia on 11 July 1629, he prays that his cause against Ralph Yeardley, apothecary of London, may be determined. (SSPC)

1630 Feb 19 The Privy Council orders Ralph Yeardley to pay 200 pounds to Edmund Rossingham. (CSPC)

Abbreviations:

 CSPC-Calendars of State Papers. American and Colonial Series 1574-1660, ed W. Noel Sainsbury.

 PRO:C0-Public Records Office, Kew, Richmond, Surrey TW 9 4 DU; England

 APC-Acts of the Privy Council of England (1613-1631)

 EEAC-English Estates of American Colonists (Vol. 1)

     The present Niemeyers are direct descendents of this Yeardley line. In Tidewater Ancestors, the noted generation should be changed as follows.

19	18	Lt. Col. William Frederic Niemeyer, C. S. A.
		m. Sarah Campbell Smith
20	19	John Frederic Niemeyer m. Lucrece Bilisoly
21	20	Antonio Bilisoly Niemeyer m. Lutie Stuart Spotts
22	21	Antonio Bilisoly Niemeyer, Jr. m. Alice Virginia Berry

23	22	William Frederic Niemeyer	Frank Berry Niemeyer	John Stuart Niemeyer
		m.	m.	m.

		Carolyn Louise Holtzhauer	Shannon Page Eadie	April Michelle Tripp
24	23	John Cameron Niemeyer	Jacob Douglas Niemeyer	John Stuart Niemeyer, Jr.
		Kyle Antonio Niemeyer		

An interesting story related to Flowerdew Hundred:

From an article by George Tucker entitled, "Jesse James' and Dolley Madison's family tree"

John Woodson and his wife, Sarah, sailed from England on January 10, 1619 aboard the ship, George, bound for Virginia. Also, on board was Governor Sir George Yeardley and his bride, Temperance Flowerdew. After a "sore voyage" the George reached Jamestown on April 19, 1619.

Yeardley had patented on a previous visit in Virginia, one thousand acres of land on the south side of the James and named it Flowerdew Hundred. It was here that John and Sarah settled and continued to live after Sir George sold this land to Abraham Peirsey in 1624.

During the 1622 massacre, Flowerdew Hundred fared better than many settlements and John and Sarah Woodson were survivors. When the Indians attacked again in 1644 John was killed. Sarah saved her two sons, John and Robert, by hiding one under a tub and one in a potato hole, thereby gaining one the nickname Tub and the other Tatorhole.

When the first Virginia census was taken in 1625, the muster showed that the Woodsons were still at Peirsey's Hundred. By 1674 the Woodson's sons were living at Curles' Neck on the James River. It is from Robert Woodson that Dolly Payne Madison and Jesse Woodson James were descended through later intermarriages between Robert's offspring and the Payne and James families.

Jesse's paternal forebears originally settled in Henrico and Goochland Counties but moved in 1811 to Kentucky. In 1842, Jesse's parents, Robert Sallee and Zeralda Cole James moved to Missouri. It was here that Jesse was born on September 5, 1847.

de Eardley

Refer to Yeardley family, generation 7

Under generation, the first column is the generation listed on page 123 of <u>Tidewater Ancestors</u> and the second column is for the de Eardley lineage. The persons from whom we are descended are in bold print.

Generation

0   1   **Oliver Yardley** m. **Margaret de Eardley**

7   2   **John Yardley** m. **Margaret Yardley**

Recap of Significant Data: de Eardley

Generation

1   Margaret de Eardley lived during the reign of Edward IV, 1461-1483.

The present Niemeyers are direct descendents of this de Eardley line. In <u>Tidewater Ancestors</u> the noted generation should be changed as follows.

19	14	Lt. Col. William Frederic Niemeyer, C. S. A. m. Sarah Campbell Smith		
20	15	John Frederic Niemeyer m. Lucrece Bilisoly		
21	16	Antonio Bilisoly Niemeyer m. Lutie Stuart Spotts		
22	17	Antonio Bilisoly Niemeyer, Jr. m. Alice Virginia Berry		
23	18	William Frederic Niemeyer m. Carolyn Louise Holtzhauer	Frank Berry Niemeyer m. Shannon Page Eadie	John Stuart Niemeyer m. April Michelle Tripp
24	19	John Cameron Niemeyer Kyle Antonio Niemeyer	Jacob Douglas Niemeyer	John Stuart Niemeyer, Jr.

Byrkes (Burkes)

Refer to Yardley family, generation 8

Under generation, the first column is the generation listed on page 123 of <u>Tidewater Ancestors</u> and the second column is for the Byrkes lineage. The persons from whom we are descended are in bold print.

Generation

1   **William Byrkes**

8   2   **John Yardley** m. **Elizabeth Byrkes**

9   3   I-Agness Abbott m. **Ralph Yardley** m. II-**Rhoda Marston**

Recap of Significant Data: Byrkes
Generation

1   William Byrkes was of Stafford County.

The present Niemeyers are direct descendents of this Byrkes line. In <u>Tidewater Ancestors</u> the noted generation should be changed as follows.

19   13   Lt. Col. William Frederic Niemeyer, C. S. A.
                    m. Sarah Campbell Smith
20   14   John Frederic Niemeyer m. Lucrece Bilisoly
21   15   Antonio Bilisoly Niemeyer m. Lutie Stuart Spotts
22   16   Antonio Bilisoly Niemeyer, Jr. m. Alice Virginia
                    Berry
23   17   William Frederic   Frank Berry   John Stuart
                    Niemeyer   Niemeyer   Niemeyer
                       m.   m.   m.
                 Carolyn Louise   Shannon Page   April Michelle
                  Holtzhauer   Eadie   Tripp

24   18   John Cameron   Jacob Douglas   John Stuart
               Niemeyer   Niemeyer   Niemeyer, Jr.
               Kyle Antonio
                 Niemeyer

Marston

Refer to Yardley family, generation 9

Under generation, the first column is the generation listed on page 123 of <u>Tidewater</u> <u>Ancestors</u> and the second column is for the Marston lineage. The persons from whom we are descended are in bold print.

Generation

| | 1 | **James Marston** m. **Catherine Chevall** |
| 9 | 2 | I-Agness Abbott m. **Ralph Yardley** m. II-**Rhoda Marston** |

Recap of Significant Data: Marston

Generation

1 James Marston was a citizen of London.

The present Niemeyers are direct descendents of this Marston line. In <u>Tidewater</u> <u>Ancestors</u> the noted generation should be changed as follows.

19	12	Lt. Col. William Frederic Niemeyer, C. S. A. m. Sarah Campbell Smith		
20	13	John Frederic Niemeyer m. Lucrece Bilisoly		
21	14	Antonio Bilisoly Niemeyer m. Lutie Stuart Spotts		
22	15	Antonio Bilisoly Niemeyer, Jr. m. Alice Virginia Berry		
23	16	William Frederic Niemeyer m. Carolyn Louise Holtzhauer	Frank Berry Niemeyer m. Shannon Page Eadie	John Stuart Niemeyer m. April Michelle Tripp
24	17	John Cameron Niemeyer Kyle Antonio Niemeyer	Jacob Douglas Niemeyer	John Stuart Niemeyer, Jr.

Chevall

Refer to Yardley family, generation 9

Under generation, the first column is the generation listed on page 123 of <u>Tidewater</u> <u>Ancestors</u> and the second column is for the Chevall lineage. The persons from whom we are descended are in bold print.

Generation

    1   **Henry Chevall**

    2   **Catherine Chevell** m. I-**James Marston**

               m. II-Thomas Saris m. III-John Hyde

9   3 I-Agness Abbott m. **Ralph Yardley** m. II-**Rhoda Marston**

Recap of Significant Data: Chevall

Generation

    1   Henry Chevall was a citizen of London. Information obtained from The Church of Latter Day Saints reports that Henricus Chevell married Alicia Robinson, 16 June 1560, St. Martins in the Field, Westminister, London but we don't know that Catherine Chevall was their daughter.

    2   Catherine Chevall first married James Marston. When he died, Catherine married Thomas Saris and had a son, John, who was an uncle to George Yeardley. John became a famous navigator and traveler and wrote books of voyages to India, China, and the Far East. Catherine's third husband was John Hyde.

    The present Niemeyers are direct descendents of this Chevall line. In <u>Tidewater</u> <u>Ancestors</u> the noted generation should be changed as follows.

19   13   Lt. Col. William Frederic Niemeyer, C. S. A.

              m. Sarah Campbell Smith

20   14   John Frederic Niemeyer m. Lucrece Bilisoly

21	15	Antonio Bilisoly Niemeyer m. Lutie Stuart Spotts		
22	16	Antonio Bilisoly Niemeyer, Jr. m. Alice Virginia Berry		
23	17	William Frederic Niemeyer m. Carolyn Louise Holtzhauer	Frank Berry Niemeyer m. Shannon Page Eadie	John Stuart Niemeyer m. April Michelle Tripp
24	18	John Cameron Niemeyer Kyle Antonio Niemeyer	Jacob Douglas Niemeyer	John Stuart Niemeyer, Jr.

Under generation, the first column is the generation listed on page 145 of <u>Tidewater</u> <u>Ancestors</u> and the second column is for the Custis lineage. The persons from whom we are descended are in bold print.

Generation

11 1 **Col Argall Yeardley** m. I-**Frances Knight**

II-Ann Custis

Recap of Significant Data: Custis

Generation

11 0 Col. Argall Yeardley married first Frances Knight of the parish of St. Giles in the Field, London. They were married 9 March 1635/6 in the Church of St. Stephen Coleman, London. She was the mother of his three children, Argoll, Rose and Frances.

Argall shipped much of his tobacco to Rotterdam. After the death of Frances Yeardley, he made a trip to Rotterdam. While there he married Ann Custis and brought her back to Virginia with him. She was the daughter of John and Joane Custis. They had two sons, Edmund and Henry.

Since we are descended from Frances Knight Yeardley the Niemeyers are not related to the Custis family.

19 0 Lt. Col. William Frederic Niemeyer, C. S. A. m. Sarah Campbell Smith

20 0 John Frederic Niemeyer m. Lucrece Bilisoly

21 0 Antonio Bilisoly Niemeyer m. Lutie Stuart Spotts

22 0 Antonio Bilisoly Niemeyer, Jr. m. Alice Virginia Berry

23	0	William Frederic Niemeyer m. Carolyn Louise Holtzhauer	Frank Berry Niemeyer m. Shannon Page Eadie	John Stuart Niemeyer m. April Michelle Tripp
24	0	John Cameron Niemeyer Kyle Antonio Niemeyer	Jacob Douglas Niemeyer	John Stuart Niemeyer, Jr.

Offley

Information compiled by: Souil W. Garner
Under generation, the first column is the generation listed on page 173 of <u>Tidewater</u> <u>Ancestors</u> and the second column is for the Offley lineage. The persons from whom we are descended are in bold print.

Generation

1   1   **Margery ...**
                      m.
        I-**John Offley** II-... Dillarne

2   2   **William Offley**
                       m.
        I-Elizabeth Dillorne   II-**Elizabeth Rogerson Wright**

3   3   Sir   John   Margaret   Elizabeth   Margery
         Thomas   m.   m.   m.   m.
           m.   Alice   I-John   Thomas   I-Thomas
         Joane   Wright Nicholls   Blower   Mitchell
         Nicholis   II-Stephen   II-James
                           Kirton   Leveson

   Robert Thomas Richard William Hugh Katherine Anne
       m.

   Mrs..Rose

4   4   **Robert**   Ursala   Elizabeth
            m.

    Anne Osborne

5   5 Robert   Anne   Robert   John   Edward   Hewett   Robert

            m.   m.

       I-...Wortman   Elizabeth

       II-Robert Hayes   Moore

Katherine **Sarah** Elizabeth Abigail Stephen Thomas Susan

m.   m.   m.   m.   m.   m.

John   **I-Adam** I-William Edward Ursala   Henry

Baker   **Thorowgood** Clark   Windham Clarke   Hastings

      II-John   II-Benoni

      Goodkin Honywood

   III-Francis

   Yeardley

6   6   **Adam**   Ann   Sarah   Elizabeth

         m.   m.   m.   m.

    Frances I-Job   Simon   John

    Yeardley Chandler Overzee Michael, Sr.

       II-Gerard Fowke

Recap of Significant Data: Offley

Generation

    1   John Offley of Staffordshire, England, born circa 1460, was the first husband of Margery ?, who married secondly a Dillarne.

    2   William Offley, son of John and Margery Offley of Staffordshire, was born circa 1490, was Sheriff of Chester in 1517 and twice mayor of Stafford. He married twice. His first wife was Elizabeth Dillorne, and secondly, he married the widow of ...Rogerson, Alderman of Chester.

    As directed by the will of his son William, a monument was erected to his memory in St. Peter's Church, Chester, no trace of which now remains; but Ashmole has fortunately preserved a copy of the inscription, viz:

"Under the East window of the South lle, is a faire Alabaster Monument Erected wth the portraiture of a Man & Woman kneeling, under whome is this inscripion cut:

'Here lyeth the body of William Offley sometymes Sheriff of this Citty, to whom by two wives, God gave for yssue 26 Children, among whom Sr Thomas Offley his eldest son by his first wife Elizabeth Dillorne, attained to the dignity of Lord Maior of London; his second son John Offley, to the Maioltie of this Citty, an° 1553, to whome also by his second wife, Elizabeth Wright among other was borne Hugh Offley, Alderman of London, who by his last will gave unto the Corporacon of this Citty, 200^{ii}, with a yearely rent of 5^{li} to the releife of young Traders, & the poore of the same. And his eldest son by the same wife Robert Offley of London by his last will gave 600^{li} to this Citty, for the like Godly uses & releife of the poore, with an yearely exhibition of 5^l towarde the trasyning of some learned divine, being the son of a freeman of this Citty, in the univsity of Oxford or Cambridge wth 5^l toward his charge commencing M^r of Arte in either of the said Schooles.'

On the right hand, under the figures of their Sons and daughters, is cut this inscripcon:

'He had also by his second wife William Offley, a wor^{ll} Cittizen of London, & Marchant of the Staple; who had by Anne Offley 15 Children; who being blessed with greate wealth, by his last will, gave 300^l to this Citty, being the place of his nativity, to the benefit of young Traders; & ordained the ereccon of this Monum^t according to the discrecon of Anne Offley his loving wife & Executrix, who faithfully accomplished the same, in the yeare of o^r Lord 1602.'"

3   Sir Thomas Offley, buried September 17, 1582; married

Joane Nicholis.

Sir John Offley, High Sheriff of Stafford; M.P. for Stafford, and Gentleman of the Bedchamber to King James I; married Anne Fuller.

Margaret Offley, married first, John Nicholls; second Stephen Kirton, Alderman of London.

Elizabeth Offley, married Thomas Blower.

Margery Offley, married first, Thomas Michell; second, James Leveson.

Robert Offley, of Gracechurch Street, London; married the widow of Nicholas Rose.

William Offley of London; his will, dated December 21, 1600, contained this clause: "Item, I will that my Executors within One yeare next after my decease shall cawse to be made and set upp in some conveniente place of the parishe of Sainte Peeter in Chester aforesaid there still to remayne one faire table of white Allyblaster and black marble which shall cost Thirtie or ffortie poundes of lawfull money of England or there aboute wherein shalbe fairely engraven as well the picture of my ffather and mother withall their children as allso such wordes and sentences wrytten in ffaire letters as shalbe thoughte meete and agreable eyther for memorie or edification to be set downe by the discretion of my Executors uppon the same monumente."

The following corrections to the data on William Offley's children was provided by:

Mrs. E. Offley Evans
36 Maidenhead Road
Stratford-on-Avon
Warwickshire, England

<u>Corrections</u>: (John and Thomas were the first 2 sons of William. All the male children of William would have died long before James I succeeded to the throne.)

The 2nd son of William Offley was John who gave up his articles in London and returned to Chester to join his father in his leather busdiness. He married his father's stepdaughter, Alice Wright. He was Sheriff of Chester in 1544 and Mayor in 1553. The "Sir John Offley" was the grandson of Sir Thomas, not his brother.

Thomas was born in 1500 plus or minus a year or so, so his father, William, would have been born about 1480, not 1490.

William was never Mayor of Stafford. Mayors of Stafford only started in 1614. Prior to this, there were two Bailiffs and William was a Bailiff in 1510.)

Mrs. Evans continues, "It has to be borne in mind that the Offley MS was not written until the reign of James I, I calculate about 1620, and though the author knew the sons and grandsons of William, he could not possibly have known personally about William's parents, for instance, he gives William's second wife as the widow of Rogerson, whereas, in fact, she was the <u>daughter</u> of William Rogerson but widow of Alderman Wright. This is born out by the will of William Rogerson who speaks of 'my sonne-in-law, Wm. Offeley and my daughter Elizabeth his wife'."

"Also, I take the view that Wm. junior, who erected the monument to his parents, would have known the name of his own mother rather better than the author of the MS, and he names her as Elizabeth Wright, i.e. her name when she was married to William."

Robert Offley of Gracechurch Street, London, Citizen and Haberdasher, Merchant of the Staple, son of William Offley,

Mayor of Stafford, was born in Chester circa 1520. He was appointed an executor of the will of his brother, Sir Thomas Offley, Knight, which was dated August 5, 1580. Robert Offley married the widow of Nicholas Rose of London. She was buried at St. Benet's Church, London, October 8, 1572 He survived her nearly twenty four years and was buried at the same church, April 29, 1596. His will, dated April 9, 1596, was proved May 11th following.

4 Robert Offley, son of Robert Offley of Gracechurch Street, London, born circa 1564, was a Turkey merchant of Gracechurch Street. He married at St. Dionis, Backchurch, February 3, 1588-9, Anne Osborne, daughter of Sir Edward Osborne, Knight, Lord Mayor of London in 1583. She was baptized in St. Dionis' Church, March 25, 1570.

Robert Offley was buried at St. Benet's Church, May 16, 1625. Administration on the estate was granted to his son John Offley, May 27, 1625. Anne, the widow of Robert Offley, was buried in St. Augustine's Church, London, January 14, 1653-4. Her will, dated March 11, 1650, was proved at Westminster, February 13, 1653-4.

Ursala Offley, married May 5, 1572, Robert Brooke, Alderman of London.

Elizabeth Offley, married by license, dated April 22, 1574, William Gamage of St. Matthew's Parish.

5 Robert Offley, baptized February 8, 1589-90 died young.

Anne Offley, baptized January 3, 1590-1. She first married ... Wortman (or Workman) and secondly, Robert Hayes. She and Robert came to Virginia about 1637 for he patented 100 acres of land in Lower Norfolk County, 10 February 1637, upon the river of Lynnhaven, for the transportation of himself and his wife. Later, on 29 August 1643, he patented 750 acres in Lower Norfolk County, at Little Creek, adjoining the lands of

John Grimsditch and Capt. Adam Thorowgood, deceased, for the transportation of 15 persons including Robert Gilbert, Ann Hayes, his wife, Ann Wortman, John Wortman, Thomas Wortman, Alex. Hayes, Nathaniel Hayes and himself. Robert Hayes evidently died in 1648, for the administration of his estate was granted to his widow, Ann Hayes, in that year. Ann Hayes died in 1650. Her will was recorded 26 March 1650.

Robert Offley, baptized March 12, 1591-2; died young.

John Offley, baptized March 5, 1592-3; died August 28, 1667 married Elizabeth Moore.

Edward Offley, baptized August 29, 1594; died March 11, 1650.

Hewett Offley, baptized November 2, 1595; buried October 23, 1610.

Robert Offley, baptized May 23, 1599.

Susan Offley, baptized October 26, 1600; married Henry Hastings.

Thomas Offley, baptized February 4, 1601-2.

Stephen Offley, married Ursala Clarke.

Abigail Offley, baptized October 4, 1604. She married Edward Windham.

Elizabeth Offley, baptized February 12, 1606-7; married first, November 9, 1631, William Clark; married second, Benoni, sixth son of Sir Thomas Honywood.

Sarah Offley, baptized at St. Benet's Church, London, April 16, 1609; married first, in St. Anne's Church, Blackfriars, London, July 18, 1627, Captain Adam Thorogood. She married second, Captain John Gookin; third, Colonel Francis Yeardley.

Katherine Offley, married, January 3, 1614-15, John Baker of the Inner Temple

Sarah Offley, thirteenth child of Robert Offley and his wife, Anne Osborne, married Captain Adam Thorowgood and came to Virginia in the ship, "Hopewell" in 1628. After the death of Capt. Adam Thorowgood, his widow, Sarah, made two more marriages. She married as her second husband, a man of Irish descent, Capt. John Goodkin. After the death of Capt. Goodkin, she married about 1645, as her third husband, Francis Yeardley, the son of Sir George Yeardley and his wife, Temperance Lady Yeardley. Francis Yeardley died without heirs, in Norfolk County, Virginia, in 1655. Sarah Yeardley appears to have died in 1657. She was buried in the Lynnhaven Churchyard by the side of her second husband. The inscription which was placed on her tombstone was printed in the Richmond Examiner, 14 December 1819, and again in the Richmond Critic, 21 September 1889, page 4. It read,

"Here lieth ye body of Capt. John Gooking and also ye body of Mrs. Sarah Yardley who was wife to Capt. Adam Thorowgood, 1st, Capt. John Gooking, Collonell Francis Yardley, who deceased August 1657."

6 Adam Thorowgood married Frances Yardley, a daughter of Col. Argoll Yardley of Northampton County, Virginia. He was a Burgess for Lower Norfolk County in 1666, Justice and Sheriff in 1669, and Lt. Col. of militia. Adam and his wife, Frances, had seven children.

Ann Thorowgood married Job Chandler, who was a friend of Governor Stone of Maryland, and who was commissioned Receiver-General of Maryland, 1 August 1651. He died in 1659 and Ann, his widow, married Gerard Fowke of Charles County, Maryland, and he died in 1669.

Sarah Thorowgood married Simon Overzee. Sarah died in childbirth, October 1658. Simon Overzee married secondly, Elizabeth …, and he died in February or March 1659/60. On 18 December 1660, his widow, Elizabeth, was granted administration of his estate.

Elizabeth Thorowgood, married John Michael, Sr. of Northampton County, Virginia. She probably died about 1670.

The present Niemeyers are direct descendents of this Offley line. In Tidewater Ancestors, the noted generation should be changed as follows.

13   13   Lt. Col. William Frederic Niemeyer, C. S. A.
            m. Sarah Campbell Smith

14   14   John Frederic Niemeyer m. Lucrece Bilisoly

15   15   Antonio Bilisoly Niemeyer m. Lutie Stuart Spotts

16   16   Antonio Bilisoly Niemeyer, Jr. m. Alice Virginia Berry

17	17	William Frederic Niemeyer	Frank Berry Niemeyer	John Stuart Niemeyer
		m.	m.	m.
		Carolyn Louise Holtzhauer	Shannon Page Eadie	April Michelle Tripp
18	18	John Cameron Niemeyer	Jacob Douglas Niemeyer	John Stuart Niemeyer, Jr.
		Kyle Antonio Niemeyer		

Refer to Offley family, generation 2

Under generation, the first column is the generation listed on page 173 of <u>Tidewater Ancestors</u> and the second column is for the Rogerson lineage. The persons from whom we are descended are in bold print.

Generation

1	1	**William Rogerson** m.
2	2	I-Alderman m. **Elizabeth** m. II-**William** Wright **Rogerson** **Offley**

Recap of Significant Data: Offley

Generation

1   William Rogerson had a daughter, Elizabeth who married twice. Her first husband was Alderman Wright and her second husband was William Offley who had also married before he married Elizabeth Rogerson Wright.

The present Niemeyers are direct descendents of this Rogerson line. In <u>Tidewater Ancestors</u>, the noted generation should be changed as follows.

13	13	Lt. Col. William Frederic Niemeyer, C. S. A. m. Sarah Campbell Smith
14	14	John Frederic Niemeyer m. Lucrece Bilisoly
15	15	Antonio Bilisoly Niemeyer m. Lutie Stuart Spotts
16	16	Antonio Bilisoly Niemeyer, Jr. m. Alice Virginia Berry

17	17	William Frederic Niemeyer m. Carolyn Louise Holtzhauer	Frank Berry Niemeyer m. Shannon Page Eadie	John Stuart Niemeyer m. April Michelle Tripp
18	18	John Cameron Niemeyer Kyle Antonio Niemeyer	Jacob Douglas Niemeyer	John Stuart Niemeyer, Jr.

Thoroughgood
Compiled by Souil W. Garner
Distributed by Mrs. Wilbur C. Garner

Under generation, the first column is the generation listed on page 194 of <u>Tidewater Ancestors</u> and the second column is for the Thoroughgood lineage.   The persons from whom we are descended are in bold print.

Generation

5	1	**William Thoroughgood** m. **Anne Edwards**			
6	2	**Adam Thoroughgood** m. **Sarah Offley**			
7	3	**Adam**	Ann	Sarah	Elizabeth
		m.	m.	m.	m.
		Frances	I-Job	Simon	John
		Yeardley	Chandler	Overzee	Michael,
			II-Gerard		Sr.
			Fowke		

Recap of Significant Data: Thoroughgood (Thorowgood)
Generation

The name of this family has been spelled variously and has appeared as Thoroughgood, Thorowgood, and Thorogood.

1   0   John Thorogood of Chelston Temple, Hertfordshire, England is the first ancestor of this line as shown by the Visitations of the counties of Essex and Norfolk.

2   0   Thomas Thorogood, son of John, was born about 1470 at Chelston Temple. He had two sons, Nicholas and John.

3   0   Nicholas Thorogood of Chelston Temple had a son, Roger.

John Thorogood of Chelston Temple was born about 1500.

4   0   John Thorogood, son of John, of Frelsted in Essex County was born about the year 1530 and married the daughter

of … Lucken.   Their children were

5   1   William Thorogood of Grimston, Norfolk, married 1st Anne Edwards, 2nd Mary Dodge (widow), 3rd Alice Holbeck (widow). He was born about 1560 and was commissary to the Bishop of Norwich in 1587.

Thomas Thorogood married … Flower of Essex, and had a son William.

Lawrence Thorogood of Stondham Parva, Suffolk; married . . .Montjoy of Essex and had sons, Edmund and John.

The town of Grimston is about seven miles east of Lynn.   In the Domesday Book it is written Grimestuna, Grunestuna and Ernestuna and takes its name from a rivulet that arises by the church.

William Thorogood's coat of arms appears in Harleian Manuscript 4756, folio I, with the following note: "A confirmation of this Armes and Crest under the hand and Seale of Sr. Wm. Seager, Garter to Willm. Thorowgood, Officiall within the Diocese of Norwich, son of John Thorowgood of Felsted in Essex, son of John, yonger brother to Nicholas Thorowgood of Chelston Temple in Co. Hertford gent. Dated 24 day of March Ao. 1620."

William and Anne Edwards were the parents of:

6   2   Edward, Sir John, Thomas, Edmund, William, Mordaunt, Adam, Frances, and Robert.

Sir John, Knight of Kensington in Middlesex; a pensioner in ordinary to King Charles First and by him knighted; later of the Privy Chamber Extraordinary to King Charles Second; married Frances.

Thomas of Grimston "B.A. from Queen's College, Cambridge, 1613-1614; M.A. 1617 (incorporated July 9, 1622); B.D. 1624; Rector of Little Massingham, 1620; of Grimston, Norfolk, 1625, and one of the assembly of Divines." Twice clerk of the Convocation.

Edmund of Markham, in Norfolk; married Frances, daughter of Edward Smith of Chelston Temple in Essex, gentleman and had issue as shown in the Visitation of Middlesex, 1663.

Mordaunt died at the Siege of Breda.

Adam Thoroughgood was born about 1603 at Grimston, Norfolk County, England. He left home when he was about eighteen years and came to Virginia from Lynn in the ship "Charles" in 1621. His home village of Grimston was about seven miles to the east of Lynn. He settled at a place on the James River called by the Indian name "Kicotan" but which is now Hampton, Virginia.

We do not know how many crossings Adam Thoroughgood made between England and Virginia but in 1627 he was back in England. On July 18, 1627, he married Sarah Offley at St. Anne's, Blackfriars, London. Sarah was the daughter of Robert Offley and his wife, Anne Osborne. She was baptized at St. Benet's, London, 16 April 1609.

Adam Thoroughgood returned to Virginia with his wife, Sarah, in the ship "Hopewell" in 1628. He became known as Captain Adam Thoroughgood, and he acquired much land by patent. He appears to have used "head rights" as a means of land acquisition and to have accumulated a considerable number of "headrights" from 1628-1634.
In "Cavaliers and Pioneers" by Mrs. Nell Marion Nugent, p. 22, we find record of the land patent granted to Adam Thoroughgood of 5350 acres of land. This patent was   granted on June 24, 1635, "at the especial recommendation of him from their Lordships and others of his Majesties most Honorable privie Councell, to the Governor and Council of State of Virginia." This land was stated to be due him as follows:
50 acres for his personal adventure

50 acres for the personal adventure of his wife, Sarah
5250 acres for the transport of 105 persons in the following ships

the Hopewell in 1628

the True Love in 1628

the Hopewell in 1628

a French ship in 1629

the Africa in 1633

the Ark in 1633

the Hopewell in 1633

the Bona Adventure in 1634

the Mr. Middleton in 1634

the Merchant's Hope in 1634

the John and Dorothy in 1634.

Adam Thoroughgood appears to have been in England in 1633 or 1634 for he and his brother in law, Edward Windham, were aboard the "John and Dorothy" when it arrived in Virginia in 1634.

The land acquired by this patent was situated in the area that was later known as Princess Anne County, Virginia. It bordered on a beautiful bay that Adam called Lynnhaven Bay. It was here he built his home. Here he amassed a large fortune and rose to much distinction. He represented Elizabeth City County in the Virginia Assembly in 1629, 1631, and 1632. In 1637, he was a member of the Virginia Council, and in the same year was presiding justice of the County Court of Lower Norfolk.

He died in the spring of 1640 at the age of 37 years. His will was dated 17 February 1639/40 and was proved 27 April 1640. It is of record in Portsmouth, Virginia. In his will he named:

Brother   Edward Windham

Brother   Robert Hayes
Godson   Adam Keeling
Godson   Jean Wheeler
Wife   Sarah
Son   Adam
Daughter   Anne
Daughter   Sarah
Daughter   Elizabeth

Edward Windham was, in fact, his brother in law who had married Abigail Offley, a sister of Sarah. Abigail was about seven years older than Sarah, she having been baptized 4 October 1602.

Robert Hayes was, also, a brother in law who had married Anne Offley, another of Sarah Thoroughgood's sisters. Anne was baptized 3 January 1590/91. She first married ... Wortman (or Workman) and second Robert Hayes. Robert and Anne appear to have come to Virginia about 1637 for he patented 100 acres of land in Lower Norfolk County, 10 February 1637, upon the River of Lynnhaven for the transportation of himself and his wife. Later, on 29 August 1643, he patented 750 acres in Lower Norfolk County, at Little Creek, adjoining the lands of John Grimaditch and Capt. Adam Thoroughgood, deceased, for the transportation of 15 persons including Robert Gilbert, Ann Hayes, his wife, Ann Wortman, John Wortman, Thomas Wortman, Alex. Hayes, Nathaniel Hayes and himself. Robert Hayes evidently died in 1648 for the administration of his estate was granted to his widow, Ann Hayes, in that year. Ann (Offley Wortman Hayes) died in 1650. Her will was recorded 26 March 1650.

Frances Thorowgood married Robert Griffith of Wales.

Robert Thorowgood "late mayor and captain in King's Lynne in Norfolk;" married Anne, daughter and heir of Edward Hawke of Norfolk, gentleman.

7 3   Adam Thoroughgood married Frances Yeardley, daughter of Col. Argoll Yeardley of Northhampton County, Virginia. He was a Burgess of Lower Norfolk County in 1666, Justice and Sheriff in 1669 and Lt. Col. of militia. Adam and his wife had seven children, six boys and one girl.

Ann Thoroughgood married Job Chandler who was a friend of Governor Stone of Maryland and who was commissioned Receiver General of Maryland, 1 August 1651. He died in 1659 and Ann married Gerard Fowke of Charles County, Maryland who died in 1669.

Sarah Thoroughgood married Simon Overzee. Sarah died in childbirth, October 1658. Simon married a second time. He died in February or March 1659/60.

Elizabeth Thoroughgood married John Michael, Sr. of Northhampton County, Virginia. She died about 1670.

Chrysler Museum

The Thoroughgood House is thought to have been built around 1680 by a grandson of Adam Thoroughgood, one of Virginia Beach's earliest settlers. Thoroughgood, born in England and the son of a clergyman, acquired more than 5,000 acres along the western branch of the Lynnhaven River in 1634.

The present Niemeyers are direct descendents of this Thoroughgood line. In <u>Tidewater Ancestors,</u> the noted generation should be changed as follows.

14   10   Lt. Col. William Frederic Niemeyer, C. S. A.
                   m. Sarah Campbell Smith.

15   11   John Frederic Niemeyer m. Lucrece Bilisoly.

16   12   Antonio Bilisoly Niemeyer m. Lutie Stuart Spotts

17   13   Antonio Bilisoly Niemeyer, Jr. m. Alice Virginia
                   Berry

18	14	William Frederic Niemeyer	Frank Berry Niemeyer	John Stuart Niemeyer
		m.	m.	m.
		Carolyn Louise Holtzhauer	Shannon Page Eadie	April Michelle Tripp
19	15	John Cameron Niemeyer	Jacob Douglas Niemeyer	John Stuart Niemeyer, Jr.
		Kyle Antonio Niemeyer		

Edwards

Under generation, the first column is the generation listed on page 194 of <u>Tidewater Ancestors</u> and the second column is for the Edwards lineage. The persons from whom we are descended are in bold print.

Generation

	1	**Henry Edwards**
5	2	**William Thorowgood** m. **Anne Edwards**

Recap of Significant Data: Edwards
Generation

Henry Edwards is of Norwich, England.

The present Niemeyers are direct descendents of this Edwards line. In <u>Tidewater Ancestors,</u> the noted generation should be changed as follows.

14	11	Lt. Col. William Frederic Niemeyer, C. S. A. m. Sarah Campbell Smith
15	12	John Frederic Niemeyer m. Lucrece Bilisoly
16	13	Antonio Bilisoly Niemeyer m. Lutie Stuart Spotts
17	14	Antonio Bilisoly Niemeyer, Jr. m. Alice Virginia Berry

18	15	William Frederic Niemeyer m. Carolyn Louise Holtzhauer	Frank Berry Niemeyer m. Shannon Page Eadie	John Stuart Niemeyer m. April Michelle Tripp
19	16	John Cameron Niemeyer Kyle Antonio Niemeyer	Jacob Douglas Niemeyer	John Stuart Niemeyer, Jr.

Mordaunt

This information furnished by Lewis Kirby

Under generation, the first column is the generation listed on page 194 of <u>Tidewater Ancestors</u> and the second column is for the Mordaunt lineage. The persons from whom we are descended are in bold print. The final proof that this family is related to the Thorowgood family has not been confirmed. It has been added only as a reference.

Generation

0	1	Osbert le Mordaunt
0	2	Eustace Le Mordaunt m. Alice de Alneto
0	3	William De Mordaunt m. Ann Onley
0	4	William Mordaunt m. Rose Wake
0	5	Robert Mordaunt m. Joan Bray
0	6	Mordaunt m. Helen Brock
0	7	Mordaunt m. Agnes Le Strange
0	8	Robert Mordaunt m. Elizabeth Holdenby
0	9	William Mordaunt m. Margaret Poeke or Peck
0	10	William Mordaunt m. Anne Huntingdon
0	11	Robert Mordaunt m. Barbara Le Strange
0	12	Henry Mordaunt m. Anne Poley

```
0    13        Sir Le Strange Mordaunt m. (1)Margaret de
                Charles   (2)Frances Sotherton

0    14

    Sir Robert Mordaunt    Anne Mordaunt   Henry Mordaunt
            m.                  m.               m.
        Mary Sotherton      Thomas Clere  Barbara Calthorpe


0    15   Sir Charles Mordaunt         Strange Mordaunt
                    m.
            Catherine Tollemache
```

Recap of Significant Data: Mordaunt
Generation

1   Osbert le Mordaunt was a Norman knight of Radwell, Beds.

2   Eustace Le Mordaunt lived from 1197-1231. Alice, his wife, was the daughter and co-heir of Sir William de Alneto.

3   William De Mordaunt was of Turvey', He died in 1243. Ann, his wife, was the daughter of Sir William Onley of Onley.

4   William Mordaunt of Turvey died in 1297. He married Rose, daughter of Sir Ralph Wake.

5   Robert Mordaunt was MP for Co Beds. in 1307. Joan Bray was his second wife.

6   Mordaunt of Turvey married Helen, daughter and co-heir of Ralph Brock by Mgt Hussey.

7   Mordaunt of Turvey died in 1372. He married Agnes, daughter and heir of John Le Strange of Brokely, Suffolk by Elizabeth, sister of William Boteler of Waldon.

8   Robert Mordaunt ESQ MP for Beds in 1412. He married Elizabeth, daughter of John Holdenby.

9   William Mordaunt ESQ of Turvey 1447 married Margaret,

daughter of John Pocke or Peck ESQ of Cople, Beds. by Agnes Winter or Vinter of Crick, Northants.

10 William Mordaunt ESQ of Turvey Prothonotary Common Pleas died in 1518. He married Anne, daughter and co-heir of Tho Huntingdon of Hempstead. They married in 1495.

11 Robert Mordaunt of Hempstead, cousin to Baron Mordaunt. He had property Lt Massingham Norfolk. Will written 1569/70, died 1572. He married Barbara, daughter and heir of John Le Strange of Lt Massingham. She was born in 1479 and living in 1569/70.

12 Henry Mordaunt of King's Lynn and Lt Massingham was the youngest son. Henry had brothers and uncles but he seems to be the only family member to have lived in Norfolk at this time. He was born about 1515. He married Anne Poley of Co Beds.

13 Sir Le Strange Mordaunt, born in 1572 was High Sheriff from 1606-1611, Bart. 1611 married (1) Margaret, daughter of Peter de Charles and married (2) Frances, daughter of Thomas Sotherton.

14 Robert Mordaunt was the son of Strange Mordaunt and married Mary, daughter of Sir Aug. Sothert

14 Anne Mordaunt, daughter of Strange Mordaunt, married Thomas Clere.

14 Henry Mordaunt, Esq. of Middleton, son of Strange Mordaunt, married Barbara, daughter of Christopher Calthorpe.

15 Sir Charles Mordaunt, son of Sir Robert and Mary Sotherton, married Catherine Tollemache.

15 Strange Mordaunt, son of Henry Mordaunt and Barbara Calthorpe, was living in 1631.

Hypothesis
A researcher in England was attempting to connect the

121

Mordaunt and Thorowgood families. He believed there was a connection because the sixth child of William and Anne Edwards Thorowgood was Mordaunt Thorowgood, who died at the Siege of Breda, and the seventh child was Adam Thorowgood.

Anne Edwards and William Thorowgood had nine children. William Thorowgood married first, Anne Edwards; second, Mary Dodge, widow; and third, Alice Holbeck, widow.

The researcher says, "So at this stage, I think we can say that Adam Thorowgood was descended from the above to Robert and Barbara Le Strange. I haven't finished on this because there must be some way of getting more definite answers. William Thorowgood was Vicar at Grimston by 1581 so must have been born before about 1556. I have found one baptized as early as 1588. This would make a birth giving span to 1613 most unlikely for one woman so we can safely say there were two wives but who and when. A Mordaunt mother to Adam would need to have been before about 1580 so this would tie in exactly when Henry and Anne were having children at Lt Massingham. I have picked up a daughter Barbara Mordaunt baptized there 1574 and the eldest son Sir Le Strange at King's Lynn in 1566. Technically then if Adam had a Mordaunt mother she could have been either a daughter of Henry and Anne or of Robert and Barbara. Alternatively if Anne Edwards provided the Mordaunt connection, her mother could have been a daughter of Robert and Barbara. I will try to see if this can be clarified."

We still need proof before we can assume a rela- tionship between the Mordaunt and Thorowgood families.

Mason

Under generation, the first column is the generation listed on page 221 of <u>Tidewater</u> <u>Ancestors</u> and the second column is for the Mason lineage. The persons from whom we are descended are in bold print.

Generation   1

1   **Francis Mason** m. I-Mary ? m. II-**Alice Ganey**

2 2   Ann   Francis   **Lemuel**   Elizabeth

                                 m.   m.

                          Ann Seawall James Thelaball

3 3

Elizabeth Lemuel George I-Thomas **Frances** Alice

m.[1]   m.   m.   m.[1]   m.[1]   m.[1]

William Mary Philia Elizabeth George Robert

Major Thilaball or ? Newton Hodges

m.[2]   Phillis m.[2] m.[2] m.[2]

Captain   ? Captain **Francis** Samuel

Thomas   Richard **Sayre** Boush

Cocke   Sanderson

Anne Margaret Dinah Mary

m.   m.   m.   m.[1]

            ? ? Walton

        Thorowgood m.[2]

              ? Cocke

```
4        4
Children of Phillis    Children of Elizabeth     Child of
and George Mason        and Thomas Mason          Frances and
                                                  Francis Sayre

Thomas George Abigail Frances              Charles
    m.                                        m.²
  Mary            Lemuel  Ann   Mary  Margaret   Margaret
  Newton                  m.    m.               Lawson
                   No   Captain                    m.¹
                   Issue  Thomas                  Captain
                        Willoughby                 John
                                                  Thorowgood


5        5
                     Arthur    Frances    Elizabeth
                       m.        m.¹         m.
                     Elizabeth  Thomas    Nathaniel
                      Walke     Lawson     Newton
```

Recap of Significant Data: Mason Generation

1   Francis Mason came to Virginia on the John and Frances with his wife, Mary, and daughter, Ann, in 1613. Some historians list his wife's name as Ann. His rank was given as lieutenant. He died in 1648.

2   Francis was born in Virginia but it is thought that both Francis and Ann died in early infancy. There are some that believe that Francis was a bridge between the Norfolk and Surry families.

Lemuel married Ann Seawall. They had ten children. Lemuel Mason was born in Virginia in 1628 and he died in 1702 at his home on Mason's Creek in lower Norfolk County. In his will, which was drawn on June 17, 1695, he remembered his sister, Elizabeth, who married James Thelaball of Norfolk. His will states "if the said Lemuel Mason die before my sister, Elizabeth Thelaball then I doe give and bequest unto my said sister soe much good Black Sarge as will make her a Mourning Gown." The will of Lemuel Mason also mentions three daughters.

The following is from the will of Ann Mason of Elizabeth River Parish in ye county of Norfolk, Gentlewoman. Book 7, page 116____dated 30 October 1705, proved 15th March 1706/5_____ ye death of my dead husband Col. Lemuel Mason____Christian buriall at ye discretion of my executors hereafter named or at ye discretion of my three sonnes, Thomas, Lemuel, and George Mason____unto my loveing Daughter Frances Sayer ye sume of Seven Pounds ten shillings without being accountable to her husband____unto my loveing Daughter Alice Boush____without being accountable to her husband_____unto my loveing Daughter Mary Cocke_____without being accountable to her husband_____ unto my loveing Daughter Dinah Thorowgood____ unto my son Thomas Mason____the pair of andirons that are in ye chimney where I commonly are myselfe my dead husband promising ye same to my said son Thomas about twenty years past____my Seale Skinned Trunks_____ said three sons_____ sole Executs.

Witnesses   (Thomas Willoughby)

(Elizabeth Newton)

(Ann Porter)

Ann Mason and Seale

In 1705 when Ann Mason died, her three sons and her daughters Frances Sayer, Alice Boush, Mary Cocke and Dinah Thorowgood were living.

3   Some sources have Frances as the oldest daughter while others list Elizabeth. Frances was born about 1661. Her

first husband, Mr. George Newton, died in 1694. A descendent
was Mr. Cincinnatus Newton. She secondly married Mr. Charles
Sayer.

George Mason died in 1710 and Thomas died in 1711.

A will on record, wherein one Robert Hodges in 1681
states that his father in law was Lemuel Mason and Alice was
his wife.

Margaret married and was living in England. Anne, also,
married.

The present Niemeyers are direct descendents of this Mason
line. In Tidewater Ancestors the noted generation should be
changed as follows.

9	9	Lt. Col. William Frederic Niemeyer, C. S. A. m. Sarah Campbell Smith		
10	10	John Frederic Niemeyer m. Lucrece Bilisoly		
11	11	Antonio Bilisoly Niemeyer m. Lutie Stuart Spotts		
12	12	Antonio Bilisoly Niemeyer, Jr. m. Alice Virginia Berry		
13	13	William Frederic Niemeyer m. Carolyn Louise Holtzhauer	Frank Berry Niemeyer m. Shannon Page Eadie	John Stuart Niemeyer m. April Michelle Tripp
14	14	John Cameron Niemeyer Kyle Antonio Niemeyer	Jacob Douglas Niemeyer	John Stuart Niemeyer, Jr.

Under generation, the first column is the generation listed on page 235 of <u>Tidewater</u> <u>Ancestors</u> and the second column is for the Seawell lineage. The persons from whom we are descended are in bold print.

Generation

1	1	**Henry Seawell**
2	2	**Henry Seawell** **Ann Seawell m. Lemuel Mason**

Recap of Significant Data: Seawell
Generation

     1   Henry Seawell's estate was located at the present Sewell's Point in Norfolk. He died in 1644.

     2   The son of Henry Seawall died without issue.

The present Niemeyers are direct descendents of this Seawell line. In <u>Tidewater</u> <u>Ancestors</u>, the noted generation should be changed as follows.

9	9	Lt. Col. William Frederic Niemeyer, C. S. A. m. Sarah Campbell Smith
10	10	John Frederic Niemeyer m. Lucrece Bilisoly
11	11	Antonio Bilisoly Niemeyer m. Lutie Stuart Spotts
12	12	Antonio Bilisoly Niemeyer, Jr. m. Alice Virginia Berry

13	13	William Frederic Niemeyer	Frank Berry Niemeyer	John Stuart Niemeyer
		m.	m.	m.
		Carolyn Louise Holtzhauer	Shannon Page Eadie	April Michelle Tripp

| 14 | 14 | John Cameron Niemeyer | Jacob Douglas Niemeyer | John Stuart Niemeyer, Jr. |
| | | Kyle Antonio Niemeyer | | |

Sayre (Sayer)

Under generation, the first column is the generation listed on page 243 of <u>Tidewater</u> <u>Ancestors</u> and the second column is for the Sayre lineage. The persons from whom we are descended are in bold print.

Generation

Thomas Sayre was a subscriber to the Second Virginia Charter for 12 pounds, 10 shillings.

1   1   **Thomas Sayre**

m.

I- ?   II-**Frances**   III-Elizabeth (Yellow ?)

m^2

Walter Bruce

2   2

Mary   **Francis**   Trustram   Ann

m.   m.^{1} m.^{2}

Richard   Martha   **Frances**

Church   (Odeon?)   **Mason**

m^2 m^1

Elizabeth   George

Newton

3   3

Richard Captain **Charles**   Mary   ?

   Thomas   m.   m.^{1} m.^{2} m.^{3} m.

          Margaret William   Captain   Dr.   Smith

          Lawson Moseley, III Adam   Robert

             m^1 m^1 Thoroughgood Kingman

          Captain John Blandinah   III

          Thoroughgood   Poole

129

4	4
Children of Capt. John and Margaret Lawson Thorowgood	Children of Charles and Margaret Lawson Sayer, her second husband

Mary	John		Arthur	**Frances**	Elizabeth
			m[1]	m[1]	m.
			Elizabeth	**Captain**	Nathaniel
			Walke	**Thomas**	Newton
			m[2]	**Lawson**	
			Samuel	m.[2]	
			Boush	? Boush	

5   5

Charles	Frances	Margaret	Mary	Elizabeth
m.	m.	m.	m.	m.
Mary	John	Peter	William	Henry
Hoggard	Hancock	Singleton	White	Woodhouse

6   6

Arthur	Mary	Diana	Eliza (Betsy)	Susanna	Frances
				m.	m.
				Francis Foster	Jasper Moran

Recap of Significant Data: Sayre, Sayer

Generation

1   Thomas Sayre or Sayer came to Virginia in the "Assurance" in 1610 according to <u>Tidewater</u> <u>Ancestors</u>. He was fourteen years old. Another source agrees he was fourteen but gives his birth as between 1616 and 1621 and that he came to Virginia in 1635. In 1637 he patented land in the Upper County of New Norfolk on the eastern branch of the Elizabeth River. He married three times. His first wife was unknown

but there was a daughter, Mary, who married Richard Church. She was born by 1650 and married before 1666. Church sued Francis Sayre for a parcel of land that he claimed in right of the daughter of Thomas Sayre. The court decided for Church.

Thomas had three children by his second wife, Frances, who died in 1650. His third wife was Elizabeth (Yellow?) who was administrator of the estate in 1658. Elizabeth married secondly Walter Bruce before 15 March 1660/61.

2 Francis Sayre was born before 1637 and died intestate by 1707. Francis married first Martha, possibly Odeon and secondly, according to Mrs. Fontaine, Frances Mason. Frances Mason had been married, firstly, to Captain George Newton who died intestate. Frances Mason was the daughter of Lemuel and Anne Seawell Mason. The wives of Francis Sayre are not positively identified. Trustam Sayre died by June 1666. Ann Sayre was born before March 1653/54. Francis Sayre had five children.

3 Charles Sayre is the son of Francis in both versions. The difference is that <u>Tidewater</u> <u>Ancestors</u> has Charles as the husband of Frances Mason while Mrs. Fontaine has Charles as the son of Frances Mason. It seems that Charles was the son of Frances Mason and Francis Sayre.

The first child born to Francis was Richard whose will was probated 15 July 1720 leaving all his land to John and Eleanor Britt. The second child was Captain Thomas Sayre of whom we know little. Charles Sayre of Princess Anne County was the third child. He was born before 1695 and married before 1712 Margaret Lawson, daughter of Lt. Col. Anthony Lawson. Margaret was born in 1676 and married first Captain John Thoroughgood, son of Adam. Frances Mason first married George Newton. Francis' fourth child was Mary Sayre who married William Moseley, III before 1699. William first married

Blandinah Poole who was the mother of his four children. Mary married secondly Captain Adam Thoroughgood, III who was born in 1663. Mary thirdly married Dr. Robert Kingman before 1716. The last child was a Sayre who married a Smith before 1716.

4   Both versions of the Sayre family agree that Charles had a daughter, Frances, who married Thomas Lawson, gentleman, son of Thomas Lawson.

Arthur Sayer was born before 1718. From 1740 to 1761 he served as clerk of the Court of Princess Anne County and in 1752 he was a vestryman of Lynnhaven Parish. Before 1740 he married Elizabeth Walke.

The present Niemeyers are direct descendents of this Sayre line. In _Tidewater_ _Ancestors,_ the noted generation should be changed as follows.

9	9	Lt. Col. William Frederic Niemeyer, C. S. A. m. Sarah Campbell Smith		
10	10	John Frederic Niemeyer m. Lucrece Bilisoly		
11	11	Antonio Bilisoly Niemeyer m. Lutie Stuart Spotts		
12	12	Antonio Bilisoly Niemeyer, Jr. m. Alice Virginia Berry		
13	13	William Frederic Niemeyer m. Carolyn Louise Holtzhauer	Frank Berry Niemeyer m. Shannon Page Eadie	John Stuart Niemeyer m. April Michelle Tripp
14	14	John Cameron Niemeyer Kyle Antonio Niemeyer	Jacob Douglas Niemeyer	John Stuart Niemeyer, Jr.

Bennett, Snayle and Saunders

Under generation, the first column is the generation listed on page 254 of <u>Tidewater Ancestors</u> and the second column is for the Bennett, Snayle and Saunders lineage. The persons from whom we are descended are in bold print.

Generation

1   **Henry Snayle** m.

1   2   **Ann Snayle** m. **Thomas Bennett**

2   3   **Mary Bennett**

                        m.

  I-Thomas   II-**Rev. Jonathan Saunders** III- Maximilian
   Ewell   Boush

3   4   **Mary Saunders** m. **Cornelius Calvert**

Recap of Significant Data: Bennett, Snayle and Saunders
Generation

     1   Henry Snayle made his will in 1655. He was living in Virginia. Henry Snayle (Snaile) was of Little Creek.

     3   Maximilian Boush was one of the first mayors of Norfolk.

     4   Mary Saunders was the daughter of Mary Bennett and the Rev. Jonathan Saunders. Mary Bennett was the widow of Thomas Ewell and daughter of Thomas and Anne (Snayle)   Bennett. Anne Snayle was the daughter of Henry.

     The present Niemeyers are direct descendents of this Bennett, Snayle and Saunders line. In <u>Tidewater Ancestors</u>, the noted generation should be changed as follows.

8   9   Lt. Col. William Frederic Niemeyer, C. S. A. m.

Sarah Campbell Smith

9	10	John Frederic Niemeyer m. Lucrece Bilisoly
10	11	Antonio Bilisoly Niemeyer m. Lutie Stuart Spotts
11	12	Antonio Bilisoly Niemeyer, Jr. m. Alice Virginia Berry

12	13	William Frederic Niemeyer	Frank Berry Niemeyer	John Stuart Niemeyer
		m.	m.	m.
		Carolyn Louise Holtzhauer	Shannon Page Eadie	April Michelle Tripp
13	14	John Cameron Niemeyer	Jacob Douglas Niemeyer	John Stuart Niemeyer, Jr.
		Kyle Antonio Niemeyer		

Under generation, the first column is the generation listed on page 263 of <u>Tidewater</u> <u>Ancestors</u> and the second column is for the Calvert lineage. The persons from whom we are descended are in bold print.

Generation

1	1	**Cornelius Calvert**	Joseph Calvert
		m.	m.
		Mary Saunders	Lucy (Hinkston) Webb

Recap of Significant Data: Calvert

Generation

1   1   Cornelius Calvert was a sea captain who settled in Norfolk. He married Mary Saunders in Princess Anne County on July 27, 1719. Mary Saunders was born before 1700 in Princess Anne County. Her father was the Rev. Jonathan Saunders who was the minister of Lynnhaven Parish in 1695 and who died about 1700. She died about 1762 in the borough of Norfolk.

Cornelius was Justice of Norfolk County from July 18, 1729 to January 17, 1729/30. He served on the Common Council of Norfolk Borough. He and his wife settled in Norfolk and on July 7, 1741 he was appointed to a committee to form a law to prevent "All persons being servants or slaves from purchasing any rum or spirituous liquors under two gallons." He died in 1748 and his will was probated on June 18, 1748.

When Cornelius was growing old, he became, if he had not already been, very pious and was always reading his Bible and writing verses in the margin. He had ten sons and two daughters. The boys were all wild and fond of sport and frolic. The old man was very strict with them and every evening he would have them called in to sit in the corners of the wide old chimney place to behave while he sat reading his Bible and writing verses in the margin.   And so wholly wrapped up would he be in the employment that some of the boys could easily manage to steal out (especially as he was a little deaf) to play pranks and return without being missed from their places.   And many pranks they played.

There was one old woman in particular that they were fond of teasing with their tricks, a poor old Mrs. Archer. She would be gone abroad and being to return, as they knew through their father's yard to her own dwelling, they would slip out while the old gentleman was pouring over his book, and stretch a string over which poor Mrs. Archer would be sure to fall sprawlin to the ground.   Suspecting them, she would go in to complain to the old gentleman against them. "Captain Calvert, I do declare you must have something done to them, indeed you must."   Then she would tell her tale, but he would answer, "Madam, I am sorry for your fall but you must be mistaken in supposing that my boys had a hand in it, for I can assure you that they have not been out of their seats all evening and here you see they are."   And so they would be, all trying to look as grave as judges and hardly able to keep from laughing out.

The old gentleman died sometime before his wife, who lived to a good old age and saw her sons grown and the Masters of vessels.   Their son Jonathan died at sea and was buried at sea.

The Calvert Family Bible was found at an exhibit of the northeastern North Carolina historical societies of Pasquotank, Currituck and Perquimans Counties by Norfolk residents.   They found that the father of the present owner had purchased a box of old books for $3.00.   The Bible was in this box.   A number of the Calvert descendents still live in this area.   One of those listed was Mrs. Helen Calvert Read (1750-1833).   Mrs.

Frances Calvert Stansbury was a great[5] granddaughter. This Bible was on loan to the Norfolk Museum by the Great Bridge Chapter of the Daughters of the American Revolution.

A page of the Bible says:

Cornelius Calvert and Mary Saunders were married 29 of July 1719 in Princess Anne County.

1- Jonathan Calvert, the son of Cornelius and Mary Calvert, was born the 23 of September 1720.

2- Maximilian Calvert, the Son of Cornelius and Mary Calvert, was born the 29 of October 1722.

3- Cornelius Calvert, the Son of Cornelius and Mary Calvert, was born the 13 of March 1723/24.

4- Thomas Calvert, the Son of Cornelius and Mary Calvert, was born the 8 of September 1726.

5- Saunders Calvert, the Son of Cornelius and Mary Calvert, was born the last day and hour of January 1728/29.

6- Joseph Calvert, the Son of Cornelius and Mary Calvert, was born the 14 of April 1732.

7- William Calvert, the Son of Cornelius and Mary Calvert, was born the 10 of June 1734.

8- Christopher Calvert, the Son of Cornelius and Mary Calvert, was born the 26 of September 1736 about 5 o'clock in the morning.

9- John Calvert, the Son of Cornelius and Mary Calvert, was born the 19 of September 1739 about 5 o'clock in the morning.

10- MARY (unlooked for), the Daughter of Cornelius and Mary Calvert, was born the last day of July 1741 about 6 o'clock.

11- Samuel Calvert, the Son of Cornelius and Mary Calvert, was born the 8 of December 1743 about 6 o'clock in the morning.

12- Elizabeth Calvert, the Daughter of Cornelius and Mary Calvert, was born the 27 of November 1746 about 10 o'clock at night.

Mrs. Louise Niemeyer Fontaine wrote the following note.

I have seen a copy somewhere in which Mary, the tenth child of Cornelius and Mary Saunders Calvert was recorded as Mary (unlooked for) which is nonsense. The Calvert Bible belonged to Fannie Tardy, born Fanny Wilson. She was the granddaughter of our great aunt, Virginia Isabella Chandler, who married Henry Harwood. When Fanny gave the Bible to the Museum she asked me to present it, which I did at a meeting in Norfolk of the descendents of Cornelius Calvert. I have read the record as I gave it above: "long looked for." Louise Niemeyer Fontaine

Cornelius Calvert secured land and established a home site called "Pomfret" on the lower eastern bank of the Elizabeth River, "facing the James River and the setting sun".

Cornelius Calvert

From the "Memoirs of Helen Calvert Maxwell Read"- his granddaughter.

My grandfather, Cornelius Calvert, came to this country, I suppose, sometime about the year 1699, in command of a vessel (for he was a sea captain) from some part of England. Here he married a girl by the name of Mary Saunders, the daughter, I believe of a country clergyman, residing somewhere about Newtown in the county of Princess Anne. He was an active, industrious man and his wife was a prudent, managing woman, and so he soon made a clever little estate and was enabled to leave off going to sea — though he still did business about vessels and had some concern in them. He owned three or four lots up town where Mr. Archer's house now stands and thereabouts, and used to employ his boys, as soon as they were big enough, to carry stones to make land in the water. He owned, too, I remember four valuable negroes who were good seamen and brought in good wages.

Shortly after his marriage, and before he left the sea, he made a voyage to England to see his mother, who, residing, I believe, in some part of the country, received him with great kindness, but having now married a second husband could not do much for him. However, on his being about to take leave of her, she accompanied him some miles driving him in her chair; and when they came to the place they must part, she said to him, "My son, we are about to separate, and I never expect to see you again in this world. I am sorry I have nothing to give you but this ball of yarn. Take it. It will serve you to mend your stockings when you get on board ship. I suppose you mend your stockings? And mind, you must unwind it yourself." So my grandfather took the ball and feeling it to be very heavy, when his mother had left him, he was very anxious to find out what might be in it, and long before he got to the ship unwound the ball, and found, to his great joy and surprise, sixty solid gold guineas.

After my grandfather left the sea and was growing old, he became if he had not already been, very pious, and was always reading his Bible and writing verses in it. To be sure, they were the roughest and hardest going verses in the world, but he took great pleasure in writing them. The very Bible is now in possession of Capt. Tucker, who married, you know a granddaughter of the old man.

He had eleven sons, ten of whom lived to grow up and to become masters of ships, and two daughters. The sons that grew up were Jonathan, Maximilian, Cornelius, Thomas, Saunders, Joseph, William, Christopher, John, and Samuel. The daughters were: Mary, who married Col. Lawson of Petersburg, by whom she had Mrs. Chandler and Mrs. Cartwright; (and Elizabeth).

The old gentleman died sometime before his wife, who lived to a good old age, and saw all her sons grownup and masters of vessels. The oldest of them, as I said, was Jonathan. I do not know that I ever saw him, but he died at sea. For I remember that one winter day when it was very cold and snowing very fast (the winters then were much harder than they are now), the vessel of which he had gone out captain came sailing into the harbour with the sails all set and frozen, and steering about in a very wild manner, which made those who saw her think that all was not right on board. So some of them went to her and found that the Captain had died at sea, and had been buried in it, and that several of the men were frozen to death, and others down with the small pox, and one of those four negroes of my grandfather's was at the helm. So they took command of her and brought her to.

Cornelius Calvert had a brother, Joseph. He married in Spottsylvania County to Lucy Webb who probably died in Norfolk County after 1773. She was the widow of George Webb whom she married in Spottsylvania on October 19, 1735 when she was Lucy Hinkston. She married a third time in Norfolk County on June 19, 1755 to Edward Pugh, a widower. Joseph Calvert died before 1755.

Two of Cornelius' sons were Mayor of Norfolk. Maximilian, 2nd son, served from 1765-1766 and from 1769-1770. Cornelius, 3rd son, served from 1768-1769 and from 1778-1779. This is according to information obtained by telephone from the Norfolk Mayor's Office in 1995.

The present Niemeyers are direct descendents of this Calvert line. In Tidewater Ancestors, the noted generation should be changed as follows.

6   6   Lt. Col. William Frederic Niemeyer, C. S. A. m.
          Sarah Campbell Smith
7   7   John Frederic Niemeyer m. Lucrece Bilisoly

```
8    8    Antonio Bilisoly Niemeyer m. Lutie Stuart Spotts
9    9    Antonio Bilisoly Niemeyer, Jr. m. Alice Virginia
              Berry
10   10   William Frederic      Frank Berry          John Stuart
              Niemeyer              Niemeyer             Niemeyer
                 m.                    m.                   m.
           Carolyn Louise        Shannon Page         April Michelle
              Holtzhauer             Eadie               Tripp
11   11   John Cameron          Jacob Douglas        John Stuart
              Niemeyer              Niemeyer            Niemeyer, Jr.
           Kyle Antonio
              Niemeyer                 _____
```

From: Memoirs of Helen Calvert Maxwell Read
24 Edited by Charles B. Cross, Jr., 1970
Pub. by: Norfolk County Historical Society of Chesapeake, Virginia

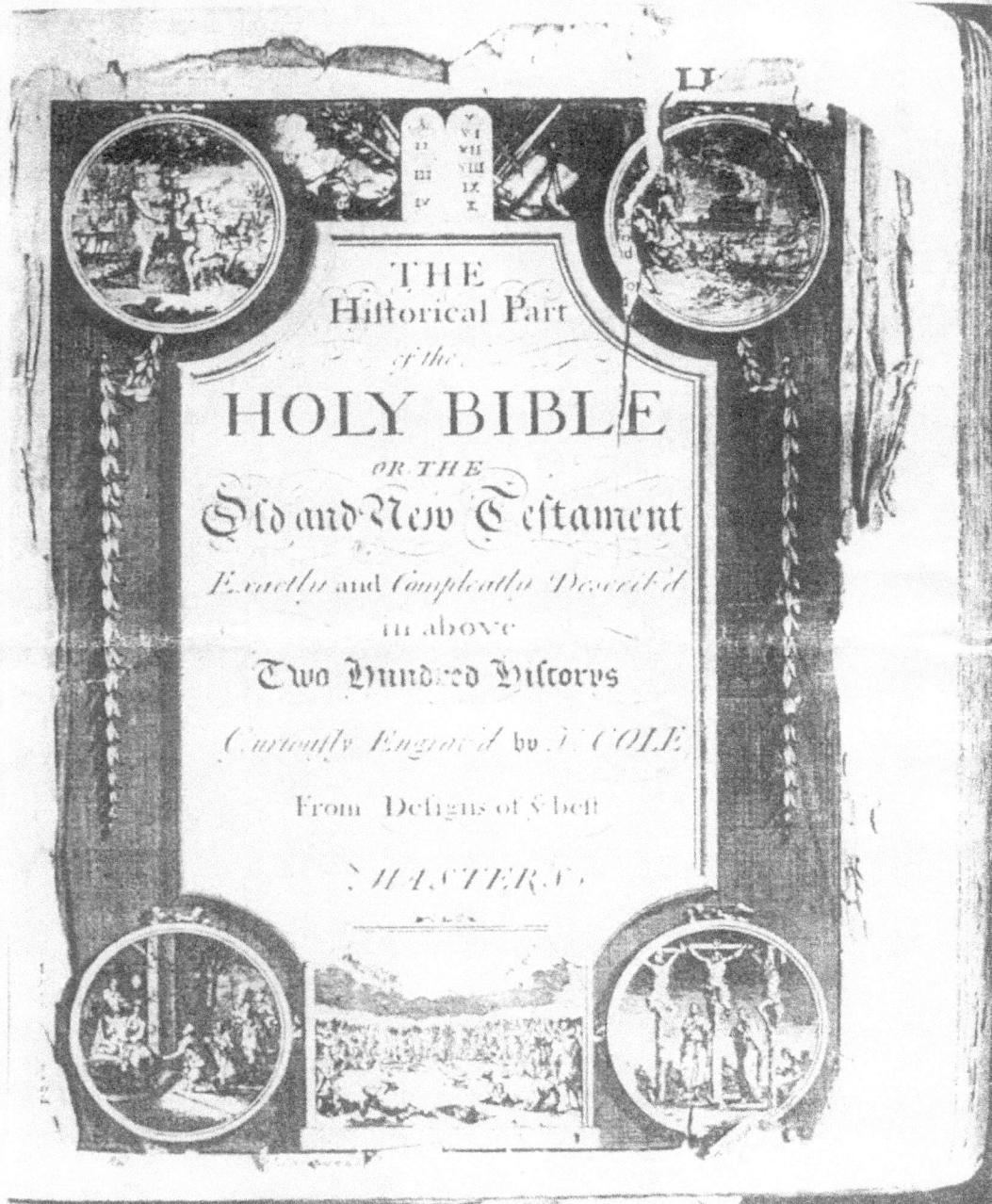

THE
Historical Part
of the
HOLY BIBLE
OR THE
Old and New Testament
Exactly and Compleatly Describ'd
in above
Two Hundred Historys
Curiously Engrav'd by J. COLE
From Designs of Sibell
MASTERS

Pages from Calvert Family Bible

Cornelius Calvert and Mary Saunders was Married
29 of July 1719 in Princess Ann County. . . . .

Jonathan Calvert, the Son of Cornelius and Mary
Calvert, was born the 23 of September. 1720. . .
Maximilian Calvert, the Son of Cornelius and,
Mary Calvert, was born the 29 of October. 1722. . .
Cornelius Calvert, the Son of Cornelius and Mary Calvert,
was born the 13 of March 1723/4. . . . .
Thomas Calvert, the Son of Cornelius and Mary Calvert,
was born the 8 of September. 1726. . . . .
Saunders Calvert, Son of Cornelius and Mary Calvert, . .
was born the last day and hour of January 1728/9. . . .
Joseph Calvert Son of Cornelius and Mary Calvert . . .
was born the 1 of April 1732. . . . .
William Calvert, the Son of Cornelius and Mary Calvert,
was born the 10 of June 1734. . . . .
Christopher Calvert the Son of Cornelius and Mary Calvert,
was born the 26 of September 1736 about 5 o Clock in the Morning
John Calvert the Son of Cornelius and Mary Calvert
was born the 19 of September 1739 about 5 o Clock in the Morning
MARY, unlooked for, the Daughter of Cornelius and Mary
Calvert was born the third day of July 1741 about 6 o Clock in the
Samuel Calvert the Son of Cornelius and Mary Calvert, was
born the 8 of September 1743 about 6 o'Clock in the Morning
Elizabeth Calvert the Daughter of Cornelius and Mary Calvert
was born the 21 of November 1746 about 10 o Clock at night

In the Name of God - Amen.

I, Cornelius Calvert of Norfolk Borough, Merchant, being in
good health of body and sensible in Mind but knowing the un-
certainity of Death, do now make this my last will and Testament
in Manner and form following.

Imprimus - I give and bequeath my immortal Soul to God in
hopes of its eternal Happiness, through the merits of Jesus Christ;
my body to be decently buried and my temporal Estate as followeth.

Item - I give and bequeath amongst all my Children and their heirs
forever as much land as will make an Alley from the Front Street
into the Back Street, the said Alley to begin at the South East
Corner of my Store House on the Front Street and run thence on a
Straight line to the South East corner of my Kitching. And from
thence along the side of the said Kitching and my Garden Pails into
the Back Street which Alley is now measured and laid out being
six feet wide and Two Hundred and Thirty four feet long or thereabouts.

Item - I give and bequeath to Mary, my wife the free use and occupation of my dwelling house (at the upper end of Norfolk Borough and
nearest the publick Landing) with the kitching, Storehouse, Smoke
House, Hen House, and new Shade joining to my dwelling house and
all the Land belonging to it (according to several courses and
distances hereafter mentioned)during her life and after her decease I give and bequeath said Land and Buildings (except for my
new Shade) to my son Cornelius and his heirs for Ever. But if he
dies without heirs I give the said Land and buildings (except by
new Shade) to my Son William and his heirs for Ever.

Item - I give and bequeath to Mary my wife the free use and occupation of my three Negro Women, Parthena, Lucy and Rose and of my

two Negro men Jeffrey and Quanano during her life and after her
decease I give and bequeath the said Parthena and Lucy and their
increase after the date thereof to be equally divided amongst my
three sons Christopher, Jonatha and Samuel and their Heirs for Ever
and the said Rose and all her Increase after the date thereof to my
son William and his Heirs for Ever. And if either of my daughters
die without Heirs I give and bequeath all her Estate to my surviving
Daughter and her Heirs for Ever.

Item - I give and bequeath to my son Christopher and his heirs
for ever my Negro girl Jenny and all her Increase to be delivered
to him at the age of twenty one years. I give and bequeath to my
son John and his heirs for ever my Negro Girl Madge and all her
increase, to be delivered to him at the age of twenty-one years.

Item- I give and bequeath to my son Samuel and his heirs forever my
Negro Girl Phillis and all her Increase to be delivered to him at
the age of twenty-one years.

Item - I give and bequeath to my Daughter Mary and her Heirs for
ever my Negro Girl Cherry and all her Increase to be delivered to
her on the day of her Marriage or when she is eighteen years old.

Item - I give and bequeath to my Daughter Elizabeth and her Heirs
for ever my Negro Girl Nancy and all her increase to be delivered
to her on the day of her Marriage or when she is eighteen years
old.

Item - I give and bequeath to Mary, my wife, the free use and
occupation of one dozen Leather Chairs, one Leather Couch, one
Large looking Glass, a large walnut Table, a chest of Drawers,
twelve silver spoons and Two Feather Beds with furniture to them
during her life and after her decease I give and bequeath the said
things to be equally divided between my Daughters Mary and Elizabeth
and their heirs forever.

Page #3 of Cornelius Calvert's Will and Testament.

Item - I give and bequeath to Mary, my wife and her Heirs for Ev
all the remainder of my household furniture, as Beds, Bedding,
Tables, Chairs, Pewter, Brass, Iron etc. both in my dwelling hou
and Kitching and also my Sloop and all appurtenances.

Item - I give and bequeath to my Daughters Mary and Elizabeth th
free use and occupation of my new Shade joining to my Dwelling
house till the day of their Marriage and after that I give the s
Shade to my son Cornelius and his heirs for Ever. But if he die
without heirs I give the said Shade to my son William and his he
for Ever.

Item - I give and bequeath to my son Maximilian and his Heirs
for ever my brick dwelling house with the Kitching, Storehouse,
Smoke House, Hen house and all land belonging to it, according
to several courses and distances hereafter mentioned.

Item - I give and bequeath to my Son Cornelius and his heirs for
Ever a small piece of Land and my Wharf joining to it (lying
between the Front Street and my son Thomas' land) to be delivere
to him after Wife's decease. But if he dies without Heirs I gi
the said Land and Wharf to my son William and his Heirs for Ever.

Item - I give and bequeath to my son Thomas and his Heirs for
Ever a piece of Land at the upper end of Norfolk Borough (according to the several courses and distances afterwards mentioned)
with the Storehouse on the same, the said Land (except that where
on the Storehouses stand) to be delivered to him when twenty-one
years old and the said Storehouse with the Land whereon they stan
to be delivered to him after my wife's decease. If he dies witho
Heirs I give the said land and storehouse to my son John and his
Heirs for Ever.

Item - I gvie and bequeath to my son Joseph and his Heirs for Eve

and distances hereafter mentioned) with a new Kitching thereon to be delivered to him at twenty-one years of age but if he dies without Heirs, I give the said Land and Kitching to my Son Samuel and his Heirs for Ever.

Item - I give and bequeath to my son Maximilan, Pools Annotations; to my son Cornelius the History of the Bible, to my son Thomas the Works of the Author of the whole Duty of Man to my wife all the rest of my books, to them and to their Heirs for ever.

Item - I give to my Grand Daughter Mary Clavert andher Heirs for Ever five pounds.

Item - I give to my brother Joseph's Daughter May Calvert and her Heirs for Ever five pounds. I give the bequeath to Mary, my wife, and her heirs for Ever, the one half of all my Cash and the other half I give to be equally divided amongst my six younger children, William, Christopher, John, Mary, Samuel and Elizabeth, to them and their Heirs for Ever. And the cash left with my wife by my son Jonathan deceased (being about ten pounds) I give to her and to her heirs for Ever.

And for the true Performance of this my last will and testament, I do appoint and constitute for my Executors, Col. Samuel Boush of the aforesaid Borough, merchant; Mr. Samuel Boush of Princess Ann County, Gentleman and my wife Mary, and in Testimony that all before mentioned is my sincere Will and Desire, I have now before Witnesses set my hand and seal this Twenty-Ninth day of May in the year of our Lord, one thousand, seven hundred and forty six.

Signed, Sealed and Delivered
in the presence of: Nichols Wonycott
                    Edward Archer
                    Hannah Eady

Cornelius Calvert and Seale.

Keeling

Under generation, the first column is the generation listed on page 301 of <u>Tidewater</u> <u>Ancestors</u> and the second column is for the Keeling lineage. The persons from whom we are descended are in bold print.

Generation

1   1   Ensign **Thomas Keeling** m **Ann** ? m II-William Jeremy

                                                      m III-Col. Robert Bray

2   2

        Adam Alexander Thorowgood Sarah **Ann** Frances Elizabeth

                                                              Edward

    m.   m.
    Ann   I-John II-John III-Colonel
    Martin   or   Okeham   **Anthony**
                                    Joel   **Lawson**
                                    Martin

3   3   Mary   John   William   **Thomas**

                                                  m.

                                            Rose

                                      Thoroughgood

Recap of Significant Data: Keeling

Generation

        1   Ensign Thomas Keeling was born in 1608 and died in 1664. Thomas Keeling was one of 105 colonists brought to Virginia by Adam Thoroughgood in 1635. His wife is unknown except for her first name of Ann. She was born in 1618 and died in 1683. They had eight children.

        Ann Keeling married secondly William Jeremy who died in 1666. She married thirdly before 1670 Colonel Robert Bray. Robert Bray had two brothers and a sister. His brothers were

John and Plomer Bray and his sister married Mr. Thompkins.

2   Ann Keeling married first John or Joel Martin. They were married by 1666. After he died she married John Okeham and they had three children. Her third marriage was to Colonel Anthony Lawson before February 16, 1670/71. They had one son, Thomas. Ann died before August 15, 1672.

Adam Keeling built his home in Princess Anne County between 1683 and 1714. It was restored about 1940. The Keeling House was known as "Ye Dudlies".

How Lynnhaven Inlet Was Formed

During Virginia's first century it was only possible to enter the Lynnhaven River by way of Little Creek. Then, at some now unknown date, but presumably during the early years of the 18th century, a member of the Keeling family who lived on the eastern side of the river grew tired of having to bring his fishing vessels home by way of the tortuous Little Creek route.

At that point he caused a canal to be dug across the narrow sandbank that then divided the Lynnhaven from Chesapeake Bay to provide an easier access for his boats. Shortly afterward, according to long standing tradition a vicious hurricane blew in from the West Indies and in no time the narrow canal became the Lynnhaven Inlet of today.

3   Thomas Lawson was born before 1672. He married Rose Thoroughgood before 1692/93.

The present Niemeyers are direct descendents of this Keeling line. In Tidewater Ancestors, the noted generation should be changed as follows.

9   9   Lt. Col. William Frederic Niemeyer, C. S. A. m.

Sarah Campbell Smith

10	10	John Frederic Niemeyer m. Lucrece Bilisoly		
11	11	Antonio Bilisoly Niemeyer m. Lutie Stuart Spotts		
12	12	Antonio Bilisoly Niemeyer, Jr. m. Alice Virginia Berry		
13	13	William Frederic Niemeyer m. Carolyn Louise Holtzhauer	Frank Berry Niemeyer m. Shannon Page Eadie	John Stuart Niemeyer m. April Michelle Tripp
14	14	John Cameron Niemeyer Kyle Antonio Niemeyer	Jacob Douglas Niemeyer	John Stuart Niemeyer, Jr.

Lawson

Under generation, the first column is the generation listed on page 313 of <u>Tidewater Ancestors</u> and the second column is for the Lawson lineage. The persons from whom we are descended are in bold print.

Generation:

1   1   **Thomas Lawson** m. **Margaret Bray**

2   2   **Anthony Lawson m. ?**

3   3   **Col. Anthony Lawson**   George Lawson

                           m.

  I-**Ann Keeling** II-Mary Gookin III-Elizabeth Westgate
     Okeham   Moseley   Conner

4   4 **Thomas** Mary Margaret Elizabeth Anthony

         m.   m.   m.

        Rose   Thomas John
   Thoroughgood Walke Thoroughgood

5   5

Anthony George Frances Ann **Captain** Thomas Anthony Mary
                       Thomas   Walke
                        m.   m.
                   Frances Katherine
                    Sayre

6   6

      Col. Anthony Thomas Charles Thomas III
          m.   m.
     Mary Calvert   Margaret Thoroughgood

7   7   Children of Colonel Anthony and Mary Calvert Lawson

Thomas   Richard   Anthony   **Mary**   Elizabeth   Helen   Frances
   m.   Henry Lee   m.   **Calvert**   m.   Sayre
Sarah   m.   (?)   m.   (?)   m.
Robinson (?)   Marvolt **George** Cartwright   Dr. Evans
   Godwin   **Chandler**

8   8
Anthony   Thomas   Tilly
 died   died   died
unmarried   unmarried unmarried

8   8   Mary Frances m. James Edward Wilson

9   9
Indiana   Katherine   Lucy   Mary   Richard   Roscoe
   E.   m.   A.   D.   T.   T.
   m.   Dr. John   m.   m.   died   died
John W.   Payne   Charles   Thomas   unmarried
 Young   D. Willard   C. Handford

10   10
Elizabeth Mary Indiana   Mary Jennie Son   Fannie
   m.   died Constance   Wilson
 John   unmarried died   m.
Paxton   unmarried   Rev. Waterfield

11   11
 Paxton
  child

Children of Anthony, the third child of Col. Anthony and Mary Calvert Lawson, who married (?) Marvolt.

8	8	Alexander	Elizabeth
		died	m.
		unmarried	James Hill
			Ramsone

9	9		one son

Children of Mary Calvert, the fourth child of Col. Anthony and Mary Calvert Lawson, who married George Chandler.

8	8	George	**John**	Mary
		Washington	**Adams**	Lawson
		died	m.	m.
		unmarried	**Sarah**	I-F. W. Boush
			Howard	II-Dr. Daniel Cary
			Woodward	Barraud

9   9

Mary	**Sarah**	Martha	Georgianna	Henrietta	Virginia	George
Eliza	**Howard**	W.	Matlack	Calvert	Isabella	McKendree
m.	m.	m.	m.	m.	m.	died
John	**William**	Dr.	Henry	Henry	Henry	unmarried
Thompson	**Angus**	Leonidas	F.	Harwood	Harwood	
Hill	**Niemeyer**	Rosser	Woodhouse			

Children of Mary Eliza Chandler and John Thompson Hill

10	10	John Thompson, Jr.	Chandler Woodward
		m.	m.
	Mary Elizabeth Bembury Collins		Fannie Gregory Collins

153

Children of John Thompson Hill, Jr. and Elizabeth Collins
11   11

William   Mary   Elizabeth Fannie   Evelyn Blanche
Collins Chandler   Gregory   Calvert Collins Baker
        The above six children died unmarried.

Children of Chandler Woodward and Fannie Gregory Collins

Richard	John	Anthony	Fannie	William	Baynham
Gregory	Chandler	Lawson		Collins	Matlack
m.	m.	Calvert	died	m.	m.
Eliza	Lottie	m.	young	Marion	Esther
Benson	Brown	Mabel	age	Hume	Almeda
Bilisoly		Vincent	two		Covington
		No Issue			No Issue

12   12

Richard	Antonio	John	Robert	Annie	Frances
Gregory	Bilisoly	Calvert	Camm	Camm	Chandler
died	died	died	died	died	Sister of
young	unmarried	unmarried	unmarried	unmarried	Charity

Children of John Chandler and Lottie Brown Hill

Chandler	Burroughs	Charlotte
Woodward	Reed	Reed
m.	m.	m.
Jessie Wilson	Ruth Beebe	Peter Campbell Hutchison

13   13

Chandler	Thomas	John	Burroughs	Peter	Polly
Woodward	Moss	Benjamin	Reed	Campbell	m.
Jr.	Wilson	Collins	Jr.	m.	Thomas
					Midge Glassburner

14   14   Thomas   Peter

12   12

Children of William Collins and Marion Hume Hill

Marion Hume	Annie Heartwell Hume	William Collins Jr.	Frances Gregory
Died Young	m. Charles Artenzen	m. Ellie (?)	m. Sam Von Kommer
	No Issue	No Issue	

13   13

Peggy   Marion   Ruth

Children of Sarah Howard Chandler and William Angus Niemeyer

10   10

William Frederic	John Chandler	Henry Victor	Sarah Howard	George McKendree	Arthur Emmerson	Crawford Hill
m.		m.			m.	m.
Sarah Campbell Smith	died unmarried	Martha Jane Hunter	died unmarried	died unmarried	Sarah Hoyt Mahan	Mrs. Pauline Ritter

Mary Chandler	John Christian	Ann McLean	Sam Watts	Herman Christain
m.	m.	m.	m.	m.
Dr. Robert Rivers Robertson	Mary Janet Wooten	Samuel Patterson Wigg	I-Mary Agnes Moore	Mary Louise Benson
			II-Lellie Land	Hook

155

Children of Martha Woodward Chandler and Dr. Leonidas
    Rosser, D.D., Methodist

10   10

John Mary Jacob McKendree   Louise   Henry Leonidas
Chandler Lawson   (Lulie)
                                 m.
                        Jesse Talbot Littleton

11   11   Leonidas

Children of Georgiana Matlack Chandler and Henry F.
    Woodhouse

10   10

Sarah   Mary Georgiana Henry Annie John Kenneth
                 m.   m.
died   died Mr. Bott died   died died   Grace
single single   single single single Hudgins

11   11   Grace   Louise   Georgiana
                          Virginia   m.   Chandler
                           m.   William J.
                        Clyde   Story, Jr. died
                        Rawls   unmarried

12   12   Clyde   Chandler   William
                        Virginia   m.   J.,III
                        Rawls   David   m.
                              Boyette   Diane
                              Dennis   T.

Children of Chandler and David Boyette Dennis

13	13				
Christopher Yeardley	John Chandler m. Susanne (?)	David Boyette Jr. m. Kim White			

Children of William J. and Diane T. Story, III

		William J.,IV m. Kim H.	Warren Hatcher m. Susan (?)

Children of Henry Harwood and his first wife, Henrietta Calvert

10	10	Fanny died young	John died young

Children of Henry Harwood and his second wife, Virginia Isabella Chandler.

10	10	Rosa m. Walter Wilson	Henry
11	11	Evelyn died unmarried	Fannie m. Walter C. Tandy no issue

Children of Mary Lawson and Dr. Daniel Cary Barraud.

9   9

Ann   Myra   Phillip   John Thomas   Mary Ann   Lelia   Courtney
 B.   Rosanna   St.   Taylor   m.   Jane   Roy   Baker   Cornelia
died   m.   George   m.   Mary   died   died   died   m.
young Samuel   died   Honoria   Baker   single young young George
        M.   young   Allmand   A.
      Wilson   Hanson

Child of Myra Rosanna and Samuel Wilson

10   10

          Catherine m. Lt. Richard Coke Marshall

11   11

    Rev. Myron Barraud Marshall m. Sarah Elizabeth Niemeyer

Children of Sarah Elizabeth Niemeyer and Myron Barraud Marshall

12   12

   Louise   Elizabeth   Catherine   Myron   Herman   Richard
  Chandler   Barraud   Wilson   Barraud   Calvert   Coke
    m.   m.   m.   m.   m.   m.
I-Robert   Dudley   Robert   Margaret   Jean   I-Martha
Craddock   Diggs   Hamill   Haddow   Scott   McKenny
II-George   II-Clara
  Hoffman
III-Edward
  McCrensky   Arthur   John   Helen
                                    Niemeyer   m.   St. Julien
                                       m.   Gladys   m.
                                     Isabel   Fawcett   Henry
                                   Montgomery   Fedgick

158

Recap of Significant Data: Lawson

Studying the genealogy of the Lawson family, we find that the information differs according to the source.

Thomas Lawson is the first member of the family to come to the New World. He married Miss Bray. Two sources indicate they had one child, Anthony Lawson who married, but died young leaving two children, Anthony and George. The third source leaves out the first Anthony and Thomas is said to have had two children, Anthony and George.

When Anthony (1st or 2nd) returned from schooling in England, he married three times. Again the sources differ: Anthony had no children by his first two marriages and five children by his third wife or he had one child by his first wife and four by his second wife and none by his third.

The study in one case lists Anthony's 3rd wife as Elizabeth Westgate Connor and their children are Thomas, Ann, Frances, George, and Thomas. In the second case, Anthony had one child, Thomas, by his first wife, Ann Keeling Okeham, and four children (Mary, Margaret, Elizabeth and Anthony) by his second wife, Mary Gookin Moseley. He had no children by his third wife, Elizabeth Westgate Connor.

Generation

1   Thomas Lawson was born in Northumberland, England in 1583 and came to Jamestown in 1610. He was shipwrecked in the Bermudas during a storm. Governor Gates and Admiral Somers had two small ships built from the wrecked one and this group continued to Jamestown. Thomas Lawson and his wife, Margaret Bray, had a son, Anthony. There is a question as to whether these Lawsons are the ancestors of the Lawsons of Lower Norfolk County. Thomas died in Jamestown in 1668 at the age of eighty-five.

2   Anthony Lawson was born near Jamestown in 1611. He married and died young. The name of his wife is unknown. There is a question as to whether this Anthony Lawson is an ancestor of Colonel Anthony Lawson.

3   Anthony Lawson was born in 1634 near Jamestown and attended school in England for several years. He returned to Virginia in 1668 when his grandfather died. He purchased several thousand acres in Lower Norfolk County, now the city of Virginia Beach.

The following is from an old unrecorded paper found in the Clerk's Office, Princess Anne County.

> In power of attorney made Dec. 1668 proved June 15th, 1669, Thomas Moncreffe of Londonderry, Alderman and Alex Tomkins and Henry Gardner of the same city made Anthony Lawson, Merchant, their attorney for Virginia "or any other part of the West Indies."   April 16, 1673 a certificate of four hundred acres of land was granted Mr. Anthony Lawson for his own importation twice and for John Canter, William Church, Garrett Really, Eliza May and Zambo and Maria, two negroes. He was married first to Mrs. Ann Okeham, relict of Mr. John Okeham, then to Mrs. Mary Moseley, relict of William Moseley and daughter of John Gookin, and then to Elizabeth. He was Justice of Lower Norfolk County from Feb. 18, 1672 to May 11, 1682 and from May 17, 1687 to May 28, 1691 and then for Norfolk County to May 16, 1693 and High Sheriff for Norfolk County from May 18, 1693 to May 7, 1695 and Justice of Princess Anne from November 4, 1696 to July 3, 1701.

This land was about five miles from the present site of Norfolk. Here he built a brick mansion he named Lawson Hall. He was a lieutenant colonel in the Virginia Militia, was prominent in the suppression of Bacon's Rebellion, was a founder of Norfolk, sheriff of Lower Norfolk County and later a justice of Lower Norfolk County. In 1688 he was a member of the House of Burgesses.

His first wife was Ann Keeling Okeham, a widow of John Okeham, whom he married before February 16, 1670/71. She died before the summer of 1672. They had one son, Thomas. His second wife was Mary Gookin Moseley, the widow of Captain William Moseley, whom he married on August 15, 1672 and by whom he had four children. She died in 1698. He and his third wife had no children. Colonel Lawson moved to Princess Anne County to live about 1694. He died before July Court in 1701.

Colonel Lawson and William Robinson purchased fifty acres of land on the Elizabeth River that was to become the city of Norfolk.

Lower) At a Court held 15th of October 1680
Norfolk) Present 18th of October 1680
19th ditto

Capt. Wm. Robinson, Maj. Francis Sayer, Lt. Col. Robt. Bray, Mr. Malachy Thurston, Mr. Henry Spratt, Mr. George Newton, Justices.

It is by this Court order that Capt. Wm. Robinson and Maj. Anthony Lawson be the feofees in trust for the disposal of the land laid out in this County for building a towne.

(Note: In 1680 Colonel Lawson secured the enactment of a law by the General Assembly establishing the town of Norfolk.)

March 16th, 1694-5 Malachy Thurston appointed "Chief and head Surveys" of the "Roads in Tanners Creek precincts from Mr. Spratt's bridge to Chichester's point at the mouth of Tanners Creek and so to the towne" in place of Lt. Col. Anthony Lawson removed to Little Creek. In a deed made and proved June 15, 1682 Anthony Lawson of Lower Norfolk County in Virginia gent. for and in Consideration of ye sume of five thousand pounds of Porke and one mare sold to Owen Grady of ye same place, planter, one parcell of land containing one hundred acres "more or less", being part of patent of seven hundred acres of land granted John Ladd 27th of May 1697 and by him sold to Lawson. On the 16th day of July 1689 he sold Henry Snayle for 3000 pounds of Tobacco and "Six thousand good oaken covering house boards" two hundred and fifty acres of land at "head of Linnhaven River upon the west side thereof".

Norfolk County July 16th, 1701, Major James Wilson appointed one of the feofees in trust for disposing of the town land in place of Lt. Col. Anthony Lawson, Deceased.

At a Court held for Princess Anne County Oct. 15th, 1701. Upon ye Petition of Elizabeth Lawson, Thomas Lawson, John Thorowgood and Lewis Conner an order for a commission of Adm. Con is granted ym on ye Estate of Lt. Col. Anthony Lawson, he dying intestate. They having pformed wt ye Law as Such cause requires.

4   Colonel Lawson's five children were Thomas, Mary who married Thomas Walke, Margaret who married John Thoroughgood, Elizabeth and Anthony. Thomas who was born in 1666 married Rose Thoroughgood in 1692/93. She was the daughter of Colonel Adam Thoroughgood. He was Justice of Princess Anne County from May 8, 1702 to September 1, 1703. They had five children.

May 4, 1702 Thomas Lawson son and heir of Lt. Col. Anthony Lawson sold to Lewis Conner for eight pounds sterling "one lott of Land" in New Towne in ye County of Princess Anne containing one halfe acre of ground. In a discharge made May 6, 1702 "Margaret Thorowgood widow and Ext. of Lt. Col. John Thorowgood Dec. and daughter of Col. Anthony Lawson decd. Released "Tho: Lawson Coe Adm of her father Colonel Anthony

Lawson of all "Legaseys" particularly "A Legacy given her by her uncle Geo. Lawson Decd and acknowledge having recc'd of the said Lawson her share of her father's estate. He was justice of Princess Anne County from May 8, 1702 to September 1, 1703. His will was made 27th of 8br 1703 witnessed by Edw. Moseley, Richard Bolton and C. Cocke and proved 4th of 9br 1703 by the oaths of Col. Edward Moseley and Christopher Cocke.

Extract from the Will of Thomas Lawson "made 27th of 8br, 1703, witnessed by Edward Moseley, Richd Bolton, and C. Cocke, and proved 9br, 1703 by the oaths of Edward Moseley and Christopher Cocke.

"It is my Will and Desire y't Great Harry Cuffee and Andrew w't ye parts I have in ye two Sloops in partnership wth Mr Joell and all so all my Part debts and To be Debts as received, be sould for money by Mr Lewis Conner and Mr Jno Richardson and Christopr Cocke for to pay ye debt I owe Mr. Walke's children and yt all my money Debts and money in England be by ye above named Lewis Conner, Jn Richardson and Christopr Cocke put to ye aforesd use if need soe require but if ye above mentioned shall not amount to what I owe yt then ye remaindr be Paid out of my Estate by my Executrs hereafter named. Riding Horse, "Rainbow", to brother in law Lewis Conner, Plantation on which he lived to son Anthony, after his wife's decease. Son George Lawson the plantation he purchased of Sim Franklin and Martha Workman; and also the tract of land his father bought of Francis Brocket. "To ye child my wife now goes with, if it be a boy ye plantat where I formerly lived in Tanner's Creek, commonly known by ye Name of Elders; and to his Heir's forever, but if it should be a Girle then ye sd land to go to ye Heire's." I give and bequeath to my Eldest Son, Anthony Lawson ye large plate punch Boull with ye Cupp thereunto Belonging wch was my Grandfather Coll. Robert Bray's. To wife

Rose Lawson, her riding horse, Forrester, w^t a Good Saddle and furniture wth one negro woman Esbell. Remainder of property to be equally divided between wife Rose, and sons Anthony and George Lawson, and daughters Frances and Ann Lawson and ye childe, my wife Now Goes with, Wife Rose whole and Sole Exct."

In a deed of gift made October 3, 1705, acknowledged in open court the same day, Mrs. Rose Lawson, Widow "for love and affection" which she bore her five children of Thomas Lawson Gent^n, late of Princess Anne County, Dec^d, gave to son Anthony "the largest bed and furniture in the hall chamber; being silk curtains and counterpaine, one paire large blankets and paire ffine sheets wth one dozen new Diaper napkins and table cloath m^{rkt} A. L. one silver Porridger m^{rkt} A. L. To second son George Lawson one Dozen New Diaper Napkins and table cloath m^{rkt} C. L. and a paire of ffine Sheets, also a plate porringer m^{rkt} T. M. To third Sonn Thomas Lawson, Three negro boyes, by name Samuel, Ned and Sam, one of them ab^t two years old, ye other two about eight and ten months old apease, with One Dozen New Diaper Napkins and one table cloath m^{kt} T. L., one paire ffine Sheets, and a plate porringer m^{kt} T. M. in the handle.

To the eldest daughter, Frances, one Dozen New Diaper Napkins and table cloath m^{kt} F. L., one silver porringer m^{kt} T. M. and one paire good ffine sheets"

"To the youngest daughter, Anne, one Negro Girle, by name of Dinah, being ab^t a month old, with one dozen Nice Diaper Napkins and table cloath m^{kt} A. L. and a hoop ring with ye posey (vertue makes love eternal) likewise one paire ffine sheets and a silver porringer m^{kt} T. M." and "further" gave "to daughter Anne a Negro woman Izbell with her first child (but not to be possest wth her tiel after her decease) all of ye rest of ye s^d Izbell's Increase except ye first child before mentioned to be equally divided among her five children, or their survivors.

Also among her five children, to be equally divided, thirty pounds of New Milled money, but in case any of her s^d children, vizt, Anthony, George, Thomas, Frances and Anne Lawson should die in their nonage, or without lawful heirs, then ye several things wch to him or them shall belong by the Deed of Gift to fall among the Surviveours of them, etc.

5   The children of Thomas and Rose Lawson were named in the will as Anthony, George, Frances, Ann and an unborn child. This unborn child became Thomas as determined by a deed made by Rose Lawson. Captain Thomas Lawson was born in 1703/04 at Lawson Hall and married Frances Sayre, daughter of Charles Sayre. Mary and Thomas Walke had three children: Thomas II, Anthony and Mary. Thomas II married Katherine. Thomas and Frances Sayre Lawson had three children. Thomas died on May 7, 1735.

On the 5th of February 1728 Thomas Lawson Gent. (Ye only surviving son and Heir of Thomas Lawson dced.) of Princess Anne County sold to Nathaniel Hutchins of the same county yeoman for twenty-seven pounds current money seven acres of land in Princess Anne County. On the 8th of October 1730 Thomas Lawson was made Captain of Horse.

His will was made March 18, 1731-2 and proved May 7th, 1735. "All his stocks of Creatures" Cattel, Sheep and Hoggs to be equally divided between his wife and his three sons. To son Anthony the plantation where he (Thomas) lived except four hundred acres; to son Thomas the place called Franklins together with ye four hundred acres above excepted but in laying off ye Said four hundred acres not to come within the old field of that part given to son Anthony, but to join on the branch of ye head hereof and so to Extend it Self into the Main woods towards Major Spratt's. Such a course as Shall lease prejudiced ye manner plantation until ye Said compliments shall be completed reserving liberty to him to get oak timber for his own use and Some pine plank to sell off his brother Anthony's Land--to "Son Charles" all his "lands and marsh to the wash track and Nannie's Creek to be equally divided". Negro woman Nannie to be sold and the money equally divided between his three sons. To son Anthony Six Slaves, "Frank, Africa, John, Amy, Jennie, and Sam, to son Thomas Six Slaves, Peg, Jacob, George, Harry, Isbell and Robin", to Son Charles "Five Slaves, Dinah, Ham, Hannah, Jonas and Rose", and the child that "that negro woman Jennie is now Bigg with. His horses and mares and plate to be equally divided between his wife and three children, to wife Frances Lawson the slaves "Jack, Nanny and Nedd"; household goods to be appraised and the amount together with what reddy money he had "in the house to be equally divided with his wife and three Sons." Wife Frances and her father Charles Sayer Exors (Joyntly and Separately).

Jan. 15, 1750 Anthony and Thomas Lawson made an exchange of some lands which had been left them by their father Thomas Lawson deceased. On the 24th of March 1760 Anthony and Charles Lawson sold to George Chapple two hundred seventy acres of land in the county of Princess Anne near Back Bay, it being a part of a larger tract of land left by Thomas Lawson to his sons Anthony, Charles and Thomas and Thomas being then dead his part descended to his heir at law Anthony. September 17, 1783 Anthony Lawson "Esquire" sold to William Robinson "Attorney at Law" for thirty pounds current money of Virginia "one hundred acres of land" in Princess Anne County, part of that tract of land, Marsh Land, Sand Banks and Flat Sands binding on the north side of Old Currituck Inlet commonly called and known by the name of the "Wash-Tract" belonging to "Anthony Lawson, Major Walke and others".

Thomas audit of Thomas Lawson made June 3rd, 1758, 3 doz. Lemmons for funeral 4s 6d pd. Mr. Dickson for Funeral Sermon 40s for punch for the appraisers they having no other allowance 6s 3d. To Mr. Staton dancing master p. rect. 10s 10d. Pd. Mr. Walke for funeral liquors 44s 11d.

Lower Norfolk County comprised all territory which now includes Norfolk and Princess Anne Counties and Norfolk and Portsmouth. Its records commence in 1637 and terminate in 1691 when it was made into Norfolk and Princess Anne counties. The first court for Lower Norfolk County was held in 1637.

"At a court houlden in the Lower Court of New Norfolk the 15th day of May 1637.

Capt. Adam Thoroughgood, Esq., Capt. John Sibsey, Mr. Francis Mason, Mr. Edward Windham, Mr. Robert Cann, Mr. William Julian".

The first Courts for Norfolk and Princess Anne Counties were held in 1691. The Norfolk County Court was composed of Colonel Lemuel Mason, Capt. Wm. Robinson, Capt John Hatton, Lt. Col. Anthony Lawson, Capt. Wm. Crafford, Major John Nichols and Mr. James Wilson.

6 Colonel Anthony Lawson, who was born in 1729 at Lawson

Hall, married Mary Calvert on June 29, 1758. He inherited Lawson Hall. He was a soldier in the Revolutionary War and died on February 16, 1785 at Lawson Hall. Mary Calvert Lawson, daughter of Cornelius and Mary Saunders Calvert, was born on July 31, 1741 in Norfolk and died on June 18, 1787 at Lawson Hall. They had seven children. Anthony Lawson was a lawyer who was admitted to the practice of law on May 15, 1750 after an examination by Peyton Randolph and George Wythe. He was justice of Princess Anne County from May 20, 1760 to November 3, 1768, from May 8, 1772 to August 10, 1775, sheriff from November 3, 1768 to November 1, 1770. He was vestryman for Lynnhaven Parish from November 14, 1769 to November 6, 1772. He was church Warden to December 14, 1773 and vestryman to November 17, 1778. He was a lieutenant colonel participating in the defense of Norfolk in 1776 when Lord Dunmore burned the city leaving only two buildings standing; St. Paul's Church and a brick house on Bermuda Street which was the town house of Anthony Lawson. Norfolk at this time had 6000 citizens. Later he was captured by the British and sent to East Florida on the Otter, Man of War, under Captain Squires, to be later paroled in exchange for an Englishman.

Thomas and Katherine Walke II had a son, Thomas III who married Margaret Thoroughgood.

The Will of Anthony Lawson
"To All Whom It May Concern"

In the name of God Amen. I, Anthony Lawson, of Princess Anne County and Commonwealth of Virginia, being sick and weak in Body but of a sound disposing mind and memory (Blessed be God) do make and Ordaine this my last Will and Testament in manner and for following.

Imprimes. I give and devise unto my Son Richard Henry Lee Lawson two hundred and fifty acres of Land, part of the Tract whereon I now live, to be laid off at the south End of the said Tract to wit, to begin at the Southern most line next to New Town and extend Northerly the whole breadth of the said Tract, that is from the Westernmost to the Eastermost side until the said two hundred and fifty acres are completed which I give unto him and His Heirs forever.

Item. I give and devise unto my son Richard Henry Lee Lawson, four hundred acres of Sand Banks and Marsh being part of the Wash Tract, to him and His Heirs forever.

Item. I give and devise unto my son Thomas Lawson the remainder of my Land Sand Banks and Marshes to him and His Heirs forever. (Except such as I have hereafter given to my son Anthony).

Item. I give and bequeath unto my said son Thomas Lawson all my silver Plate marked AIE (except two cups and two Salvers which I have hereafter given to my son Richard Henry Lee Lawson). I also give unto my said son Thomas my Clock, Books and Book-case, a young horse (his choice) my best Saddle and Bridle and my Silver Mounted Gun.

Item. I give and bequeath unto my Son Richard Henry Lee Lawson, two Silver Cups and two Salvers marked AIE as aforesaid, also one gun which was given to me by my Kinsman William Wishard in his last Will and Testament.

Item.   I give and devise unto my Son Anthony Lawson two hundred acres of Land at the place commonly called the Logg House bounded by the road that leads from the Cross Roads of Norfolk to the northward of the said tract, to the westward on Nathaniel Hoggard's Lane by a line to be run to the southward, to the Eastward by the main Road that leads to the New Town, to complete the said two hundred acres which I give unto him and his Heirs forever.   I also give unto my said Son Anthony Lawson one Gun such as shall be judged to be a neat and genteel Fowling piece.

Item.   I give and bequeath unto my Daughter Frances Sayer Lawson one good young horse, one saddle and bridle well mounted.

Item.   It is my Will and Desire that after my wife's Dower is set apart, the remainder of my slaves be Equally divided amongst all my children as aforesaid and after my wife decease it is my will and desire that no division shall be made of my slaves until my Son Thomas arrives at the age of twenty-five years, but be kept and employed on the Manor Plantation and the profits after all expenses are paid to be applied to the Maintenance and Education of my children unless any one or more of my Daughters in the meantime should marry in that case I desire that such Daughter or Daughters so marrying may have her or their Proportion of my Slaves set apart immediately.

Item.   I desire that my three Sons Thomas, Richard Henry Lee and Anthony Lawson may have a liberal Education.

Item.   I give and bequeath unto my wife and seven children the residue of my personal Estate to be equally Divided amongst them, reserving the use of my furniture, riding chair and Horse to my Wife during her Widowhood.   It is also my Will and Desire that not any Article or thing given to my Children shall be Sold but at the Discretion of their Guardian or

Guardians.

Item.   If in case any British Debt shall come against the concern of William White and Company, more than can be paid by the same concern, I do then and in that case leave as much Land given to my Son Thomas to be sold for payment of my proportion of the same, except he (my Son Thomas) will undertake to pay it.   Lastly, I do hereby nominate constitute and appoint my Kinsmen Charles Sayer and Thomas Wishart sen[r] Guardian to all my children and Executors of this my last Will and Testament.   In witness Whereof I hereunto set my Hand and Seal this fourth Day of February in the year of our Lord one thousand seven hundred and eighty-five.

Signed Sealed Published and Declared

William White   In the presence of

Lucretia Gordon

William Russel   Anthony Lawson

7   The seven children of Anthony and Mary Calvert Lawson are Thomas who married Sarah Robinson, Richard Henry Lee who married (?) Godwin, Anthony who married (?) Marvolt, Mary Calvert who married George Chandler on March 20, 1793 at Lawson Hall, Elizabeth who married (?) Cartwright, Helen and Frances Sayre who married Dr. Evans.

Mary Calvert was born in November 1767 and died on April 17, 1859 in Norfolk.   George Chandler, a son of John and Elizabeth Matlack Chandler, was born in 1760 in Chester County, Pennsylvania and died in Norfolk.   They married in 1793.

Mary Calvert Lawson Chandler

8   Thomas and Sarah Robinson Lawson had three children none of whom married.   Anthony was born August 14, 1787. Thomas, who was born on August 29, 1789 and died May 14, 1861, served in the War of 1812.   He was commissioned a surgeon mate by James Madison and commissioned Surgeon in Infantry to rank as such from November 30, 1836.   For meritorious service in the field before and during the Mexican War he was promoted to Brevet Brigadier General dated March 3, 1849 to rank as such from May 30, 1848.   He died in the residence of Dr. Daniel Cary Barraud in Norfolk.   General Thomas Lawson willed twelve mahogany chairs which had belonged to his great grandfather, Cornelius Calvert, to Sarah Chandler Niemeyer. Tilly Robinson, the third child, was born June 8, 1793.

Richard Henry Lee Lawson and his wife, a daughter of

Joseph Godwin, had one daughter, Mary Frances. She married James Edward Wilson.

Anthony Lawson married (?) Marvolt and had one son, Alexander, who did not marry and one daughter, Elizabeth, who married James Hill Ransome. Elizabeth was born December 23, 1805 and James Hill Ransome was born April 19, 1795 and died April 17, (?). They were married November 29, 1844 and had one son.

John Adams Chandler was born on August 26, 1795 in Norfolk and died March 31, 1848 in Portsmouth. He married Sarah Howard Woodward on April 30, 1817. She was born in Norfolk on September 10, 1801 and died in Portsmouth on July 3, 1876. John Adams Chandler was a lawyer in Portsmouth.

John Adams Chandler   Sarah Howard Woodward

John Adams Chandler's brother was George Washington Chandler who died unmarried. His sister, Mary Lawson Chandler married first F. W. Boush who was a member of the legislature of Virginia and died without children and married secondly on September 18, 1819 Dr. Daniel Cary Barraud.

9   John Thompson Hill, who was born on January 6, 1813 and died on February 6, 1842, was the adopted son of John Thompson (1768-1847) who married Elizabeth Cutler (1776-1851). John Thompson Hill was the infant son of Shadrack Hill who married Margaret Cutler, sister of Elizabeth. Shadrack Hill died in a boating accident at sea in 1813 and Margaret died shortly afterwards. John Thompson Hill married Mary Elizabeth Chandler who was born on January 28, 1819 and died on August 31, 1893. Her sister, Sarah Howard Chandler married William Angus Niemeyer, a son of John Christian and Ann McLean Niemeyer. Another sister, Henrietta Calvert Harwood, died of

yellow fever in 1855.

William Angus Niemeyer   Sarah Howard Chandler

Children of Mary Lawson Chandler and Dr. Daniel Cary Barraud were cousins of Mary Elizabeth Hill. Two of them were involved in the military. John Taylor Barraud was a lieutenant in the U.S.Navy who died on October 29, 1860. He married Honoraria Allmand on May 25, 1857. Thomas Barraud died at the battle of Bristow Station on October 14, 1863. He was a captain in the 16th Regiment of Mahone's Brigade in the Confederate Army. Courtney Cornelia Berraud married George A. Hanson who died August 4, 1871.

The fourth child of John Adams and Sarah Howard Woodward Chandler was Georgianna Matlock Chandler who married Henry F. Woodhouse. They had seven children of whom two married.

Henrietta Calvert married Henry Harwood. They had two children who died young. Henrietta died during the yellow fever epidemic of 1855. After her death Henry Harwood married Henrietta's sister, Virginia Isobella Chandler. They had two children, Rosa and Henry.

10 Mary Elizabeth Bembury Collins, who was born on December 18, 1841, was the daughter of Dr. William (1804-

1855) and Frances Gregory Collins. Elizabeth Bembury Collins died on July 29, 1926. She married John Thompson Hill, Jr. who was born on February 5, 1839 and died July 29, 1903. Fannie Gregory Collins was the sister of Elizabeth Collins. She was born on June 24, 1849 and died on September 24, 1931. She married Chandler Woodward Hill who was born on October 15, 1841 and died on August 14, 1896. He was a judge of the Hustings Court of Portsmouth and later judge of the First Circuit Court of Virginia.

The Niemeyers were cousins of John Thompson and Chandler Woodward Hill. William Frederic Niemeyer was killed in the Battle of Spotsylvania Courthouse on May 12, 1864. He was born in Portsmouth on May 12, 1840. He was a lieutenant colonel in the 61st Virginia Regiment, Confederate Army. He married Sarah Campbell Smith, the daughter of William Campbell and Martha Elizabeth Smith. They married in 1861. John Chandler Niemeyer was killed at Gettysburg on July 3, 1864. Henry Victor Niemeyer married Martha Jane Hunter of Portsmouth on September 8, 1874. Sarah Howard Niemeyer died unmarried on January 13, 1899. George McKendree Niemeyer was born on November 19, 1849 in Portsmouth and he died unmarried on October 11, 1906. Arthur Emmerson Niemeyer married Sarah Hoyt Mahan of Memphis, Tennessee in February 1878. Crawford Hill Niemeyer married Mrs. Pauline Ritter of Little Rock, Arkansas. Herman Christian Niemeyer married Mary Louise Hook of Baltimore, Maryland. Sam Watts Niemeyer married twice. He first married Mary Agnes Moore of Deep Creek in Norfolk County in 1893 and secondly married Lellie Land of Emporia, Virginia.

Other cousins of the Hills and Niemeyers are children of Martha Chandler Rosser. There were two Rosser brothers. One of the brothers moved to Alabama and there are descendents in

Alabama. There were descendents in Virginia but there are none left.

The youngest son of Georgianna Matlock Chandler and Henry F. Woodhouse was Kenneth Woodhouse who married Grace Hudgins.

Rosa Harwood married Walter Wilson and had two daughters. There is no evidence that Henry Married.

11   John Thompson, Jr. and Mary Elizabeth Bembury Collins Hill had six children, one boy and five girls, none of whom married. William Collins Hill was born on April 15, 1868 and died on October 26, 1934. Mary Chandler Hill was born on November 4, 1869 and died on November 4, 1947. Elizabeth Gregory Hill was born on April 1, 1871 and died on July 6, 1957. Frances Calvert Hill was born on July 2, 1873 and died January 21, 1958. Evelyn Collins Hill was born on May 19, 1877 and died on November 22, 1965 and Blanche Baker Hill was born May 7, 1879 and died December 11, 1949.

Chandler Woodward and Fannie Gregory Collins Hill, sister of Mary Elizabeth, had six children, five boys and one girl. Richard Gregory Hill who was born on November 18, 1872 and died on November 13, 1956. He married Eliza Benson Bilisoly who was called Bennie. She was born on May 23, 1874 and died on October 17, 1953. John Chandler Hill was born on December 16, 1874 and died on September 2, 1960 at the age of eighty-five years and was buried in Elmwood Cemetery in Norfolk. He married Lottie Brown who was called Daisy. She was born on November 18, 1878 and died at the age of ninety-four on January 20, 1973. They were married in 1905. Anthony Lawson Calvert Hill married Mabel Vincent. They had no children. Fannie Hill died young. William Collins Hill was born on September 12, 1879 and died on June 16, 1971. He married Marion Hume who was born on December 26, 1881 and died on April 3, 1962. Baynham Matlack Hill was born on August 27, 1882. He married

Esther Covington who was born on October 11, 1895.

Mary Lawson Chandler, sister of John Adams Chandler, married Dr. Daniel Cary Barraud. They had nine children of whom only four married. Myra Rosanna Barraud, one of the four children, married Samuel Wilson and their daughter, Catherine Wilson married Lt. Richard Coke Marshall a great grand-son of John Marshall, Chief Justice of the Supreme Court of the United States. Catherine and Richard Marshall's son, the Rev. Myron Barraud Marshall, was a priest in the Episcopal Church. The Rev. Marshall was born on September 12, 1883 and married July 21, 1907. His wife, Sarah Elizabeth Niemeyer (Bessie) was an artist who painted wildflowers in watercolor. The Petersburg Garden Club, in 2000, had some of her paintings "With Paintbrush & Shovel Preserving Virginia's Wildflowers" published by the University Press of Virginia.

Kenneth and Grace Hudgins Woodhouse had three daughters, Grace Virginia, Louise and Georgiana. Grace Virginia married Clyde Rawles and Louise married William J. Story, Jr. Georgiana did not marry. All three of these girls were educators and William J. Story, Jr. was a coach and educator.

The daughters of Rosa Wilson were Evelyn who did not marry and Fannie who married Walter Tandy. They had no children.

12 Richard Gregory and Eliza Benson Bilisoly Hill had six children, none of whom married. Frances Chandler Hill took orders in the Sisters of Charity and became at one time Sister Louise. She was born on February 8, 1915. Richard Gregory Hill, Jr. was born on April 3, 1906. He suffered with heart disease and died on February 18, 1925. Robert Camm Hill was born on January 8, 1911 and died June 3, 1911. Antonio Bilisoly Hill was born December 30, 1907 and died August 3, 1998. John Calvert Hill was born May 28, 1909 and died January 10, 1997. Annie Camm Hill was born June 10, 1912.

She died March 5, 2003 at Thornton Hall.

John Chandler Woodward and Lottie Brown Hill had three children. Chandler Woodward Hill was born on June 19, 1906 and married Jessie Lewis Wilson who was born on September 12, 1913. They married on February 27, 1938. Their son, Chandler Woodward Hill, Jr. was born on July 10, 1939. Burroughs Reed Hill was born on September 30, 1907 and married Ruth Beebe. Their son was Burroughs Reed Hill, Jr. Charlotte Reed Hill was born on April 4, 1909. She married Peter Campbell Hutchison who was born on October 9, 1900 and died October 21, 1972. Their children were Polly Hutchison and Peter Campbell Hutchison, Jr.

William Collins and Marion Hume Hill had four children. Marion Hume Hill was born November 4, 1910 and died April 30, 1913. Annie Heartwell Hume Hill married Charles Artenzen and had no issue. William Collins Hill, Jr. married Ellie ? and had no issue. Frances Gregory Hill married Sam Von Kommer and had three daughters.

Grace Virginia and Clyde Rawles had a daughter, Clyde Virginia Rawls and Louisa and William J. Story, Jr. had two children, William J. Story, III who married Diane (?) and Chandler who married David Boyette Dennis.

The present Niemeyers are direct descendents of this Lawson line. In Tidewater Ancestors, the noted generation should be changed as follows.

15	15	Lt. Col. William Frederic Niemeyer, C. S. A. m. Sarah Campbell Smith
16	16	John Frederic Niemeyer m. Lucrece Bilisoly
17	17	Antonio Bilisoly Niemeyer m. Lutie Stuart Spotts
18	18	Antonio Bilisoly Niemeyer, Jr. m. Alice Virginia Berry

19	19	William Frederic Niemeyer	Frank Berry Niemeyer	John Stuart Niemeyer
		m.	m.	m.
		Carolyn Louise Holtzhauer	Shannon Page Eadie	April Michelle Tripp
20	20	John Cameron Niemeyer	Jacob Douglas Niemeyer	John Stuart Niemeyer, Jr.
		Kyle Antonio Niemeyer		

From The Virginian Pilot, Sunday January 12, 1964
PAST LIVES IN BOXWOODS
Katharine Syer

It is amazing to discover that as long as 1668, a brick manor house was built in old Lower Norfolk County (later Princess Anne County and now the City of Virginia Beach) which has the elegance of a formal boxwood garden.

And it is more amazing that the trees, now 30 feet tall, are still handsome and strong.   Today these boxwood trees outline the garden of Mr. and Mrs. Charles Hodgman, who own this estate, called Lawson Hall.

Manor House

Unfortunately, the manor house burned before 1900, during a Christmas party, shortly after it had been beautifully restored by Mr. Hodgman's grandparents, Mr. and Mrs. Carl Fernstrom.

The long entrance land is alive with the spirits of former visitors.   Many distinguished men have been entertained here. As you approach the grounds, hoary old trees firmly established a mood of awe.   An oak on the right is judged to be a truly virgin tree.

Formally planted in front of a rebuilt dwelling are two heroic beech trees.   The bottom limbs arching down from the massive trunks, reach out a distance of 125 feet.

Old Gardens

Think of the time, 300 years ago, when the boxwood garden was planned and planted.   There were Indians still in the woods.

Col. Anthony Lawson, the original builder and gardener had been born on a plantation near Jamestown in 1634.   He was the grandson of the Lawson immigrant, Capt. Thomas Lawson, who was in the shipwreck of the Sea Venture in the Bermudas in 1609.

Captain Thomas Lawson's young wife, Margaret Bray Lawson, wrote home to England from her Jamestown plantation that she could keep a better house in Virginia on 100 pounds a year than she could in England on 500 pounds.

If you remember the English game of Bowles, which Sir Francis Drake played so enthusiastically as the Spanish Armada approached England, you will appreciate the bowling green at Lawson hall. It is lined with giant boxwood.

Here again you feel the company of the ten generations that have lived their lives here. It is a great privilege to experience the perspective that comes with a visit to Lawson Hall.

Lawson Hall Near Cape

"Seven miles from Norfolk, on the road leading toward Cape Henry is Lawson Hall; an avenue one half mile long, connects the house itself with the thoroughfare. The plantation, until a few years ago, contained over 1000 acres of land, and the lovely formal garden, the oldest in this section, and one of the oldest in America, was laid out by Anthony Lawson, who sailed to this country in 1609 and of whom it is said was one of the company who sailed in the ship of Sir George Somers which was caught in a gale off the Bermudas and driven to these shores, and from which setting even Shakespeare obtained the material for his "Tempest."

"Formerly ships came from the sea through Little Creek and landed their stores near the site of the present house. Of these merchant ships the Lawsons had many and brought in them, so the story goes, some of the bricks and much of the carved gray marble of which the original dwelling was constructed. The walls of this house were two feet thick and the drawing room was 36 feet square and every room was finished in handmade wainscoting. Unfortunately this fine old landmark was destroyed by fire several years ago and the residence we now see was built a few years ago by the late C. F. Hodgman, Sr., who built with appreciation and sympathy for the older home.

"However, it is the garden which interests us most. Here are great beeches and laurel, oaks with a spread of over 100 feet, and many boxwood trees in formal rows; these are among the largest in America. The boxwood and the rows of cedars make it a scene as if summer were here the whole year round.

English Garden Reproduced

"One feels in looking at the old place that one of these Lawsons brought with him the memory of some loved garden in England and reproduced it here. For many years the estate suffered decay, being officers' headquarters during the War Between the States, by both armies. Yet, during all these trying times, no one cut down the beautiful boxwood or harmed the larger trees.

"After entering from the long avenue, the road divides and circles to the marble walk which leads to the entrance of the house. On this front lawn within the circle are the very largest trees—beech, laurel, oak and maple. Across the front of the house and along the two sides are planted boxwwod trees, those in front kept low and clipped, but at the sides have been allowed to grow as trees will, until now they reach the eaves of the house.

"On the left of the house is a terrace with fine old box trees on its edge. Going down from the terrace by two stone steps and on for some 40 feet, one comes upon a little stream with box trees on either side, whose tops mingle above. This spot is a veritable bird sanctuary for here the year round birds of some kind may be found. In summer the mocking bird, the cardinal and the wren make it their own.

Box Trees Lined

"Across a little bridge on the other side of the stream after another level of some 40 feet is terraced again. Here, too, are box trees in line with the trees of the other terrace. On this the orange day lily runs wild and in June is a glowing mass of beauty. This is not seen until one comes upon it suddenly upon descending the first terrace. There, two, (sic) the white narcissus is naturalized. Other native wild flowers have been moved here—blood root, trailing arbutus, lady slipper, and the atamasco lily.

"Several years ago when the boxwood trees had their first clipping, 1300 pounds of short clippings were cut and never missed, showing the number andsize of the stately trees of England that have found a home here and seem to like it.

"These Lawsons and their kinsmen, the Walkes, who occupied Lawson Hall so many years, identified themselves with all that was fine in the history of the new country. One of them was always a vestryman in that now ancient and most interesting church, known as Old Donation, as well as the little church which preceded it at Church Point. Anthony Lawson helped select the site of Norfolk. There were women, too, of charm and beauty. One, Mary Calvert Lawson, has had her name handed down from generation to generation.

"When the moonlight streams over this garden and lingers lovingly there, one feels that much of interest has happened in it. That these wonderful trees through their several generations have been revered is truly evident in that during these more than two centuries they have never been harmed, keeping their foliage green and making of a lovely spot, a perpetual summer."

Lawson Hall

This description and story of Lawson Hall is interesting especially because it was given by its former owner, who was a most enthusiastic lover of and worker for beautiful gardens.

Under generation, the first column is the generation listed on page 369 of <u>Tidewater</u> <u>Ancestors</u> and the second column is for the Matlack lineage. The persons from whom we are descended are in bold print.

Generation

1   1   **William Matlack** m. **Mary Hancock**

2   2   Mary Haines m¹ **Timmy Matlock** m² **Martha Burr Haines**

3   3

Priscilla Letitia Achsob Abigail

Sybil **Elizabeth** Timothy II Titus Josiah Seth White

m

John Chandler

4   4   Sybil   **George**
                  m.   m.
          Elijah Coffing   **Mary Calvert**
                                   Lawson

Recap of Significant Data: Matlack

Generation

2   2   Timothy Matlack was born in 1695. His first wife, Mary Haines was born in 1701 and died in 1728. He married secondly Martha Burr, widow of Josiah Haines on January 12, 1730. She was the daughter of Henry and Elizabeth Burr.

3   3   Timothy Matlack was the father of four children by his first wife and the father of seven children by his second wife. Priscilla was born in 1722, Letitia in 1724, Achsob in 1726 and Abigail on November 11, 1728. Sybil, the first child

by Martha Burr Haines, was born in 1730; Elizabeth was born in Haddonfield, New Jersey on April 12, 1734. She married John Chandler of Chester County, Pennsylvania. He was born in 1731. Elizabeth died in Norfolk, Virginia in 1793. Timothy II was born in Haddonfield, New Jersey in 1736. Various dates were given for his birth. He died in Hornsburg, Pennsylvania on April 14, 1829. His tombstone says he was ninety-nine years old.

Timothy was a Revolutionary patriot, a state official and a member of the Society of Friends who moved to Philadelphia to follow in his father's footsteps as a merchant. He was married on October 5, 1758 to Ellen, daughter of Mordecai Yarnell, a leading Quaker preacher, but was disowned by the Quakers in 1765 for "frequenting company in such manner as to neglect business whereby he contracted debts, failed and was unable to satisfy the claims of his creditors."

In May 1775, he joined the Philadelphia Associators and in the same month was employed as an assistant to Charles Thomson, secretary of the Continental Congress. A few of the minutes are in Matlack's handwriting and he wrote the commission for Washington as commander in chief. The following year, it is probable; he was employed to engross the Declaration of Independence.

Congress appointed him a storekeeper for military supplies. He was elected colonel of a battalion of Associators raised early in 1776 and in the same year was a member of the Constitutional Convention for Pennsylvania, in which he served on the committee to prepare the draft. On July 24, 1776, he became a member of the Council of Safety and on the adoption of the new state constitution, he was made secretary of the Executive Council.

In the military operations around Trenton and Princeton, he

took the field with other Pennsylvania militia as colonel of a rifle battalion. Returning from this campaign, he devoted himself to the offices of secretary of the council, keeper of the great seal and keeper of the register of persons attainted.

In 1779, he was designated a trustee of the newly created University of Pennsylvania. In 1780 he was elected a member of the Continental Congress serving for two years. On the formation of the Bank of North America by Robert Morris in 1781 he was one of the first members on the board of directors. From 1780 until his death he was a member of the American Philosophical Society and served as one of its secretaries.

In 1782 he was removed as secretary of the Supreme Executive Council on charges of irregularities in his accounts. Judgment was obtained against him and for a time he was jailed for debt. He vigorously resented these charges and in 1783 the Council of Safety gave him a silver urn for the many valuable services he had rendered the cause of Independence.

After a brief residence in New York, he returned to Philadelphia in 1784. He was one of the commissioners appointed under the act of September 28, 1789 "to view the navigable waters" of Pennsylvania. He was assigned to the Delaware River. Later he resided as a minor official of the state government.

After the death of his wife he married on August 17, 1797, Elizabeth, sister of David Claypoole, the printer and widow of Norris Copper. In 1813 he was elected an alderman of the city and served until 1818 when he retired from public life.

He was active in forming the Society of Free Quakers, which was composed of those who had been disowned or who had resigned from the Society of Friends on account of their wartime activities. On his death he was buried in the Free Quaker burying ground in Philadelphia, the bodies from which were later removed to Matson's Ford across the Schuylkill River from Valley Forge. By his first marriage he had five children; through the three daughters and one son who lived to maturity, he left numerous descendents.

"At the time when Thomas Jefferson wrote the Declaration of Independence Timothy Matlack was secretary to Benjamin Franklin. His handwriting was so excellent that it was he who made the copy of the Declaration now kept under glass in the Congressional Library at Washington, D.C. An armed guard always stands beside it.

This Timothy was the brother of our ancestor, Elizabeth Matlack, who married George Chandler."

Louise Niemeyer Fontaine

Titus was born in 1738, Josiah in 1742, Seth in 1744 and White in 1745.

4   4 Sybil Chandler married Elijah Coffing in 1777 and her brother, George Chandler, who was born in 1760, married Mary Calvert Lawson of Lawson Hall in Princess Anne County, Virginia.

The present Niemeyers are direct descendents of this Matlack line. In Tidewater Ancestors, the noted generation should be changed as follows.

8   8   Lt. Col. William Frederic Niemeyer, C. S. A.
            m. Sarah Campbell Smith

9   9   John Frederic Niemeyer m. Lucrece Bilisoly

10   10   Antonio Bilisoly Niemeyer m. Lutie Stuart Spotts

11   11   Antonio Bilisoly Niemeyer, Jr. m. Alice Virginia
            Berry

12   12   William Frederic   Frank Berry   John Stuart
            Niemeyer   Niemeyer   Niemeyer
               m.   m.   m.

		Carolyn Louise Holtzhauer	Shannon Page Eadie	April Michelle Tripp
13	13	John Cameron Niemeyer	Jacob Douglas Niemeyer	John Stuart Niemeyer, Jr.
		Kyle Antonio Niemeyer		

Agreed That the Committee of safety be requested to lend this Committee 800 Swivel shott which this Committee will repay them as soon as possible

Extract from the minutes

T Matlack Secy

Timothy Matlack, a Pennsylvania Quaker who New York autograph dealer Charles Hamilton believes penned the Declaration of Independ-

ence, is at left. A sample of Matlack's handwriting, which was compared to the historic document, is at right.—AP Wirephoto.

Declaration Penned By 'Fighting Quaker'

NEW YORK, July 4 (AP).—An autograph dealer says he has just made a timely discovery—who penned the Declaration of Independence.

The dealer, Charles Hamilton, said yesterday that by comparing the Declaration with another newly discovered document he has established that the Declaration was penned by Timothy Matlack, a "fighting Quaker" from Pennsylvania.

Mr. Hamilton said he recently acquired a document handwritten by Matlack in a collection of family papers, where it had been for more than 100 years.

It is a large octavo sheet dealing with the proceedings of the Naval Committee on January 2, 1776, and concerns a loan of "600 swivel shott" or ammunition from the Committee of Safety. Matlack was a member of the latter committee, and later attended the Continental Congress.

The autograph dealer said Matlack as assistant to Charles Thompson, clerk of the Continental Congress, whose handwriting was "not elegant," and that Thompson undoubtedly delegated the penning of the Declaration to Matlack.

Mr. Hamilton said comparison of the flourishes in the Declaration of Independence and the Matlack letter leave "not the slightest doubt" that the same man wrote both.

The dealer said there had been speculation by some historians that Matlack may have

penned the document but the newfound Matlack document proves it.

The document he credits Matlack with writing is the engrossed parchment copy, signed by members of the Continental Congress, which is now on display in the National Archives Building and most frequently reprinted.

The original draft written by Thomas Jefferson and edited by the Congress was lost after it had been sent to a printer, but there are several copies in Jefferson's handwriting in existence, as well as copies made by John Adams and other members of the Congress.

THIS is A photo of the ORIGINAL oil painting of TIMOTHY MATLACK BY

Burr

Under generation, the first column is the generation listed on page 369 of <u>Tidewater Ancestors</u> and the second column is for the Burr lineage. The persons from whom we are descended are in bold print.

Generation

1   1   **Henry Burr** m. **Elizabeth**

2   2   Mary Haines m^1 **Timmy Matlack** m^2 **Martha Burr Haines**

3   3   **Elizabeth Matlack** m **John Chandler**

4   4   **George Chandler** m **Mary Calvert Lawson**

Recap of Significant Data: Burr

Generation

   2   Martha Burr, widow of Josiah Haines, married Timothy Matlack on January 12, 1730.

   3   Timothy had 4 children by his first wife and with Martha had 7 children. Their daughter, Elizabeth, married John Chandler of Chester County, Pa. in 1758. Elizabeth died in Norfolk, Va. in 1793. Elizabeth and John had 2 children, Sybil and George.

   4   George married Mary Calvert Lawson of Lawson Hall in Princess Anne County, Va. in 1783.

The present Niemeyers are direct descendents of this Burr line. In <u>Tidewater</u> <u>Ancestors</u>, the noted generation should be changed as follows.

8 8 Lt. Col. William Frederic Niemeyer, C. S. A.
         m. Sarah Campbell Smith

9 9 John Frederic Niemeyer m. Lucrece Bilisoly

10 10 Antonio Bilisoly Niemeyer m. Lutie Stuart Spotts

11 11 Antonio Bilisoly Niemeyer, Jr. m. Alice Virginia Berry

12 12	William Frederic Niemeyer	Frank Berry Niemeyer	John Stuart Niemeyer
	m.	m.	m.
	Carolyn Louise Holtzhauer	Shannon Page Eadie	April Michelle Tripp
13 13	John Cameron Niemeyer	Jacob Douglas Niemeyer	John Stuart Niemeyer, Jr.
	Kyle Antonio Niemeyer		

Under generation, the first column is the generation listed on page 369 of <u>Tidewater Ancestors</u> and the second column is for the Hancock lineage. The persons from whom we are descended are in bold print.

Generation

1   1   **William Matlack** m. **Mary Hancock**

2   2   Mary Haines m[1] **Timmy Matlock** m[2] **Martha Burr Haines**

Recap of Significant Data: Hancock

Generation

    1   William Matlack emigrated to West New Jersey and located on a piece of land which became the boundary line for the counties of Burlington and Gloucester. There he married Mary Hancock.

The present Niemeyers are direct descendents of this Hancock line. In <u>Tidewater Ancestors</u>, the noted generation should be changed as follows.

8   8   Lt. Col. William Frederic Niemeyer, C. S. A.
         m. Sarah Campbell Smith
9   9   John Frederic Niemeyer m. Lucrece Bilisoly
10   10   Antonio Bilisoly Niemeyer m. Lutie Stuart Spotts
11   11   Antonio Bilisoly Niemeyer, Jr. m. Alice Virginia
         Berry

12	12	William Frederic Niemeyer	Frank Berry Niemeyer	John Stuart Niemeyer
		m.	m.	m.
		Carolyn Louise Holtzhauer	Shannon Page Eadie	April Michelle Tripp
13	13	John Cameron Niemeyer	Jacob Douglas Niemeyer	John Stuart Niemeyer, Jr.
		Kyle Antonio Niemeyer		

MacLean

Under generation, the first column is for the MacLean lineage. <u>Tidewater Ancestors</u> has no genealogical chart listed for the MacLean clan. The persons from whom we are descended are in bold print.

Generation

1   **Duncan MacLean** m. **Ann**

2   **Ann MacLean** m. **John Christian Niemeyer**

3 Eliza Ann   **William Angus**   Virginia Margaretha
       m.   m.
Dr. Samuel Crawford   **Sarah Howard Chandler**

Recap of Significant Data: MacLean
Generation

1   Duncan and Ann MacLean were of the "Red MacLeans of Ross Shire, Scotland."

2 Ann MacLean was married on August 15, 1813 at Moyock, North Carolina. John Niemeyer died on October 20, 1820 when Eliza Ann was six and William Angus was four years old. Ann married a second time to a Mr. Smith. She died on April 14, 1824 leaving her two children. Eliza was eight and William was six.

Upon hearing of the death of Ann MacLean Niemeyer, her brother, Duncan, came to America from Scotland and offered to take the children back to Scotland with him, but they did not wish to leave their half-brothers so their uncle returned to Scotland without them.

The present Niemeyers are direct descendents of this MacLean line. In <u>Tidewater</u> <u>Ancestors</u>, the noted generation should be as follows.

4   Lt. Col. William Frederic Niemeyer, C. S. A.
      m. Sarah Campbell Smith

5 John Frederic Niemeyer m. Lucrece Bilisoly

6 Antonio Bilisoly Niemeyer m. Lutie Stuart Spotts

7 Antonio Bilisoly Niemeyer, Jr. m. Alice Virginia Berry

8

William Frederic Niemeyer	Frank Berry Niemeyer	John Stuart Niemeyer
m.	m.	m.
Carolyn Louise Holtzhauer	Shannon Page Eadie	April Michelle Tripp

9

John Cameron Niemeyer	Jacob Douglas Niemeyer	John Stuart Niemeyer, Jr.
Kyle Antonio Niemeyer		

Woodward

Under generation, the first column is the generation listed on page 403 of <u>Tidewater</u> <u>Ancestors</u> and the second column is for the Woodward lineage. The persons from whom we are descended are in bold print.

Generation

0   1

Edward Woodward

2

Christopher Woodward 1

m^1 m^2

Margarett   **Elizabeth Westwood**

3

(four   Susan Salerna?   **Christopher 2**

daughters)   m^1 m^2 m^3

Catherine **Margarett** Dorothy

Audley   **Clay**   Wilkinson

4   Children of Christopher 2 and Catherine Audley

Thomas   William   Katherine   Susan   Mary   Anne   Elizabeth

m.   m.   m.

Katherine   Roger   Edward

Fountain   Ashe

Children of Christopher 2 and Margarett Clay

Christopher 3   George

Child of Christopher 2 and Dorothy Wilkinson

Samuel

m.

Sarah Holloman

5   Children of Thomas and Katherine Woodward
Thomas Katherine Elizabeth Mary Rochelle Philerita John
                                                m.   m.
                                            ? Giles ? Pierce

                    Children of William
        3 sons   Martha
                      m¹   m²
                    Gideon Nathaniel
                    Macon   West

        Children of Mary Woodward and Roger Fountain
                    Roger   Robert   Mary

        Child of Samuel Woodward and Sarah Holloman
                    Samuel, Jr.

            Child of Christopher 3 Woodward
                      George
                        m.
                Elizabeth Honiwood

6   Child of Martha Woodward and Gideon Macon
            Martha Macon m. Orlando Jones.

Child of Martha Woodward and Nathaniel West   Unity
            West m. William Dandridge

        Child of John Woodward who married ? Pierce
                    Henry Woodward
        m¹   m²   m³
    Elizabeth Yeardley   Margaret ?   Mary Godfrey

Children of George and Elizabeth Honiwood
Lancelot   John   George   Samuel
m.
Elizabeth Cocke

7   Child of Martha Macon and Orlando Jones
Frances Jones m. Col. John Dandridge

Child of Henry Woodward and Elizabeth Yeardley
Francis Woodward

Children of Lancelot Woodward and Elizabeth Cocke
Jeremiah   William   Richard   **Lancelot**

8   Child of Frances Jones and John Dandridge
Martha Dandridge
m^1 m^2
John Parke Custis   George Washington

A descendent of Lancelot
William Woodward m. **Sarah Howard**
(This generation number may not be correct.)

9
Children of Martha Dandridge and John Parke Custis
George Washington Parke Custis   Martha Custis
m.
Mary Lee Fitzhugh

Child of **William Woodward** and **Sarah Howard**
Sarah Howard Woodward m **John Adams Chandler**

200

10   Child of John Parke Custis and Mary Lee Fitzhugh
Mary Ann Randolph Custis m. Robert Edward Lee

Child of Sarah Howard Woodward and John Adams Chandler
Sarah Howard Chandler m. **William Angus Niemeyer**
(NOTE: Again there is no proof that this is the tenth
generation of my descendency.)

Recap of Significant Data: Woodward
Generation
   1   Edward Woodward, the father of Christopher 1, was of
Shropshire Co., England. He died about 1550 in England.
   2   Christopher 1 Woodward had four daughters by his first
wife, Margarett, and by his second wife, Elizabeth Westwood
of Oldbury, had a further issue of two daughters and a son,
Christopher 2.   Christopher 1 came to Virginia in the ship,
Gifte, in 1618. He was at Martin's Hundred on the north side
of the James River in 1620.   During the Indian uprising of
1622 he and 75 other men, women and children were massacred.
   3   Christopher 2 Woodward was born in Worcestershire,
England and married Catherine Audley on June 20, 1603 in St.
Magnus-Martyr, London Bridge, Middlesex, England. He came
to Virginia in the ship, Trial, in 1620.   Another source
indicates that he was from Lambet Surry (near London) England
and married three times. His first wife, Catherine Audley,
died before 1625. His second wife, Margarett Clay, died
before November 9, 1635 and he had married the third wife,
Dorothy Wilkinson, before March 6, 1636.
   He was a burgess of the Assembly convened in Jamestown
on October 16, 1629. In 1635 he received a land grant of 300
acres on the Appomattox River. He, later, received a land
grant of 350 acres on the Appomattox and in 1637 a land grant

of 600 acres on the Appomattox River. Christopher 2 died in 1650 in Charles City County, VA.

en children.

Thomas, one of these children was born in 1605 and his brother, William, was born in 1611. William was awarded a land grant of 2100 acres in New Kent County, Virginia on February 23, 1664 by the Governor and the Council. He lived in New Kent County on the north side of the York River.

The following was copied from a contributor to the Genforum.genealogy.com/woodward/messages/2120.html

Land Grant 23 Feb 1664

William Woodward, 2100 acres in New Kent Co VA

"To all &c. Now Know yee that I the said Sir Wm. Berkeley Knt. Govr. &c. give and grant unto Mr WM WOODWARD two thousand one hundred acres of Land Lying in the county of New Kent upon the North side of Yorke river and Bounding as follows beginning at the mouth of a Creeke called Mr. JOHNs Creeke from thence running up the river and bounding by the said River including on neck of sunken grownd and soe continuing the bounds above the said sunken grownd by the river unto a Creeke nere against Capt BASSETTs now dwelling house to a marked Hickory that stands by the said Creeke side which Creeke is the Lower bounds of Mr SAMUELL SNEAD senior his Land where hee now dwelleth from thence southerly up the said Creeke 320 pole bounding upon the said Devident of mr SNEADs, from thence East So. East Easterly 220 pole from thence So East Easterly 200 pole, from thence So So East Easterly 210 pole from thence East and by So Southerly 130 pole from thence So East and by East 90 pole to the aforesaid Mr JOHNs Creeke, from thence down the said Creeke to the mouth thereof 320 pole to the place where it first began, The said Land being purchased by the said Mr WOODWARD of Coeka Coeske Queene of Pomunke as by a sale appears bearing date the 27th September 1664 and upon desire of the said Queene that the said Mr WOODWARD might seate upon the said Land by her assigned and sett over unto him the said Woodward, It was accordingly granted by order of the Govr and Councell dated the 24 of November 1664 to have & to hold&c. To bee held &c. Yeilding & paying&c. Dated the 23d ffebruary 1664"

Thomas was a Royalist. He was a founder of Mineralogy and settled on Pagan Creek in Isle of Wight County and had large land holdings in Isle of Wight and Gloucester Counties.

Mary, the sister of Thomas and William, married a Huguenot, Roger Fountain, who established a colony on the Cape Feare River of North Carolina. Roger Fountain, Sr. became demented and a missionary to the Indians.

Sons, Christopher and George, were descended from Christopher and his second wife. Christopher was born in 1633 and died in 1665. George was born in 1635. He patented 2000 acres of land in 1677 on the north-east side of Dyascund Swamp in James City County in the parish of Wimbleton.

By his third wife, Christopher had a son, Samuel. This Samuel was born in 1637 and in 1704 he owned the six hundred acres originally belonging to his father. Samuel, Sr. died in 1704.

5   Thomas Woodward had seven children. His son, John, married a Pierce. The other children were Thomas, Katherine, Elizabeth, Mary, Rochelle, and Philartia.

William's daughter, Martha, married twice. Her first husband was Gideon Macon and her second was Nathaniel West.

Christopher had a son George.

Samuel, Sr. was the first husband of Sarah Holloman. Her

second husband was John Sturdivant. Samuel and Sarah had a son, Samuel, Jr. When his father died Samuel, Jr. sold his 1/3 of 1000 acres and moved to Boston, Massachusetts. The Maine Woodwards are descended from this Samuel.

Roger, Robert and Mary Fountain moved to Virginia.

6   John Woodward had a son, Henry, who married Elizabeth Yeardley.

Martha Woodward Macon had a daughter, Martha, who married Orlando Jones. She became an ancestress of the Custis and Lee families of Virginia. By her second husband, Martha West had a daughter, Unity West, who married William Dandridge.

George Woodward had four children: Lancelot who was born in 1685 and married Elizabeth Cocke in 1705; John, who was born in 1692; George and Samuel. Elizabeth Cocke was the daughter of William Cocke. Lancelot and Elizabeth Woodward became the ancestors of most of the Woodwards living in Virginia. Lancelot died in 1750.

4   Frances Jones married Colonel John Dandridge.

Henry Woodward and Elizabeth Yeardley had a son, Francis.

8   Martha Dandridge married twice. Her first husband was John Parke Custis and her second was George Washington who added his name to Martha's son, George Washington Park Custis.

9   George Washington Park Custis married Mary Lee Fitzhugh.

10 Mary Ann Randolph Custis married Robert E. Lee.

Note: It has not been proven how many generations of Woodwards there are between Lancelot, born in 1683 a son of George Woodward of the 5th generation, and Sarah Howard Woodward who was born in 1801.

An hypothesis is that Lancelot, of the 6th generation, married Elizabeth Cocke in 1705. They had a son, Richard (generation 7). This Richard married and had a son, Richard, who married Ann Watts (generation 8). In generation 9, a son, Richard, married R. H. Collier. Their son was William Woodward (generation 10) of Norfolk who married Sarah Howard.

Their daughter, Sarah Howard Woodward (generation 11), married John Adams Chandler. Sarah Howard Chandler (generation 12) was born August 4, 1821 in Norfolk. She married, on July 31, 1839, William Angus Niemeyer who was born on April 28, 1816. They had twelve children. Sarah Howard Woodward Chandler Niemeyer died on October 21, 1904.

William Angus was the grandson of Hans Heinrich Niemeyer who was born in Hoya, Germany in 1734. His father was John Christian Niemeyer who was born in Verdon, Germany in 1776. John Christian died in Norfolk County, Virginia in 1820. William Angus' mother was Ann McLean, born of Scottish parents on Staten Island, New York in 1796. She died in Portsmouth, Virginia in 1822.

The present Niemeyers are direct descendents of this Woodward line. In <u>Tidewater</u> <u>Descendents</u> the noted_generation should be changed as follows.

7	12	Sarah Howard Chandler m. William Angus Niemeyer
8	13	Lt. Col. William Frederic Niemeyer, C. S. A. m. Sarah Campbell Smith
9	14	John Frederic Niemeyer m. Lucrece Bilisoly
10	15	Antonio Bilisoly Niemeyer m. Lutie Stuart Spotts
11	16	Antonio Bilisoly Niemeyer, Jr. m. Alice Virginia Berry
12	17	William Frederic Niemeyer Frank Berry Niemeyer John Stuart Niemeyer

		m.	m.	m.
		Carolyn Louise	Shannon Page	April Michelle
		Holtzhauer	Eadie	Tripp
13	18	John Cameron	Jacob Douglas	John Stuart
		Niemeyer	Niemeyer	Niemeyer, Jr.
		Kyle Antonio		
		Niemeyer		

Under generation, the first column is the generation listed on page 403 of <u>Tidewater</u> <u>Ancestors</u> and the second column is for the Cocke lineage. The persons from whom we are descended are in bold print.

Generation

1

Colonel Richard Cocke m^1 Temperance Baily m^2 Mary Aston

2

Captain	Richard	William	John	Richard	Edward
Thomas	"The Elder"			"The Younger"	
m.	m.	m.			
^{1}-Margaret	Elizabeth	^{1}-Jane			
Wood	Hartwell	Flower			
^{2}-Margaret		^{2}-Sarah			
Powell		Dennis			

3

Mary	Elizabeth
m.	m.
Obadiah	Lancelot
Smith	Woodward

Recap of Significant Data: Cocke
Generation

1   Richard Cocke was born ca. 1600 in England and married1, in 1637 in Virginia, to Temperance Bailey who was born about 1617 in Charles City County. Her mother was Ciceley Reynolds. Richard Cocke, of "Bremo", secondly married Mary Aston and died about 1665 in Henrico County, Virginia.

2   William Cocke of the "Lowground" was born in 1655, married in 1689 and died in February 1693. His father was Col. Richard Cocke and his mother was Mary Aston. His wife was Jane Flower who was born before 1635 and died after 1690. Jane Flower had a brother, John Flower, who owned land in James City County. William Cocke married a second time to Sarah Dennis. He had five brothers.

Captain Thomas Cocke married twice. His first wife was Margaret Wood and his second wife was Margaret Powell. He was born ca. 1638 in Henrico County, married in 1663 and died in Henrico County in 1697.

Richard "The Elder" Cocke was born on December 10, 1639 in Henrico County and died there in 1706.

3   Elizabeth Cocke inherited land in James City County from her uncle, John Flower. Mary and Elizabeth Cocke were raised either by their uncle, Richard "The Younger" or their grandmother, Mary (Aston/Cocke) Clarke, both of whom lived in Charles City County not far from Christopher Woodward's plantation. Elizabeth Cocke married Lancelot Woodward in 1708. She died after this year.

Mary and Elizabeth Cocke were sisters. Mary married Obadiah Smith. She died in 1754.

The present Niemeyers are direct descendents of this Cocke line. In Tidewater Ancestors the noted ancestors are in doubt.

8   Lt. Col. William Frederic Niemeyer, C. S. A. m. Sarah Campbell Smith

9   John Frederic Niemeyer m. Lucrece Bilisoly

10   Antonio Bilisoly Niemeyer m. Lutie Stuart Spotts

11   Antonio Bilisoly Niemeyer, Jr. m. Alice Virginia Berry

| 12 | William Frederic Niemeyer m. Carolyn Louise Holtzhauer | Frank Berry Niemeyer m. Shannon Page Eadie | John Stuart Niemeyer m. April Michelle Tripp |
| 13 | John Cameron Niemeyer Kyle Antonio Niemeyer | Jacob Douglas Niemeyer | John Stuart Niemeyer, Jr. |

Chandler

Under generation, the first column is the generation listed on page 431 of <u>Tidewater</u> <u>Ancestors</u> and the second column is for the Chandler lineage. The persons from whom we are descended are in bold print.

Generation

	1		**John Chandler**		
	2		**John Chandler**		
	3		**John Chandler**		
	4		**Nicholas Chandler** m. **Edyth Spratt**		
	5		**Thomas Chandler** m. **Ann Downham**		
	6		**John Chandler** m. **Ann**		
1	7		**George Chandler** m. **Jane**		

<table>
<tr><td>2</td><td>8</td><td>William Chandler
m.
Ann Bowater</td><td>George Chandler
m.
Ruth Bezer</td><td>2 sons</td><td>3 daughters</td></tr>
</table>

3	9		**George Chandler** m. **Esther Taylor**
4	10		**John Chandler** m. **Elizabeth Matlack**

<table>
<tr><td>5</td><td>11</td><td>Sybil Chandler
m.
Elijah Coffing</td><td>George Chandler
m.
Mary Calvert Lawson</td></tr>
</table>

Children of George and Mary Calvert Lawson Chandler

6	12	George Washington Chandler	**John Adams Chandler** m. **Sarah Howard Woodward**	Mary Lawson Chandler m¹ W. F. W. Boush m² Dr. Daniel Cary Barraud

7	13	Mary Elizabeth Chandler m. John Thompson Hill	**Sarah Howard Chandler** m. **William Angus Niemeyer**	Martha W. Chandler m. Rev. Leonidas Rosser	Georgiana Chandler m. Henry F. Woodhouse	Henrietta Calvert Chandler m. Henry Harwood

George McKendree Chandler

Virginia Isobella Chandler
m.
Henry Harwood

Recap of Significant Data: Chandler

Generation

1   John Chandler, Chaundler or Chaundeler of Oare in the parish of Wilcot, Wiltshire, England was living in 16 Henry VIII (1521).

2   John Chandler of Oare was living in 35 Henry VIII (1543).

3   John Chandler of Oare was living in 35 Henry VIII (1543).

4   Nicholas Chandler of Oare was buried at Wilcot Church on November 15, 1604. He married Edyth Spratt who was buried on February 23, 1623-24.

5   Thomas Chandler of Oare was a churchwarden from 1619-1629. He was buried in Wilcot Churchyard on 20 June 1629. He married Ann Downham who was buried at Wilcot on 25 June 1620.

6   John Chandler of Oare was churchwarden of Wilcot from 1630 almost continuously until his death in March 1684. He married Ann who was buried in Wilcot on 8 April 1633.

7   George Chandler was baptized at Wilcot on the 8 April 1633 and left England for America but died during the voyage and was buried at sea on December 13, 1687. His wife, Jane, and children reached Pennsylvania and during their residence endured many hardships. At first, they lived for several months in a cave. They had seven (4 boys and 3 girls) children. Jane was living in Philadelphia in 1717.

8   George Chandler II was born June 14, 1671 in Wiltshire England. He, his mother, brothers and sisters reached Pennsylvania in 1687 or 1688. In 1698 he married Ruth Bezer of Wiltshire, England. He died in Chester County, Pennsylvania in 1715.

9   George Chandler III, was born about 1700 and died August 16, 1799. He married Esther Taylor in 1724.

10   John Chandler was born in Chichester Township, Chester County, Pennsylvania on May 7, 1731. His birth, the name of his parents, his marriage and death are recorded on the flyleaves of "The History of the People Called Quakers by William Sewel", published in London in 1725. The record in

this book states that on August 6, 1758, he married Elizabeth Matlack who was born in Haddonfield, Gloucester County, New Jersey on June 12, 1734. She was the daughter of Timothy and Martha Matlack of Pennsylvania who were members of the Society of Friends.

10   Their daughter, Sybil, was named after her aunt, Sybil Cooper. Sybil married Elijah Coffing in 1777. George, their son, was born in 1760 and married, on March 20, 1793, Mary Calvert Lawson, daughter of Colonel Anthony Lawson of "Lawson Hall", Princess Anne County, Virginia and settled in Virginia. They had three children.

11   Their second son was John Adams Chandler who was born in Norfolk in 1795. He served in the U. S. Army in the War of 1812 and married Sarah Howard Woodward in 1817. She, too, was from Norfolk.

He went west of the Ohio in 1822. He rode as far as the Mississippi River and picked a location for his home. On the way back to Virginia Indians attacked the party he traveled with and several men were killed. The rest drove off the Indians after killing a number of them. This made him decide against taking his family to this part of the country and he remained in Norfolk.

He studied law, was admitted to the bar and became prominent in his profession. He was Commonwealth's Attorney for the judicial circuit which is formed of Norfolk and Portsmouth and the counties of Norfolk, Nansemond and Isle of Wight. He served a number of terms in the Virginia Legislature and introduced a bill for the emancipation of slaves but the bill was defeated. He was president of the Bank of Virginia in Portsmouth. He died in 1848. He was survived by his wife, six daughters and one son. The son, George McKendree Chandler, was preparing to be a doctor when he died of tuberculosis.

John Adams Chandler   Sarah Howard Woodward

13 The second daughter, Sarah Howard Chandler, was born on August 4, 1821 in Norfolk. She married William Angus Niemeyer July 31, 1839. They had twelve children, the first of whom was

The present Niemeyers are direct descendents of this Chandler line. In <u>Tidewater</u> <u>Descendents</u> the noted generation should be changed as follows.

7 13 Sarah Howard Chandler m. William Angus Niemeyer

  8 14 William Frederic Niemeyer C. S. A. m. Sarah Campbell Smith

9 15 John Frederic Niemeyer m. Lucrece Bilisoly

10 16 Antonio Bilisoly Niemeyer m. Lutie Stuart Spotts

11 17 Antonio Bilisoly Niemeyer, Jr. m Alice Virginia Berry

12	18	William Frederic Niemeyer	Frank Berry Niemeyer	John Stuart Niemeyer
		m.	m.	m.
		Carolyn Louise Holtzhauer	Shannon Page Eadie	April Michelle Tripp
13	19	John Cameron Niemeyer	Jacob Douglas Niemeyer	John Stuart Niemeyer, Jr.
		Kyle Antonio Niemeyer		

Bezer

Refer to the Chandler family, generation 8.
Under generation, the first column is the generation listed on page 431 of <u>Tidewater Ancestors</u> and the second column is for the Bezer lineage. The persons from whom we are descended are in bold print.

Generation

7	1	**Edward Bezer**
8	2	**Ruth Bezer** m. **George Chandler II**
9	3	**George Chandler, III** m. **Esther Taylor**
10	4	**John Chandler** m. **Elizabeth Matlack**
11	5	**George Chandler** m. **Mary Calvert Lawson**

Recap of Significant Data: Bezer

Generation

1   Edward Bezer was living in Wiltshire, England around 1680.

3   George Chandler, III married Esther Taylor ca1724.

4   John Chandler married Elizabeth Matlack in 1758.

5   George Chandler married Mary Lawson in 1783.

The present Niemeyers are direct descendents of this Bezer line. In <u>Tidewater</u> <u>Ancestors</u>, the noted generation should be changed as follows.

8   Lt. Col. William Frederic Niemeyer, C. S. A.
       m. Sarah Campbell Smith
9   John Frederic Niemeyer m. Lucrece Bilisoly
10   Antonio Bilisoly Niemeyer m. Lutie Stuart Spotts
11   Antonio Bilisoly Niemeyer, Jr. m. Alice Virginia
       Berry

12 William Frederic	Frank Berry	John Stuart
Niemeyer	Niemeyer	Niemeyer
m.	m.	m.
Carolyn Louise Holtzhauer	Shannon Page Eadie	April Michelle Tripp
13 John Cameron Niemeyer	Jacob Douglas Niemeyer	John Stuart Niemeyer, Jr.
Kyle Antonio Niemeyer		

Niemeyer

Under generation, the first column is the generation listed on page 453 of <u>Tidewater</u> <u>Ancestors</u> and the second column is for the Niemeyer lineage. The persons from whom we are descended are in bold print.

Generation

1   1   **Hans Heinrich Niemeyer**

2   2

George Friedrich m. Clara Deecks	Anna Margaretha Sophie m. John Frederich Dierking	Friederich Victor	**John Christian** m. I-Catherine Adams Keys II-**Ann McLean**	William F. m. Mary ?	Sophie m. G. Christ Wellhausen

Recap of Significant Data: Niemeyer
Generation

    1- Hans Heinrich Niemeyer was born in Hoya, Germany in 1734 and died in 1806 at the age of seventy-two years. He had six children of whom only four had descendents.

    2- George Friederich Niemeyer was born in 1767 and died in Verden in 1850. He married Clara Deecks of Celle, Germany.

    Anna Margaretha Sophie Niemeyer was born in 1769 and died in 1837. She married John Frederich Dierking of Burgwedel, Germany.

    Friederich Victor Niemeyer was born in 1771 and died in 1785.

    John Christian Niemeyer was born in Verden on September 9, 1776 and emigrated from Bremen to Virginia on September 8, 1794. He arrived at Baltimore, Maryland on November 15,

1794. He married Catherine Adams Keys in Norfolk, Virginia on March 27, 1800. She was born in 1782 on Staton Island, New York and died September 20, 1812. She was thirty years old and they were the parents of four children.

Anne McDowell, half sister of Catherine Keys, married Henry Woodis. They had two children, Sarah Ann who wed Mr. Hunter and William Henary who was lost at sea. Anne died in December 1831.

John Christian secondly married on August 15, 1813 in Moyock, Currituck County, North Carolina Ann McLean who was born on Staten Island of Scottish parents, Duncan and Ann McLean of the "Red McLeans" of Ross Shire, Scotland. She was born in 1796 and died on April 14, 1824 in Portsmouth. After the death of her husband she married a second time to Mr. Smith. John Christian died at his home on the Western Branch of the Elizabeth River in Norfolk County on October 20, 1820.

William F. Niemeyer was born in 1781 and died in 1834. He married Mary ? in Baltimore, Maryland. There are no known living descendents.

Sophie Niemeyer was born in 1782 and died in 1843. She married G. Christ Wellhausen who was born in 1774 in Hanover, Germany.

Copy of a letter from Lewis Kirby to Louise Fontaine

"As I reported to you, Mr. Rudolf H. Buenz is the stain glass artisan … He was born in Hamburg, Germany and recently returned to visit his sister. Just as he was leaving, it occurred to me to ask him if he would have the opportunity to see if he could discover the proper and correct Niemeyer Coat of Arms! He is a kind man … He said he would be delighted.

I gave Mr. Buenz my copy of Uncle Sam's booklet and the page from your letter from Bob Niemeyer as well as the drawing of the shield and the arms, from 'Reitstap Heraldry'. As you know both of these shields show an arm issuing from a cloud holding in one hand a sheaf of wheat, and in the other, three sworts, BUT these are arms for Niemeyer of Wuerttemburg, and Bavaria, which are a long way from Hanover!

Well- Mr. Buenz went to the library in Hamburg and they told him that a complete set of the heraldic books for an area and Germany would be in Bremen. In Uncle Sam's booklet he speaks of our relatives named Dierking who lived in Bremen in the middle of the last century. So, Mr. Buenz went to Bremen, and there he found the proper book with the Niemeyer arms of the Niemeyer family of Hanover (the city) in Hanover, Germany.

It appears that the head of the family was a prosperous leather merchant whose shield is an elephant (where could he get more leather?) on a blue shield, and whose sons were all given separate shields of arms (which is not uncommon in German heraldry), and all lived in and around the little towns of Celle, Verden and Hoya, from which we know John Christian Niemeyer immigrated in the early nineteenth century.

Mr. Buenz then went to Hoya and Verden. He found a beautiful seventeenth century church in Hoya with thirteen coats-of-arms behind the altar, but no Niemeyer. In Verden, on the stairwell of the pulpit, was the Niemeyer shield, showing a red arm issuing from a cloud holding a tree and the name spelled Niemeyr. The minister appeared and said that the church had the records of the family back into the seventeenth century, and he would be glad to have copies made and sent to me.

… None of the shields showed the eagle crest, but I think there can be no authenticity of the shield to which the Niemeyers of Portsmouth are entitled and I suspect that John

Christian Niemeyer took the eagle for his own crest which is done frequently in German Heraldry."

Later "Christian Eberhard Niemeyer was a wealthy and successful leather merchant. After the Thirty Years War, he had the opportunity to buy seven large farms in the vicinity of Hanover and Bremen, around the towns of Celle, Hoya and Verden. Mr. Buenz feels that the farms extended to thousands of acres.

Herr Niemeyer then gave the farms to his sons and you see the similarity in their shields, and the symbolism of the heraldry. A red hand reaching down from the clouds (like manna from heaven) giving to each son a farm symbolized by a sheath of wheat, or a sickle, or in the case of our branch of the family- a tree. His own crest is a seventeenth century farmer holding a scythe. The story could not be more obvious even without knowledge of heraldry.

John Christian Niemeyer obviously gets his Christian middle name from Christian Eberhard Niemeyer who was either his father or more probably his grandfather. … Mr. Buenz does not believe that there is any Niemeyer manor house, although there are castles in the area, but rather that Christian Eberhard bought the farms for the land, and the farmhouses in which the different branches lived have subsequently been destroyed in ensuing wars.

HANS HEINRICH NIEMEYER (young)
HANS HEINRICH NIEMEYER (older)

CHRISTIAN EBERHARD NIEMEYER
WHEAT + LEATHER MERCHANT ✠
LARGE LANDHOLDER — FARMING ET.C.
NEUSTAEDTER KIRCHE · BORN · 10-11-1675.
✠ HANOVER ✠   †   27-8-1757.

JOHAN NIEMEYER.
ST. JOHANNIS KIRCHE IN
VERDEN — HANOVER.
PART OF DECOR ON
CHANCEL

INFORMATION ✠ FROM BOOKS OF
DEUTSCHE GESCHLECHTER — NIEDERSACHSEN · 12
BAND · 158 -
BREMEN — BREITENWEG — 27. TOWN · LIBRARY

St. Johannis in Verden
* im Wandel der Zeit *

Church of St. Johannis of Verden, Germany. The oldest
church register of St. Johannis (St. John) carries the
date of the year 1659. The pulpit of the church of
St. John was erected under the government of the Bishop-
Prince Philipp Sigismund, present in Verden from 1586
to 1623.

On the stairwell of the pulpit was the Niemeyer shield,
showing a red arm issuing from a cloud holding a tree
and the name spelled Niemeyr.

Niemeyer
Seal
~ from impression - brought from Germany ~
by 1800
OF HANOVER, GERMANY AND VIRGINIA

The Niemeyer family seal was owned by John Christian Niemeyer and brought by him to America:

Crest: An eagle rising reguardant proper, wings displayed and inverted

with his initials below in an oval.

Wax impression of the Niemeyer seal and records in possession of James L. Kirby, Jr.

GEORGE FREDERICH NIEMEYER
CLARA DEECKS (his wife)

JOHN CHRISTIAN NIEMEYER
CATHERINE ADAMS KEYS (his first wife)

Generation

2   2

George   Anna   Friederich   **John**   William Sophie
Friederich Margaretha   Victor   **Christian**   F.   m.
    m.   Sophie   m.   m.   G.
Clara   m.   I-Catherine Mary   Christ
Deecks   John   Adams   ?   Wellhausen
            Frederich   Keys
            Dierking   II-**Ann**
                                       McLean

3   3

Children of George Friederich   Children of Anna Margaretha
   Niemeyer who married   Sophie Niemeyer who
     Clara Deecks   married John Frederich
                                        Dierking

Heinrich   George   Elizabeth Annette   George   Auguste
Bernhard   Friedich   m.   Friederich
                      Daniel   m.
                      Hetzer   Dorothea
                                          Burns

3   3

   Children of John Christian   Children of John Christian
Niemeyer and Catherine Adams Keys Niemeyer and Ann McLean

Charles   Anne Washington Henry Eliza   **William** Virginia
Friederich Matilda Augustus Victor   Ann   **Angus** Margaretha
   m.   m.   m.   m.
Mary Ann   I-Jane   Dr.   **Sarah**
   Peed   Benthall Samuel   **Howard**
                         II-Martha Crawford   **Chandler**
                            Vaughn

CEDAR GROVE CEMETERY, PORTSMOUTH, VA
NIEMEYER FAMILY PLOT
CHARLES FREDERIC NIEMEYER

3   3   Children of Sophie Niemeyer and Christ Wellhausen

Caroline	Dorette	Louise	George	Clara	Sophie	Anna
	m.	m.	m.	m.		Niemeyer
	I-N.Vogeler	John Gerk	Clara	N.Jordan		
	II-N.Meyer	Limpen	Knollman			

Recap of Significant Data: Niemeyer

Generation

3- Heinrich Bernhard Niemeyer was born in 1804.

George Friedrich Niemeyer was born in 1809 and died in 1821.

Elizabeth Niemeyer was born in 1810 and married Daniel Hetzer of Hildershein. They had five children. She died in 1850.

Annette Niemeyer was born in 1819.

George Friederich Dierking was born in 1802. He married Dorothea Burns who was born in 1803.

Auguste Dierking was born in 1810 and died in 1853.

Charles Friederich Niemeyer was born in Norfolk, Virginia on April 11, 1801 and died at 10:00 o'clock Sunday night on September 21, 1834. He married Mary Ann Peed of Princess Anne County who was the daughter of Lemuel and Susan Peed on December 23, 1823. Mary Ann was born on January 31, 1802 and died at 10:00 o'clock on January 29, 1883 in Portsmouth at 81 years of age. She was buried on January 31, her birthday. They had been married on a Thursday evening by a Methodist minister, the Rev. Charles Moseley. They were counted in the census of 1830 in Portsmouth, Norfolk County.

Anne Matilda Niemeyer was born on December 28, 1803 and died on October 15, 1831 at the home of her aunt,   Anne

McDowell Woodis, soon after she returned from a visit to relatives in Germany. She said the relatives lived in a beautiful home and used a gold coffee service. She was buried on the grounds of the Catholic Church. The new St. Mary's Catholic Church was erected over her grave.

Washington Augustus Niemeyer was born on March 21, 1805 and died in 1824 at the home of his brother, Charles, located on the southeast corner of Washington and King Streets in Portsmouth.

Henry Victor Niemeyer was born on December 3, 1808 in Norfolk and died on August 23, 1883 in Portsmouth. He married twice. His first wife was Jane Frances Benthall, daughter of Captain William Benthall. Jane was born in 1815 and died in 1843. They were married on May 11, 1837, by the Reverend William Neal, in Portsmouth. His second wife was Martha Caroline Vaughn of "Walnut Hill" Southampton County, Virginia. They were married April 20, 1852, at "Walnut Hill", by the Reverend Dr. George D. Armstrong of the Presbyterian Church in Norfolk. They had no children. Martha Caroline Vaughn was the only member of her family who was not murdered in the Nat Turner massacre. Her Negro nurse hid with her in the woods and saved her. She was a baby in arms. Henry Victor was counted in the census in either Jefferson or Jackson Ward, Portsmouth, Norfolk County.

Eliza Ann Niemeyer was born on October 1, 1814 and married Dr. Samuel M. Crawford, of Orange County, New York, on April 28, 1836. She died on May 31, 1866. He was born February 5, 1810 and died February 25, 1886.

APRIL 28, 1816   FEBRUARY 3, 1900

William Angus Niemeyer

THIS is sent to you as a memorial of William Angus Niemeyer, who was born in Norfolk, Virginia, just one hundred years ago, April twenty-eight, eighteen hundred and sixteen.

His grandfather was Hans Heinrich Niemeyer, born in Hoya, Germany, in 1734; his father was John Christian Niemeyer, born in Verden, Germany, in 1776, emigrated to America and died in Norfolk County, Virginia, in 1820; his mother was Anne McLean Niemeyer, born of Scottish parents on Staten Island, New York, in 1796, died in Portsmouth, Virginia, in 1822.

His first work was as a clerk in his brother's general store in Portsmouth in 1829; he entered the service of the Seaboard and Roanoke Railroad in 1833; this was the second railroad in the United States and began operating in 1831; he became bookkeeper in the Bank of Virginia in Portsmouth and remained in the service of the bank until its close during the Civil War. In 1866 he engaged in farming for one year. In 1867, the Bank of Portsmouth was established and he became bookkeeper until 1869, when he became a member of the firm of Niemeyer, Etheredge & Brooks, General Commission Merchants, and conducted a successful business until he retired in 1879, on account of ill health.

His clean life's record, his high character and strict integrity we will ever remember as a precious heritage.

We recall his cares, struggles, love of home and family, his cheerfulness under the burdens of life which we as children could not fully appreciate.

His long and useful life of eighty-four years filled with sunshine and shadow, disaster and success is a sweet memory to us now.

Looking backward through the years all that was best in his life is brought home to us and we would like for our children to think of us as we do of him; we would love for them to be like him.

He came into the world in the year unique in history; we have no record of any other year like it (eighteen hundred and sixteen), for in this year there was no summer.

In January and February the weather was so mild fires were unnecessary except for cooking; most of the time the weather was warm and springlike. March came in windy as usual, the first few days in April were warm but soon became colder; by the first of May the temperature was like winter, with a plenty of snow and ice. The young buds were frozen, ice formed an inch thick on ponds and rivers. Corn was killed, cornfields were replanted until it became too late to raise a crop. By the last of May every green thing had been killed by the cold.

June was still colder, snow fell in all parts of the country; in the Middle and New England States, the snow storms were as severe as any in midwinter. People were lost and frozen in attempting to make their way through the snow. On the fourth of July, ice formed as far south as Georgia, in Virginia and Tennessee, creeks and rivers were frozen over. In Virginia and other Southern States, farmers made fires in the fields, trying to make a crop of corn; these industrious workers were the only ones to make even a part of a crop.

August proved to be the worst month of all; almost every green thing in this country and in Europe was blasted with frost.

In the Northern States no crops were made and thousands would have perished but for the abundance of fish and wild game.

Born in this disastrous year, William Angus Niemeyer was soon to face graver troubles. His father died when he was four years of age; two years later his mother passed away, leaving him and a sister two years older to the care of his half-brothers.

He was forced to shift for himself almost from the beginning; he obtained a fair education and grew to manhood, strong, self-reliant and wonderfully well informed.

July 31, 1839, he was married to Sarah Howard Chandler. In every respect she was an ideal wife and mother, a helpmate worthy of any man.

Twelve children born to them lived to be grown and there are living at this time five sons, two daughters, twenty-one grandchildren, twenty great-grandchildren and one great-great-grandchild, a total of forty-nine descendants; may their record be as good as that of their ancestor. The old home on Swimming Point, Portsmouth, Virginia, where the family lived for about fifty years, has passed to strangers.

About the old place there lingers a charm of mingled joy and sadness.

The writer of this on his last visit there, finding the house vacant, wrote on the wall in the dining room:

> "I feel like one who treads alone some banquet hall deserted,
> Whose lights are fled, whose garlands dead, and all but he departed."

With best wishes to all of our name and clan,

S. W. NIEMEYER,
Senate Office Bldg., Washington, D. C.

April 28, 1916.

William Angus Niemeyer   Sarah Howard Chandler

William Angus was born on April 28, 1816 and died on February 3, 1900. He married Sarah Howard Chandler, daughter of John Adams Chandler and his wife Sarah Howard Woodward Chandler, on July 31, 1839. William Angus and Sarah Howard Chandler Niemeyer lived in the Niemeyer house on Swimming Point on Crawford Bay. William Angus was born in Norfolk, VA and was reared by his half brothers as his father had died when he was 4 years old. Two years later his mother died and her brother came from Scotland to take the children home with him. They did not want to leave their brothers and stayed in Portsmouth. Sarah Howard Chandler was also born in Norfolk.

Later, the William Angus family moved to the Hewlett Farm on the old Deep Creek Road about 5 miles from Portsmouth. It is now known as the Lindsay Silvester Farm. After living for a short time in the country, they returned to their Swimming Point home and in 1854, built the larger 4-story home adjoining on the south. This house was razed in 1909.

Virginia Margaretha Niemeyer was born in 1818 and died in 1820.

Caroline Wellhausen was born in 1809.

Doretta Wellhausen was born in 1811 and married, firstly, N. Vogeler and secondly N. Meyer of Hanover. She had a son, George Vogeler who was born in 1843.

Louise Wellhausen was born in 1814 and married John G. Limpen. He was born in 1811. They lived in Hanover.

George Wellhausen was born in 1816 and married Clara Krollman. They had two children, Ida and Anne. Ida was born in 1851 and died in 1852. Anne was born in 1852.

Clara Wellhausen was born in 1818 and married N. Jordan. They had three children, George, Friederich and Anne.

Sophie Niemeyer Wellhausen was born in 1820.

Anna Wellhausen was born in 1823.

Generation

3   3   Elizabeth Niemeyer m. Daniel Hetzer

4   4

        George   Arthur   Adolph   Marie Ann   Elise
        Wilhelm   Bernhard Alexander Dorothea   Clara
        Hetzer   Hetzer   Hetzer   Hetzer   Hetzer

3   3   George Friederich Dierking m. Dorothea Burns

4   4   Hermann Heinrich Bernard Dierking

3   3   Charles Friederich Niemeyer m. Mary Ann Peed

4   4

        Catherine   Charles   Virginia   Susan   Henry
        Adams   Henry   Adams   Matilda   Woodis

```
Niemeyer     Niemeyer   Niemeyer   Niemeyer Niemeyer
                                                m.
                                             Alexina
                                             Constantia
                                             Wilson
```

3   3   Henry Victor   m.   I- Jane   II-Martha
              Niemeyer   Benthall Caroline Vaughn
4   4   No Issue

3   3   Eliza Ann Niemeyer m. Dr. Samuel Crawford

4   4

Eliza Susan Alexander Mary Henry Elizabeth Jane Martha
 Ann Virginia   m.   Victor   m.   m.
Matilda   Ella   m.   Miles   Charles
   m.   Hill   Sarah   Beardsley   Hinkley
 John   Brown   Montgomery
 Church
Wilber, II

3   3   **William Angus Niemeyer** m. **Sarah Howard Chandler**

4   4

William John   Henry Sarah George   Arthur Crawford
Frederic Chandler Victor Howard McKendree Emmerson Hill

237

	m.		m.		m.	m.
Sarah	Martha				Sarah	Mrs.
Campbell	Jane				H.	Pauline
Smith	Hunter				Mahan	Riter

	Mary	John	Ann	Sam	Hermann
	Chandler	Christian	McLean	Watts	Christian
	m.	m.	m.	m.	m.
	Dr. Robert	Mary	Samuel	I-Mary	Marie
	R.	Janet	Patterson	Agnes	Louise
	Robertson	Wooten	Wigg	Moore	Hook
				II-Lellie	
				Land	

3 3 Dorette Wellhausen m. I-N. Vogeler II-N. Meyer

4 4   George Vogeler

3 3 Louise Wellhausen m. John Girk Limpen

4 4 Christian   George   Hermann   Gerhard
         Limpen   Limpen   Limpen   Limpen

3 3 George Wellhausen m. Clara Krollman

4 4   Ida   Ann
            Wellhausen   Wellhausen

3 3 Clara Wellhausen m. N. Jordan

4 4 George   Friedrich   Anna
         Jordan   Jordan   Jordan

Recap of Significant Data: Niemeyer

Generation

4   George Wilhelm Hetzer was born in 1837. He lived in Verden and Hildeshein, Kingdom of Hanover.

Arthur Bernhard Hetzer was born in 1839.

Adolph Alexander Hetzer was born in 1841.

Marie Ann Dorothea Hetzer was born in 1846.

Elise Clara Hetzer was born in 1850.

The Hetzers lived in Verden and Hildeschein in the kingdom of Hanover. Dr. Fritz Hetzer wrote the Lord Mayor of Orange County, New York in the 1940s to see if he could make contact with the Niemeyers.

Herman Heinrich Bernard Dierking was born in 1828. He sent the names of the relatives in Germany to William Angus Niemeyer. He lived in Bremen, Germany.

Catherine Adams Niemeyer was born on January 23, 1825 in Portsmouth, Va. and died on March 22, 1825.

Charles Henry Niemeyer was born on March 18, 1826 in Portsmouth, Va. and died on July 21, 1886.

Virginia Adams Niemeyer was known as "Cousin Ginny" and was born on August 7, 1827 in Portsmouth, Va.

Susan Matilda Niemeyer was born on December 15,1830 in Portsmouth, Va. and died in 1875.

Henry Woodis Niemeyer was born on May 30, 1833 in Portsmouth, Va. and was in the Confederate Army. He was killed at Island no. 10 in April 1862 at twenty-nine years of age. He married Alexina Constantia Wilson and they had one son, Charles Frederic, who was born on January 12, 1860 and died on December 13, 1862 of scarlet fever. The baby's mother, Alexina Constantia Wilson Niemeyer, died of scarlet fever on December 17, 1862 at her father's residence, "Campostella" in

Norfolk County.

Eliza Ann Matilda Crawford married John Church Wilber, II on November 23, 1859. She was born on March 16, 1837 and died on June 21, 1902. John was born on July 18, 1837 and died on November 16, 1923. They lived in Suny Ford, New York with their nine children.

Susan Virginia Crawford was born on October 2, 1838 and died on September 5, 1908. She did not marry.

Alexander Crawford was born on March 17, 1840 and married Ella Hill Brown on January 26, 1871. She was born on April 16, 1842. They had three children.

Mary Crawford was born on January 25, 1842 and died on December 20, 1859. She did not marry.

Henry Victor Crawford married Sarah Montgomery of New York City. They married on June 12, 1869. They had two children, Sam and Bob.

Elizabeth Davy Crawford married Miles Beardsley. She was born on March 8, 1847 and died on November 28, 1878. They had two children, Kate and (?). She was called Lizzie.

Jane Thompson Crawford was born in 1853 and died June 4, 1866. She never married.

Martha Niemeyer Crawford was called Mattie. She was born on July 29, 1855, married Charles Hinkley in 1875 and died on November 19, 1899.

William Frederic Niemeyer was born in Portsmouth, Virginia on May 12, 1840. He was killed at Spotsylvania Courthouse on May 12, 1864, his twentieth-fourth birthday. He was a lieutenant colonel in the Army of the Confederate States. He married Sarah Campbell Smith.

John Chandler Niemeyer was born in Portsmouth, Virginia on October 5, 1842. He attended The Virginia Military Institute. He was a lieutenant in the Army of the Confederate

States and was killed at Gettysburg on July 3, 1863 at the age of twenty years nine months. On the fatal field he was conspicuously brave, three times his brigade halted under a line of galling fire. After the last "halt and dress", when the regiment began to advance, Lieutenant Niemeyer turned to a comrade and brother lieutenant and said with a bright smile on his face 'John what a beautiful line'. A few minutes later he fell dead pierced through the head with a bullet. His body was never recovered but is in one of the many unmarked graves on the battlefield. He was counted in the census of 1860 under the name of James C. He lived in Portsmouth and Montgomery, New York.

Henry Victor Niemeyer was born in Portsmouth on February 24, 1845; entered the Confederate Army at the age of sixteen. He was a prisoner of war at Point Lookout, Maryland from July 1864 until the following March after which he returned to his brigade and served until the surrender at Appomattox on April 9, 1865. He married Martha Jane Hunter on September 8, 1874 at the residence of her father on North Street in Portsmouth. They lived in St. Louis, Missouri.

Sarah Howard Niemeyer was born on March 17, 1847 and died January 13, 1899. She never married.

George McKendree Niemeyer was born on November 19, 1849 and died October 11, 1906. He never married.

Arthur Emmerson Niemeyer was born in Norfolk on January 19, 1852. He married Sarah H. Mahan of Memphis, Tennessee and they lived in Memphis.

Crawford Hill Niemeyer was born in Portsmouth on January 25, 1854. He married Mrs. Pauline Riter and they lived in Little Rock, Arkansas. He died February 27, 1928. They had no children.

Hermann Christian Niemeyer was born in Portsmouth on

February 21, 1856 and married Marie Louise Hook a daughter of Maria Benson and Henry Ferdinand Hook. Chris died on July 17, 1899 and Marie Louise died on May 18, 1928.

Sam Watts Niemeyer was born in Portsmouth on October 28, 1858, married twice and died in 1942. His first wife was Mary Agnes Moore who died on January 24, 1896 at age 27 years and 4 months. They had two children and his second was Lellie Land with whom he had one child who died young.

Ann McLean Niemeyer was born in Portsmouth on November 4, 1860 and died November 7, 1926. She married Samuel Patterson Wigg.

John Christian Niemeyer was born in Portsmouth on June 4, 1863 and died May 13, 1933. He married Mary Janet Wooten.

Mary Chandler Niemeyer was born in Portsmouth on August 6, 1865 and died November 29, 1952. She married Dr. Robert Rivers Robertson of Petersburg. They lived in Portsmouth.

F. M. Institute—
Lexington Va
May 6th

Dear Friend.

I am not certain whether I have directed this right or not. Though I suppose you are now Widow more. You see I am waiting sometime for you to inform me that you had married — ed safe at home, married and house keeping. I suppose your highness has forgotten such a favor as my my ever or — or that you have — let me tell you that they call me also, sometimes "Bachelor" and

That I am now at the Va Mil Institute from which place I send you an invitation to The Ball to be given here on the 4th July. Now after telling... my mane, and fearing this That you do most remember me, let me bring to your mind some little reminiscences. I suppose you haven't forgotten how I used to, about once a week, bring three little epistles from the Post office to Mr. & Matilda Crawford and how on the same day I used to take one to the P.O. directed to... — no matter who! You know well enough. And then another thing. Don't you remember how you used

Letter from John Chandler Niemeyer to
Eliza Matilda Crawford – May 6, 1860

Pa says she has and sorry your leading. I could have been at the wedding and know the Bride(s) you know I have done many a time). Let me congratulate on becoming Mrs. Wilder and to wish you long life, happiness prosperity and a houseful of — I hope your baby boys on according to take any notice of this little effusion you would on for and everlasting obligation in your affectionate cousin Jno.

P.S. Love to all the folks and tell Cousin Lee that this invitation Consider that this invitation my answer to invitation for her too) Cousin Jno.

to blow me up whenever I mention anything about those dam cutters? and also how I had to beg you before I could get you to show me a certain picture which you had in your bosom time? the said picture has a rather a handsome face & long beard and at which I verily believe you look at not or not less than a dozen times a day all these & many other little facts ought to keep you from forgetting me. I intend to leave this place at-... and if Pa will let me I am coming to pay you a visit. You... me to come when you were...

Porto Rico
July 27 / 1866

Dear Cousin

Your letter was received This morning after I got home and I have only been waiting to know whether or not I could come before writing. We were going to start (Parraguay) last Wednesday but when the time came I decided we could not leave. I reckon we will leave here in about two weeks. We will stop in New York a day or two from which place I will write you so as to let you know when I will be in Eastern Tenn. You mustn't make any extra preparation for me for I shall expect to be treated as "home folks" all the time I stay.

I scarcely know what to write about as this is just about the dullest little town in The world. Since I have been home I have been busy doing nothing and Therefore can't tell you any thing about my business, but I occupy my time fishing, loafing & seeing the girls. I expect to get a situation about the first of September and I am sorry to say I will be obliged to make my visit to you a short one. I reckon it will be impossible to get me to come on as she is busy worth the Lanel fry — it. She can't leave there. There are so many of them here That I leave & count them every day so as to be able to recollect how many there are. Sam, the young'un is one of the finest looking little fellows you ever saw. He is decidedly the flower. (Yours)

Letter from John Christian Niemeyer to
his cousin, Eliza Matilde Crawford.
July 27, 1860.

Personal Recollections

by Henry V. Niemeyer

I was born on Swimming Point, Portsmouth, Virginia, February 24, 1845, in the house north of the Niemeyer mansion where most of the children were born. My father built this house, in which my sister Sallie, and brother, George, were born. He afterwards built the large house in which he lived until his death.

When the War between the States began in April, 1861, I was sixteen years and two months old. Every boy in town was anxious to fly to arms, and become a hero before the war would end, which was set down at six months maximum. Many companies were being organized and drilled. In the town there was no lack of volunteers. I never knew of a conscription in Portsmouth. My brother Fred came on from West Point, where he had just completed his four-year course. He was appointed a lieutenant in the regular army, and put to drilling troops. My brother John came from the Virginia Military Institute, at Lexington, and was made a sergeant in the Old Dominion Guards, and also helped in training the soldiers.

At first young men under the age of eighteen were refused enlistment, but not to be outdone, they raised what was known as "a boy company", young fellows from fourteen to eighteen years of age. It was the custom at that time to adopt high-sounding names for the companies. The word "Light" was considered necessary to impress its admirers. "Blues" was also a favorite name at that time. So we called ourselves "The Blanchard Light Infantry Blues", named for General Blanchard, in command of Portsmouth troops.

"Light" was probably intended to denote something "quick" and strategical, that would enable us to land quickly on the flanks of the enemy and get away before they could recover from their surprise. The name "Blues" has never been made very clear to me, but I have no doubt it was intended for something very terrifying. Then there was a company called the "Dismal Swamp Rangers" from the Deep Creek section of the county.

Our boy company elected my brother John, from the Old Dominion Guards, as one of our lieutenants. The Blanchard Light Infantry Blues were never mustered into service, as the boys could brook no delay, and begged the captains of the other companies to accept them. Capt. Kearns, of the Old Dominion Guards, afterwards Company K, 9th Virginia Infantry was kind enough to consent to my joining him. We were quartered at Pinner's Point, in charge of the fort at that place for the protection of the Elizabeth River.

Another company, known as the Craney Island Artillery Blues, was also quartered there. This Blues company was never to enjoy the firing off of their artillery. They were merged into the 9th Regiment, along with the Old Dominion Guards, and called Company I, given a musket instead of a cannon, and did valiant service as infantry until the end of the war. My brother John, first sergeant of Company K, was elected lieutenant of this company, and was with them in the charge of Pickett's Division at Gettysburg, where he was killed July 3, 1863. He was not twenty-one years old, and had seen two years of service. His body was never recovered. We remained around our home until May 10, 1862.

General McClellan, with 120,000 Union soldiers, was within 10 miles of Richmond, attacking our army of half its numbers, under General Joseph E. Johnston. Reinforcements were necessary, and the ten thousand men in defense of Norfolk and Portsmouth were compelled to abandon these two cities and hurry to Richmond.

Our mothers had packed our knapsacks with clothes enough to last a long time. We were soon in the swamps at Seven Pines, fighting, sometimes in water knee deep. Our knapsacks, with clothes, bibles, and many precious articles, began to feel so heavy on the tired men, that we took them off and laid them under a tree, expecting to return and get them. But we were doomed to disappointment, and there was seldom a time after that when I could boast of an extra pair of socks or shirt. I have often stopped long enough to wash my thin cotton shirt in a ditch, wring it out as dry as I could, put it on, and let it dry the best way possible.

General Johnston was severely wounded at Seven Pines, and President Davis rode out from Richmond, with General Lee, near where we were, and placed him in command of the army. There was to be no more retreating from that time.

General "Stonewall" Jackson was called from the valley with his troops, and with Longstreet's men, and the cavalry of General J. E. B. Stuart, the offensive against McClellan began. McClellan was forced back to Malvern Hill, on the James River, under the protection of his gunboats. He was on his way to Harrison's Landing on the north side, in order to place his army on the transports to go up the Potomac River. General Lee did not intend to fight a battle at Malvern Hill, but one of his subordinates, a Major General, brought on the battle on his own responsibility. McClellan had 120 cannon and most of his army ready to defend this position. Captain Carey Grimes, of Portsmouth, climbed a steep hill with his battery of artillery, and opened fire on the Union army. The Federal cannon soon began to feel him out, and getting the range, swept his men and guns from the field. Our brigade, Armistead's, was lying on the ground behind him in support. I can remember Grimes as he looked, in his shirt-sleeves, mounted on his horse, showing no concern as to the danger. At the battle of Sharpsburg, he showed the same reckless spirit, was wounded, and placed on a litter. While in that position, he received his second wound, which proved fatal. After our artillery was silenced at Malvern Hill, the infantry was ordered forward. A Louisiana brigade was sent in, Mahone's and Armistead's brigades, Wright's Georgiana, and possibly others that I cannot remember.

It was up hill and down dale with us. We would run to the top of a hill, and down the next, re-form, climb the next hill and fight with our mus-

These heretofore unpublished recollections of Henry Victor Niemeyer, CSA were dictated to his daughter and later typed by his granddaughter June G. Benson (Mrs. Gerald W.) of the Pisgah Chapter #2375, Brevard, North Carolina.

kets, then forward again to the next protection. In this way we were soon close up under the Union guns. The twilight was falling, and with the smoke of the black powder of that time, we could scarcely see the enemy, except when the flame from their guns brightened the field. The fighting against these artillery and infantry was terrific. In addition, the gunboats in the James River would fire their large shells over the bluff and onto us. I remember a great shell burst within a foot of me, but scattered without striking me. The concussion was so great that it seemed to loosen my ear drums. A grapeshot came plowing through the ground, rose above the surface, struck me a glancing blow, as if someone had struck me with a brick, and went on its way. I can remember that I felt that our next rush would bring us into a hand-to-hand encounter. I did not relish having a fellow punching at me with a bayonet, so I stopped firing, and with a bullet and three buckshot in my gun, felt that this would give me some advantage before a bayonet could strike.

Just then I saw banks of infantry coming from behind their guns to receive the final charge. Everything stopped, and all firing ceased. That night we remained on the field, shivering in the summer night and drizzling rain, and sleeping the best way we could. Seeing a little fire down in the ravine made from a few twigs, Arthur Harvey of Company G and I went down to investigate. We noticed four men standing around, and we tried to crowd in and join them. The smallest of them was a little man weighing about 100 pounds. Then there was a big man and two medium-sized men. The little fellow said to Arthur, "Come up here and get warm, and then go up on the hill, and tell all the boys to come down to the fire, and then we will have a damned fine line of battle up there." The little fellow who was trying to be funny was General Mahone; the big one was General Wright. The others were General Armistead, and another that I cannot recall. They were holding a council of war.

The next morning, much to my delight, we discovered that the Union army had fallen back on their march to Harrison's Landing, and left us in possession of the field. I walked over the ground that morning, and saw great numbers of dead and wounded from both armies. I saw Captain Den-

nis Vermillion of our company, lying dead from a bullet wound. Melzer Fiske, a boy of 16, was dead. John Bennet, of our company, was mortally wounded with a bullet through his thigh. I found two men carrying a litter, and we placed John upon it and took him to the rear. He was sent to the hospital where he died a few days later.

We remained around Richmond for several weeks and were then started off to oppose General Pope, who had been given another army sent out from Washington. Our regiment was engaged in the battle of Warrenton Springs, and we could see the hotel, which had been set on fire, burning. One of our pickets had been left in a dangerous position, and it was difficult to withdraw them from the field. We had captured a woman in man's clothes, who proved to be Dr. Mary Walker. Colonel White of Portsmouth put a piece of cloth on a stick as a flag of truce, and took his prisoner to the Union lines. The pickets took advantage of this and escaped.

We marched all night, and the next day appeared on the battlefield of Second Manassas or Bull Run. When we were going forward we met our friend Mahone lying on a litter, wounded and being brought to the rear by four men. We told the men to let one of them take the general under his arm, and go get the surgeon, and the others must go back where they came from. Pope was defeated in this battle, and driven back across the Potomac river.

1862—We went into camp at Winchester; and in September, my father came from Portsmouth through the Union lines, and asked for my discharge from the army, as I was under eighteen. In a short time, orders came from the Secretary of War ordering my discharge. I went to Richmond by railroad and after remaining out of service a short time, re-enlisted in the Signal Service before I had reached the eighteen year limit.

I was sent to a signal station on the lower James river to get information, and passed it by flag signal to Petersburg. I was more than a year doing service around the Chickahominy River, where it empties into the James. We were many times shelled out by gunboats, and our line temporarily broken. But we would get back to work as soon as the boats would go away. Finally the Union fleet with warships and transports bearing

"The Army of the James", under General Butler, came along, and we made our escape to the south side at night, in a rowboat, with a piece of blanket tied around the oars to muffle the sound.

Our squad of six men was put on watch for troops that might be landed from transports. While there I was captured by two companies of Indiana cavalry, who had come down from City Point, and were running a telegraph wire to connect with Fortress Monroe. A boat was signaled, and I was put on board and sent to the prison at Point Lookout, Maryland. There were fourteen thousand of us divided into fourteen divisions and crowded into tents. Our rations were very scarce, a half loaf of bread, a tin cup full of bean soup, and a pie of salt meat each day. We were never given any vegetables, and as a consequence, scurvy prevailed to a great extent. I know that the doctors would at times write in a prescription a diet of potatoes or onions or vinegar.

In reconstructing the sewers, I at one time saw hundreds of rats killed by the prisoners which were cooked and eaten. My hunger never led me to this extreme, but I have been offered a piece of this kind of food.

The northern people were incensed at what they called "starvation rations" to their men in southern prisons. I believe they did not know that the Confederate army was subsisting on corn meal and strong bacon, mainly. With our ports closed and our crops destroyed, we were doing the best we could by the prisoners and our own men. The southerners were constantly pleading for a general exchange of prisoners, but the northern generals concluded that it was better judgment to let their men stay in prison and suffer than to send back a large army, and prolong the war. This may have been a wise conclusion, but it was what General Sherman said it was.

I was in prison from June, 1864, to March, 1865. No exchange of prisoners would be permitted, but in order to get some of their sick from the southern prisons, the Union people would agree to parole a boatload of Confederates, for a like number of their own men. The complaints from their own people compelled some action. This at last relieved us of the care of many thousand prisoners, and at the same time released our own men from northern prisons. In

(continued next page)

March 1865, I was included in a boatload of men, and sent up the James River under a flag of truce. When we landed at Rocketts, we were enthusiastically received by a dilapidated brass band, and orators chosen for the occasion. We were called "Patriots" and praised to the utmost degree. We marched up Main street, the ladies waving to us from the windows, and a joyous welcome was given. We were told that a substantial banquet had been arranged, and were escorted to a tobacco warehouse where planks had been placed for tables. There were no seats, but we stood up, and soon the waiters appeared with large sheets of iron pans with a big slab of cornbread. The waiters told us it was good and hot, and they passed us a canteen of sorghum molasses, and invited us to take as much as we wanted. Things had been sagging down gradually in the food line, and those good friends of ours thought everything was just right. It was easy to see that the Confederacy was on its last legs. We were given passes to our homes if we could get there, but mine being in the enemy lines, I spent my furlough in Richmond. In about two weeks things began to happen. Sunday afternoon, April 2, 1865, I walked through Capitol Square, and much to my surprise, I saw men bringing bank notes, arms full, and piling them on a fire. There must have been a carload and more coming. This was money that our printing presses had been pounding out for four years, all duly signed in pen and ink by an army of women and bearing such names as "Susan Smith" for Treasurer, and "Mary Jones" for Registrar. One of the men informed me that General Lee was evacuating Richmond, and everything of that kind that could not be carried away was being destroyed. Truly, I have seen "money to burn" in my time.

It was with intense sadness that we gave up Richmond. We had been fighting four long years to keep out the enemy, and at last it had to be surrendered. I recalled the death of my brother John, who had been killed, and my brother William Frederic, lieutenant colonel of the 61st Virginia, who was killed at Spotsylvania, May 12, 1864, on his 24th birthday.

I left Richmond at about three o'clock in the morning and ran over the bridge to Manchester, which had been set on fire to cover our retreat.

Then commenced the march of the Confederate army in the direction of Appomattox Courthouse. In the seven days from Richmond to Appomattox, I did not draw a ration. We were constantly burning our wagons to escape capture. Sometimes we would find an ear of corn that was intended for a mule. We would roast the grains in the hot ashes, or else eat it raw. The men had begun to struggle and look out for themselves, and when they were hard pressed by the calvary, would band together of their own accord and fight off pursuers. Every man had become a general in experience and knew just what to do.

Several times I saw General Lee entirely alone, riding on his horse, Traveler. If he had any worries he did not betray it. I remember his calm, handsome face to this day. We finally reached Appomattox Courthouse. It was the intention to march until we could form a junction with General Joseph E. Johnston, who was coming through North Carolina to meet us. Our ammunition was exhausted, and food, too, and with our twelve thousand men we accepted General Grant's liberal terms. General Grant and General Lee had met at the home of Mr. McLean in the village to discuss terms. We were to be disbanded and permitted to return to our homes. This was Sunday, the ninth of April, 1865.

The men did not wait for the promised rations. Those living in distant states would get their bearings and start to walk in the general direction of their homes. I wended my way over many a mile of mud and rain until I arrived at City Point. I had not drawn any food since leaving Richmond, but the Union soldiers were good to us and would give us coffee and hard tack. At City Point I found many new recruits who had not been uniformed or armed, and called "One Hundred Day Men". They had enlisted for that length of time. Somehow the impression prevailed among them that General Lee had surrendered to General Grant under an apple tree, and that some of the Confederates had pieces of that tree for souvenirs. They were anxious to possess such a valuable relic, and were willing to trade a generous supply of hard tack for a piece. The old "Rebs" were quite quick to catch on, and they invaded the orchards of City Point and were ready to supply the demand for a piece of honest-to-goodness apple tree.

I got aboard a steamboat and went down the James river to Norfolk. I found my father waiting to see if I was among the men. With him were my three brothers, George, Arthur, and Crawford. We crossed over on the ferry, and arrived home after dark, where I met my mother after three years of absence. She could not keep back her tears for her two other boys who did not return.

It was thought that many of our soldier friends might return with me and a bountiful supper had been provided. But I came home alone, and I remember the piles of hot biscuits, sure enough coffee with sugar, a great bowl of stewed oysters, and a Virginia ham. I have thought since that I must have been at the point of starvation without being aware of it. I certainly would have consumed all of the ham, along with the other food, if my father had not stopped me. They were afraid that I would gorge myself to death. It was the first time in three years that I had had enough to eat. I was twenty years old and weighed 120 pounds, and so inured to hardship that my system seemed proof to anything. I went to my room and got into a real bed, but I could not sleep; so I lay down on the floor and soon dropped off to sleep, feeling so well and strong in the morning when I awoke.

(NOTE: On the site of the Old Point Lookout prison, where Henry was imprisoned during the war, with 14,000 other Confederate prisoners, the United States Government has, within recent years, erected a magnificent monument to the Confederate soldiers who died there during the war. This demonstrates that we are again one country—no North, no South, East or West, but all for the common good. S. W. N.)

Generation 5

5   5

    Child of Henry Woodis and Alexina Constantia Wilson

             Charles Frederic Niemeyer

5   5

Children of Eliza Ann Matilda Crawford and John Church
Wilber, II

Mary	Sarah	Samuel	John	Caroline	Moses	Eleanor
Crawford	Peters	Crawford	Church	Virginia	McMonagle	Thompson
m.					m.	m.
William				Charles	Bernice	
Eager				S.	Ainsley	
				Powell		

                          Henry   Margaret

                        Niemeyer   Bauyn

                                  m.

                              William A.

                               Wood

5   5

    Child of Lt. Col. William Frederic Niemeyer and Sarah
              Campbell Smith

           John Frederic Niemeyer
                  m.
           Lucrece Bilisoly

5   5

Children of Henry Victor Niemeyer and Martha Jane Hunter

Henry Hunter   Martha McLean   Carmi Ann   Frederic Lawson
Niemeyer   Niemeyer   Niemeyer   Niemeyer
m.   m.
Margaret Post   Hugh Scott
                                        Graves

5   5

Children of Arthur Emmerson Niemeyer and Sarah Hoyt Mahan

William Angus   Jessie Chandler
Niemeyer   Niemeyer
                                m.
                             Lester Rose
                              Graves

5   5

Children of Hermann Christian Niemeyer and Marie Louise
Hook

Louise   Sarah   Henrietta   Helen   Margaret
Adelaide Elizabeth Victoria   Eugenia   Brighton
Niemeyer   Niemeyer Niemeyer   Niemeyer   Hook
m.   m.   m.   m.   Niemeyer
Berkeley Rev. Myron James   Charles   m.
Minor   Barraud   Green   Monroe   John
Fontaine Marshall   Martin   Nash   Gordon
                                                  Ennes

5   5

Children of Sam Watts Niemeyer and Mary Agnes Moore

Mary Agnes   Nell Moore
Niemeyer   Niemeyer
m.
Maj. Charles A.
Etheridge

5   5

Children of Ann McLean Niemeyer and Samuel Patterson Wigg

Sarah   Virginia   Dorette   Samuel
Chandler   Ruggles   Niemeyer   Patterson
Wigg   Wigg   Wigg   Wigg, Jr.
m.   m.   m.   m.
Walter Lee   Maurice Rudolf   James Lewis I-Roberta Burkett
Darden   Junbeck   Kirby   II-Josephine Jackson
                                          III-Ivonne Liebman

5   5

Children of Mary Chandler Niemeyer and Robert R. Robertson

Robert Angus   Dorothy
m.   m.
Dorothy   Maj. Harry K.
Pickerall   Pickett

Recap of Significant Data: Niemeyer

Generation 5

Charles Frederic Niemeyer was born on January 12, 1860 and
died on Saturday morning December 13, 1862 at 8:30 of scarlet

fever.   His mother, Alexina Constantia Wilson Niemeyer died, also, of scarlet fever on Wednesday morning December 17, 1862 at 7:20 a.m.

Mary Crawford Wilber was born on December 21, 1860 and died in 1947. She married William Eager on September 30, 1908.

Sarah Peters Wilber was born on April 30, 1862 and died March 6, 1937. She never married.

Samuel Crawford Wilber was born on January 12, 1865 and died on December 11, 1915.

John Church Wilber, III was born on November 28, 1866.

Caroline Virginia Wilber married Charles Skrine Powell in 1903 in Hamburg, Germany. She was born on July 19, 1868 and died in 1938 while Charles was born on July 15, 1870 and died in 1918.

Moses McMonagle Wilber was born on July 29, 1871 and married Bernice Ainsley. There was no issue.

Eleanor Thompson Wilber was born on May 10, 1873 and died in May 1959. She never married.

Margaret Bruyn Wilber was born on January 11, 1876 and married William A. Wood on July 24, 1900.

Henry Niemeyer Wilber was born on September 7, 1881 and died on October 8, 1902 at sea of typhoid on the way home from the Philippines.

John Frederic Niemeyer was born on December 3, 1864 in Orange County, Virginia seven months after the death of his father. He married Lucrece Bilisoly, daughter of Dr. A. L. Bilisoly and Annie Camm on October 5, 1886. He died on April 17, 1930 in Portsmouth, Virginia at the home of his son, William Campbell, on Dinwiddie Street.

Henry Hunter Niemeyer was born on January 22, 1877 in Portsmouth. He served in the Spanish American War and was a Y.M.C.A. worker in France with the American Expeditionary Force during World War I. He married Margaret Post of St. Louis. He died in July 1940.

Martha McLean Niemeyer was born in St. Louis on December 6, 1879. She died in St. Louis on December 27, 1967. She never married.

Cami Ann Niemeyer was born in St. Louis in June 1882. She was interred on October 30, 1953. She married Hugh Scott Graves of St. Louis on June 1, 1904. He died on February 7, 1962.

Frederic Lawson Niemeyer was born in St. Louis, Missouri on December 13, 1889. He served throughout World War I in the Army and was badly wounded in the arm. He died unmarried in 1987 and was interred on September 19, 1987.

William Angus Niemeyer was born in Memphis, Tennessee on February 27, 1879 and died unmarried on September 12, 1958.

Jessie Chandler Niemeyer was born on July 20, 1890 in Memphis, Tennessee and married Lester Rose Graves on April 20, 1918. He was a captain in the Army in World War I. He was born in 1888 and died on March 5, 1959. Jessie died February 22, 1920.

Louise Adelaide Niemeyer was born on September 28, 1883 in St. Louis, Missouri. She married Berkeley Minor Fontaine, son of Richard Maurice and Kate Meade Minor Fontaine on June 10, 1913. He was from Beaver Dam, Hanover County, Virginia. Louise died while living with her daughter in Riner, Virginia.

Sarah Elizabeth Niemeyer was born on December 25, 1884 and married the Rev. Myron Barraud Marshall, son of Richard Coke and Catherine Wilson Marshall, on July 2, 1907. He was a great, great grandson of Chief Justice John Marshall and was born on September 12, 1883. He died on January 9, 1946. Sarah Elizabeth was called Bessie and died on February 14,

1960.

Henrietta Victoria Niemeyer was called Dixie. She was born on May 1, 1886 and married James Green Martin, son of Judge William Bruce and Elizabeth Starke Martin on January 6, 1909.

Helen Eugenia Niemeyer was born on February 3, 1888 and married Charles Monroe Nash, son of Captain Charles Francis Nash of the United States Coast Guard and Rebecca Monroe Nash on June 29, 1908. He was born in Alexandria, Virginia.

Margaret Brighton Hook Niemeyer was born on February 17, 1891 and married John Gordon Eanes, son of Dr. John and Gertrude Eanes on January 23, 1915.

Mary Agnes Niemeyer was born on June 6, 1894 and married Major Charles A. Etheridge of the United States Marine Corps who served in both World War I and II.

Nell Moore Niemeyer was born on August 12, 1895 and died in November 1914.

Sarah Chandler Wigg was born on July 18, 1889 and died in July 1952. She married Walter Darden.

Virginia Ruggles Wigg was born on August 17, 1891 and married Maurice Rudolf Jungbeck who served as an officer in the Army through World War I.

Dorette Wigg was born on September 22, 1893. She married James Lewis Kirby on February 16, 1922. He was born on August 28, 1883 and died March 4, 1963.

Samuel Patterson Wigg was born May 17, 1899 and served in the Army throughout World War I.

Christine Louise Niemeyer was born on February 21, 1899 and died unmarried in 1947.

John Wooten Niemeyer was born on April 28, 1901 and served as a Captain in the United States Coast Guard in World Wars I and II. He was decorated for heroism. He never married.

Dorothy Robertson was born March 8, 1893 in Portsmouth, Virginia. She married Major Harry K. Pickett who was in the Marine Corps in World War I and was a general in World War II. They lived in Washington, D.C. He died on October 27, 1997 in Palm City, Florida. They had lived in Jensen Beach, Florida.

Robert Angus Robertson was born February 23, 1895. He served in the Army in World War I. He married Dorothy Pickerall. He was called Honey.

Generation 6

6   6

    Children of Caroline Virginia Wilber and Charles Skrine
                                                  Powell

Virginia	Charles Skrine Powell, Jr.
m.	m.
Francis Perkins	Marguerite Bryant
Bruce	Shannon

6   6

    Children of John Frederic Niemeyer and Lucrece Bilisoly

Marie Antonia	Raymond Frederick	William Campbell	Oscar Vincent	Antonio Bilisoly	Robert Prescott
m.	m.	m.	m.	m.	m.
Alfred Liebler	Marie Layne	Mary Daugherty	Cleo Farley	I-Lutie Stuart Spotts	Edith Louise Jones
				II-Mary W. Keefe	

6   6

    Child of Henry Hunter Niemeyer and Margaret Post

             Henry Hunter, Jr.

6   6

Children of Carmi Ann Niemeyer and Hugh Scott Graves

Martha Hunter	Hugh Scott	Emily Preston	Henry Victor	June Richie
m.	m.		m.	m.
Paul Baker	Mildred Force		Mary Ann Weir	Gerald W. Benson

6   6

Child of Jessie Chandler Niemeyer and Lester Rose Graves

Jessie Chandler m. George William Nash

6   6

Children of Louise Adelaide Niemeyer and Berkeley Minor Fontaine

Katherine Berkeley   Grace
m.   m.
I- Lee Crawford Syer   Thomas Fuller
II- Elliot Heath

6   6

Children of Sarah Elizabeth and Rev. Myron Barraud Marshall

Louise Chandler	Elizabeth Barraud	Catherine Wilson	Myron Berraud	Herman Calvert	Richard Coke	Helen St.Julian
m.	m.	m.	m.	m.	m.	m.
I- Robert Craddock	Dudley Diggs	Robert Hamill	Margaret Haddow	Jean Scott	I- Martha McKenny	Henry Fedzick
II- George					II- Clara	

258

Hoffman
III- Edward
McCrensky

                                        Arthur   John
                                    Niemeyer
                                          m.   m.
                                      Isabel   Gladys
                                    Montgomery   Fawcett

6   6
    Children of Henrietta Victoria and James Green Martin

William James Henrietta Margaret Louise Elizabeth Marianne
Bruce Green Calvert Marchant Niemeyer Starke   Reade
      m.   m.   m.   m.   m.
    Elizabeth Donald   Henry   William   William
      Weiss Bartlett   Forbes   Capehart Cole
                                   Harney Worthington

6   6
    Children of Helen Eugenia and Charles Monroe Nash

    Elizabeth   Charles   Helen   James
    Monroe   Francis   Eugenia   Monroe, Jr.
      m.   m.   m.
I- Henry Clay   I- Lt. Robert   Elsie
    Hudgins   Warren   Cary
II- John Ashton   McWhinney   Nelms
    MacKenzie   II- Charles
                                     Halcomb

6   6

Children of Margaret Brighton Hook and John Gordon Ennes

        John Chandler   Norborne Sutton
                                        m.
                         I- Virginia Duggen Newton
                        II- Helen

6   6

Child of Mary Agnes Niemeyer and Charles A. Etheridge

                Charles Antonio, Jr.

6   6

Children of Sarah Chandler Wigg and Walter Lee Darden

       Sarah Chandler   Anne McLean
         m.
   Kenneth Sterling Brown

6   6

Children Virginia Rivers Wigg and Maurice Rudolf Jungback

Duncan McLean	Alan Lockhart	Alice Mary Catherine	Margaret Patterson	Dorothea Ann
		m.	m.	m.
		Robert	David	Roland
		Leslie	Davidovitch	Casperson
		Melvin	Burleuk	

6   6

Child of Dorette Niemeyer Wigg and James Lewis Kirby, Sr.

James Lewis Kirby, Jr. m. Ann Sutherland Kirby

6   6
Children of Samuel Patterson Wigg, Jr. and Josephine Jackson
Niemeyer

Anne Virginia   Helen Jackson

6   6
Children of Dorothy Robertson and Harry K. Pickett

Dorothy Chandler   Harry K., Jr.
m.   m.
Gordon Sharpe   Jane

6   6
Children of Robert Angus Robertson and Dorothy Pickerell

Mary Chandler   John Pickerell
m.
Walter Vernon Gresham, Jr.

Recap of Significant Data: Niemeyer

Generation 6

Virginia Powell was born on May 6, 1904 and married Francis Perkins Bruce who was born on August 27, 1906 and died in September 1959.

Charles Skrine Powell, Jr. was born on April 29, 1906 and died on December 22, 1990. He married Marguerite Bryant Shannon on September 13, 1930. She was born on April 2, 1906. Marguerite Bryant Shannon was the daughter of Lenna Belle Proctor who was born on November 22, 1878 and died January 9, 1962. Her father was Clarence Downing Shannon. He was born on August 27, 1878 and died March 25, 1950.

Marie Antonia Niemeyer was born on July 24, 1887 in Portsmouth, Va. and died October 27, 1979 in Sarasota, Florida. She married Alfred Liebler. Marie worked for the Seaboard Airline Railroad. She lived with her daughter, Eloise, and Eloise's husband, Edwin Maxwell Dale.

Raymond Frederick Niemeyer was born on October 1, 1889 in Portsmouth and died in Portsmouth on June 2, 1964 and is buried in Olive Branch Cemetery. He and three of his brothers served in the 111th Field Artillery in World War I. "Dutch" (nickname) was employed by the Seaboard Airline Railroad and was assigned to Bluefield, Va. where he met and married Marie Layne on April 5, 1920. She was born on September 2, 1892 in Roanoke, Virginia and died July 31, 1970 in Portsmouth. They had one son who did not marry.

William Campbell Niemeyer was born on February 19, 1892 in Portsmouth and was baptized by Father Brady on February 20th. He married, on May 30, 1918, Mary Elicia Daugherty of Portsmouth where they made their home. He joined his brothers in the Grimes Battery and was sent to France in World

War I while his wife assisted the families and wives of navy personnel when those in the armed services were in the Naval Hospital. He later was a food broker. "Bill" died on Augst 20, 1944 at his home in Portsmouth and is buried with his wife in Evergreen Cemetery. Mary was a daughter of James P. and Ella Watson Daugherty. She was born on December 1, 1892 and died on February 21, 1953 at her home in Portsmouth.

Oscar Vincent called O.V. was born on April 13, 1894. He was a sergeant in the Grimes Battery and served in France during World War I. On his return he married Cleo Farley from whom he was later divorced. O.V. died at the home of William Campbell Niemeyer in Portsmouth on February 6, 1950. He is buried in Evergreen Memorial Park in Portsmouth.

Antonio Bilisoly was born on January 25, 1896 in Portsmouth and died on April 18, 1973 in Allston, Ma. He firstly married and divorced Lutie Stuart Spotts who was born on August 22, 1899 and died on October 23, 1986 while living with her son and his family. "Tony" moved to Boston and was employed by the Duplex Envelope Company and later Christmas Club. In Boston, he met and married Mary W. Keefe. He married secondly Mary O'Keefe.

Robert Prescott Niemeyer was born on February 7, 1898 in Portsmouth. Prescott married on February 22, 1923, Edith Louise Jones whom he later divorced. Edith was born on March 25, 1905 and died in Richmond, VA on March 22, 1986. He died at the home of Gregory Hill on Baldwin Place in Norfolk, Virginia on March 2, 1942.

Martha Hunter Graves was born on September 6, 1905. She married Paul Baker.

Hugh Scott Graves was born in 1908 and died in 1967. He married Mildred Force. They lived in Delray Beach, Florida.

Emily Preston Graves was known as Mimi. She was born

in 1910 and died July 19, 1990. She did not marry. She was interred in St. Louis on July 21, 1990.

Henry Victor Graves was born in 1912 and died in 1970. He married Mary Ann Weir and they lived in Louisville, Kentucky.

June Richie Graves was born on June 30, 1916. She married Gerald W. Benson and they lived in Brevard, North Carolina.

Jessie Chandler Graves was born on January 22, 1919. She married George William Nash, son of Isaac Thomas and Bertha Ellen Nash of Memphis, Tennessee on May 20, 1939. He was born on February 22, 1910 and died January 1, 1978. They lived in Memphis, Tennessee. Later Jessie moved to Pensacola, Florida.

Katherine Berkeley Fontaine was born November 27, 1914 in Hartford, Connecticut. She first married Lee Crawford Syer who was the son of Charles and Grace Watts Syer on October 1, 1938 by whom she had three children. After Crawford Syer died she married Elliott Heath.

Grace Fontaine was born July 6, 1916 in Glastonbury, Connecticut. She married Thomas Fuller who was a Lt. In the U. S. Navy. He was the son of Willard Perin and Elizabeth Channing Fuller of Milton, Massachusetts. They were married November 22, 1941 and had two children.

Louise Chandler Marshall was born June 24, 1908 in Saltville, Virginia. She was married three times.

Elizabeth Barraud Marshall was born in 1909 in the Philippines.

Catherine Wilson Marshall was born December 12, 1912 in Norfolk, Virginia.

Myron Barraud Marshall, Jr. was born in 1914.

Herman Calvert Marshall was born in 1916 and married Jean Scott.

Richard Coke Marshall first married Martha McKenny and later Clara ?.

264

Helen St. Julien Marshall married Henry Fedzick. They lived in Hampton, Virginia.

John Marshall married Gladys Fawcett.

Arthur Niemeyer Marshall died January 18, 1980 at 56 years of age.

William Bruce Martin was born October 18, 1909 in Norfolk, Virginia and died April 15, 1911 at the age of eighteen months.

James Green Martin, Jr. was born April 27, 1912 in Norfolk, Virginia. He served as a Major in the Army during World War II and married Elizabeth Weiss of Baltimore, Marlyand.

Henrietta Calvert Martin was born January 5, 1913 and married Donald Bartlett of Dartmouth, New Hampshire.

Margaret Marchant Martin was born November 25, 1914 and married Henry Forbes. She lives in Pawley's Island, South Carolina.

Louise Niemeyer Martin was born March 29, 1917 in Norfolk, Virginia. She attended St. Mary's Junior College in Raleigh, North Carolina and graduated from Randolph Macon Woman's College in Lynchburg, Virginia. She married William Capehart Harney who was an executive of EXXON and lived for 29 years in Somerville, South Carolina. She died November 3, 2003 in Durham, North Carolina. He was born April 12, 1917 in Edenton, North Carolina and was the son of William Selby and Clara Cotton Capehart Harney. He grew up in Norfolk and graduated from the University of North Carolina in Chapel Hill. William Harney died December 22, 2000 in Somerville, South Carolina.

Elizabeth Starke Martin was born April 3, 1919. She married William Cole Worthington.

Elizabeth Monroe Nash was born April 30 and married first Henry Clay Hudgins, a Major in the U. S. Air Force who was killed flying over Germany during World War II.

She and Henry had two children. Secondly, she married John Ashton MacKenzie who was a Lt. in the Coast Guard during World War II and retired as a U. S. Federal Judge.

Charles Francis Nash was born March 25, 1920 and was killed flying with the Canadian Air Force during World War II.

Helen Eugenia Nash was born July 6, 1922 and married Lt. Robert Warren McWhinney on July 6, 1945. They had five children. They divorced. She secondly married Charles Halcomb from whom she also is divorced.

James Monroe Nash was born December 4, 1929 and married Elsie Cary Nelms on October 23, 1954. They had three children. Elsie died on October 12, 2003 at their home in Virginia Beach. She was the daughter of Elsie Curtis and James Archibald Nelms.

John Chandler Ennes was born July 26, 1918.

Norborne Sutton Ennes was born October 18, 1920 and married, first, Virginia Duggan Newton. After her death he married Helen ?.

Sarah Chandler Darden of Nashua, New Hampshire, was born in December 1919 at King's Daughters Hospital in Portsmouth, Virginia. She married Kenneth Sterling Brown of Mystic, Connecticut on October 9, 1940. He was a commander in the United States Navy and was born on October 25, 1914 in Pinson, Alabama.

Anne McLean Darden was born on July 16, 1915 in Portsmouth and died on August 25, 1976 in Norfolk, Virginia.

Duncan McLean Jungbeck was born on October 13, 1921 in Portsmouth and lived in New York City. He was killed on July 31st in Normandy, France.

Alan Lockhard Jungbeck was born on March 8, 1923 in Portsmouth. He lived in Las Vegas, Nevada.

Alice Mary Catherine Jungbeck was born on December 2, 1924 in Portsmouth. She married Robert Leslie Melvin on January 15, 1953 in New York, New York. They divorced and she live in Hialeah, Florida.

Margaret Patterson Jungbeck was born on December 6, 1926 in Portsmouth and married David Davidovitch Burleuk of Long Island, New York.

Dorothea Ann Jungbeck was born on August 27, 1935 in Portsmouth and married Roland Casperson of Long Island on July 9, 1957 at Huntington, Long Island, New York.

James Lewis Kirby, Jr. was born in Portsmouth, Virginia on July 13, 1923. He was married on May 29, 1954 in Madison, New Jersey, to Ann Sutherland Kirby. She was born on August 16, 1928 in Wilkes-Barre, Pennsylvania, the second daughter of Allan Price and Marian Grace Sutherland Kirby, of 'Graymar Farm', Morris County, New Jersey.

Anne Virginia Wigg married Howard Eugene Kerpelman of Middlebury, Connecticut. He was a bank president born on February 26, 1937 in Suffolk, Virginia. She was born on December 14, 1937 in Wilmington, North Carolina. They divorced.

Helen Jackson Wigg of St. Louis, Missouri was a graduated of North Carolina State university and an officer of a pharmaceutical company. She was born June 13, 1941 in Wilmington, North Carolina and never married.

Dorothy Chandler Pickett died in 1988 or 1989. She lived in Durham, North Carolina.

Harry K. Pickett, Jr. died on October 27, 1997 in Palm City, Florida. Harry was a native of Portsmouth and lived in Arlington, Va. before moving to Jensen Beach, Florida.

Robert Angus Robertson was known as Honey Robertson and was Commissioner of Revenue for Norfolk County, Va.

Generation 7

7   7

Child of Charles Skrine Powell, Jr. and Marguerite Bryant
Shannon

Ann Proctor m. Richard Arnon Mathews

7   7

Child of Marie Antonia Niemeyer and Alfred Liebler

Eloise Lucrece m. Edwin Maxwell Dale

7   7

Child of Raymond Frederick Niemeyer and Marie Layne

Raymond Frederick, Jr.

7   7

Children of William Campbell Niemeyer and Mary Daugherty

Lucrece Bilisoly   Mary Camm   William Campbell, Jr.
m.   m.   m.
Franklin Edward   Lewis Leonard   Joanne McCurry
Truax   Pembroke Smith

7   7

Children of Oscar Vincent Niemeyer and Cleo Farley

Gloria Marie
m.
George C. Hudgins, Jr.

Oscar Vincent, Jr.
m.
I – Gail O'Connor
II – Annie Makuck

7   7

Children of Antonio Bilisoly Niemeyer and
I – Lutie Stuart Spotts   II – Mary W. Keefe

Eleanor Stuart   Antonio Bilisoly, Jr.   Edwin Brooks
m.   m.
Alice Virginia   I – Karina Aura Hagman
Berry   II – Hinda Rose
                        III – Suzanne Pernoy

7   7

Children of Robert Prescott Niemeyer and Edith Louise Jones

Robert Prescott, Jr.
m.
I – Nancy Narvel
II – Barbara Reedy

Nancy Adele
m.
Lewis Franklin
Baxter, Jr.

7   7

Child of Henry Victor Graves and Mary Ann Weir

James Edwin m. Lucy Bosley

7   7

Children of Jessie Chandler Graves and George William Nash

Judy Chandler   Mary Margaret   George Arthur   Nancy Elizabeth
      m.   m.   m.   m.
Finley Clarke   William Thomas   Kathy Hughes   Andrew Scott
   Holmes   Reid   Neely

7   7
      Children of Katherine Berkeley Fontaine and Lee Crawford
                                                              Syer

Lee Crawford, Jr.   Katherine Berkeley Fontaine   Charlotte

7   7
            Children of Grace Fontaine and Thomas Fuller

      Joan Channing   Berkley Fontaine

7   7
      Children of Louise Niemeyer Martin and William Capehart
                                                           Harney

      Thomas Capehart   Anne   Helen
                                m.   m.
                                     Cox   Conrad

7   7
   Children of Elizabeth Monroe Nash and Henry Clay Hudgins

         Elizabeth Nash   Henry Clay
              m.   m.
      I - Bryant Bonner Hamaker   Marie Bible

270

II - Michael Pitt

7 7

Children of Helen Eugenia Nash and Robert Warren McWhinney

Julia Woodward	Helen Nash	Charles Robert	Samuel Saxon	James Monroe
m.	m.			m.
Wilfred Magann	Halley Moriyama			Felicity Steffes

7 7

Children of James Monroe Nash and Elsie Cary Nelms

Charles Monroe	Elizabeth	James Nelms
m.	m.	m.
Donna White	I-Nigel Dyche	Cindy Ringer
	II-Harrison Taylor	

7 7

Children of Charles Antonio Etheridge, Jr.

Charles Layton   Elizabeth Lewis   Robert Niemeyer

7 7

Child of Dorothy Chandler Pickett and Gordon Sharpe

Sandra

7 7

Children of Harry K. Pickett, Jr. and Jane

William   Paul   Dorothy   Donna

7   7
        Children of Mary Chandler Robertson and Walter Vernon
                                            Gresham, Jr.

        John Robertson   Walter Vernon, III

7   7
Children of Sarah Chandler Darden and Kenneth Sterling Brown

        Kenneth McKinnon   Sarah Chandler
             m.   m.
        Janet Marie Davis   George Merritt Stabler

7   7
    Child of Alice Mary Catherine Jungbeck and Robert Leslie
                                                Melvin

                Duncan McLean

7   7

            Children of Margaret Patterson Jungbeck and David
                                        Davidovitch Burleuk

David Duncan   Ian Alan   Virginia Courtney   Lili Donan
   McGregor   Patterson   McLean

7   7

Child of Dorothea Ann Jungbeck and Roland Casperson

Jason Roland

7   7

Children of James Lewis Kirby, Jr. and Ann Sutherland Kirby

Wade Howard   Annette   Roger Hillersdon
  Osborne   Sutherland   Wigg
    m.
Linda Loretta Taylor

7   7

Child of Anne Virginia Wigg and Howard Eugene Kerpelman

Keith David

Recap of Significant Data: Niemeyer

Generation 7

Anne Proctor Powell was born on July 17, 1932. She married Richard Arnon Mathews on July 24, 1954. They lived at 709 B Ocean Avenue, Avon by the Sea, New Jersey. He was born on July 16, 1932. His parents were Susanne Hanten who married Gustave Xavier Mathews, Jr. on June 9, 1931. Susanne was born on October 20, 1910 and died on June 11, 1972 while her husband was born on September 9, 1907 and died on December 28, 1966. The younger Mathews had three children; Gustave Xavier Mathews, III, Charles Powell Mathews and Julia Isles Mathews.

Eloise Lucrece Leibler was born on August 29, 1908. She married Edwin Maxwell Dale who was born on November 25, 1907 on October 10, 1931. Mac died on June 19, 1987 and is buried in Sarasota, Florida. They had no children.

Raymond Frederick Niemeyer, Jr. was called Little Dutch and was born on March 6, 1921 in Portsmouth, Va. He was one of the early men called into the Army in 1940 and spent the war years in Australia and New Zealand. After the war Dutch graduated from The College of William and Mary and served as a state auditor. He died on September 15, 1995 and is buried in Olive Branch Cemetery, Portsmouth. He did not marry.

Lucrece Bilisoly Niemeyer was born in Portsmouth on December 19, 1920. She married Franklin Edward Truax of Rockford, Minnesota on September 8, 1945. Ed was born on February 25, 1912 and died on April 7, 1985. They had three children.

Mary Camm Niemeyer was born on July 7, 1925. She married Lewis Leonard Pembroke Smith of New Jersey on December 15, 1950 in Brooklyn, New York. Smitty was born on December 10,

1922 and died on December 27, 1993. They had three children.

William Campbell Niemeyer, Jr. was born in Portsmouth on May 25, 1929 and died on June 21, 1998. He is buried in Evergreen Cemetery, Portsmouth. Buck, as he was called, married Joanne McCurry on October 13, 1951 in Portsmouth and they had two children. Joanne was born on August 27, 1933 in Mecklenburg County, VA.

Gloria Marie Niemeyer was born in 1922. She married George C. Hudgins, Jr. in 1944. Gloria died June 22, 1991 and her husband died December 28, 1994 in Annapolis, Maryland. They had two children.

Oscar Vincent Niemeyer, Jr. was born on August 22, 1928 and married Gail T. O'Conner in January of 1950. They had three children. In 1990 he married Annie Makuck.

Eleanor Stuart Niemeyer died young.

Antonio Bilisoly Niemeyer, Jr. was born on April 13, 1928 in St. Vincent's Hospital in Norfolk, Va. He married Alice Virginia Berry of Skipwith, Virginia on November 20, 1965. She was born on November 24, 1932. They were both Science Teachers and had three children.

Edwin Brooks Niemeyer was the son of Antonio Bilisoly Niemeyer and Mary W. Keefe. He was born on August 7, 1939 in Allston, Massachusetts. He first married Karina Aura Hagman (2 children), secondly Hinda Rose (one son) and later Suzanne Pernoy (no issue).

Robert Prescott Niemeyer, Jr. was born in Portsmouth. He was a graduate of the University of Delaware, was a veteran of World War II and retired as a librarian for Armed Forces Staff College. He was born on June 5, 1925, died on March 30, 1973 and is buried in Olive Branch Cemetery. He married Nancy Jane Narvel, had one son and divorced. He secondly married Barbara Reedy and had a son and a daughter.

Nancy Adele Niemeyer was born on November 18, 1928. She married Lewis Franklin Baxter, Jr. on April 28, 1962. He was born on March 16, 1919. Nancy died in Portsmouth on May 25, 1999, Lewis died in Virginia Beach on May 26, 2000 and they are buried in Westwood Cemetery, Virginia Beach.

Judy Chandler Nash was born on April 16, 1943 and married Dr. Finley Clarke Holmes on June 4, 1966. He was born on December 25, 1939. They have three sons and live in Pensacola, Florida.

Mary Margaret Nash was born on October 21, 1945 and married William Thomas Reid on August 5, 1967. He was born on July 3, 1944. They had one son and lived in Birmingham, Alabama.

George Archer Nash was born on September 11, 1948 and married Kathy Hughes on April 12, 1980. She was born on October 3, 1955. They had two daughters and lived in Madison, Mississippi.

Nancy Elizabeth Nash was born on January 27, 1952 and married Andrew Scott Neely on June 27, 1975. He was born on October 21, 1952. They had one daughter.

Jessie Graves Nash and Family

Tommy Reid, Judy Nash, George Nash, Kathy Nash, Jamie Nash, Jessie Nash, Jennifer Neely, Nancy Neely, Bill Reid, Peggy Reid, Chandler Holmes, Jodie Holmes, John Holmes, Finley Holmes, Jr., Judy Holmes, Finley Holmes

Jessie's children: George Nash, Nancy Neely, Peggy Reid and Judy Holmes

Lee Crawford Syer, Jr. was born November 2, 1943 and was called Lee. He had no issue.

Katherine Berkeley Fontaine Syer was born June 15, 1947 and was called Fontaine. Had no issue.

Charlotte Syer was born August 31, 1951. Had no issue.

Joan Channing Fuller was born December 1, 1942.

Berkeley Fontaine Fuller was born August 17, 1947.

Thomas Capehart Harney lives in Atlanta, Georgia.

Anne Harney, with her husband (a Cox), lives in Columbia,

South Carolina.

Helen Harney and her husband (a Conrad) live in Durham, North Carolina.

Elizabeth Nash Hudgins was born on October 11, 1940 and married, and divorced in 1988, Bryant Bonner Hamaker. He was born on July 30, 1940. They had two children. She married secondly, Michael Pitt. She was elected Chairman of the Portsmouth School Board and lives on Swimming Point, Portsmouth.

Henry Clay Hudgins was born on June 30, 1945 and married Marie Bible who was born August 4, 1943. They had a daughter and were divorced in 1988. He is a tugboat captain.

Julia Woodward McWhinney married Wilford Magann and they had two children.

Helen Nash McWhinney married Halley Moriyama and they had two children.

James Monroe McWhinney was born on December 4, 1928 and married Felicity Steffes and they had one son.

Charles Monroe Nash was born on December 12, 1955 and married Donna White. They have Donna's son and their daughter.

Elizabeth Nash is called Liza and married Nigel Dyche from whom she was divorced in 1992.

James Nelms Nash married Cindy Ringer and they had a daughter.

Kenneth McKinnon Brown was born on October 27, 1946 in Honolulu, Hawaii and married Janet Marie Davis, daughter of Earl and Jean Davis of Auburn, New Hampshire on February 2, 1968 in Manchester, New Hampshire. He resides in Hollis, New Hampshire. Janet Marie was born on August 27, 1946 in Auburn.

Sarah Chandler Brown was born on July 27, 1943 in Norfolk and married George Merritt Stabler of Nashua, New Hampshire. He was born on June 6, 1943 in Williamstown, Massachusetts.

They were married in Nashua in June 1977. They are divorced.

Duncan McLean Melvin was born on February 26, 1957 in Sarasota, Florida.

David Duncan McGregor Burleuk was born on June 27, 1952 in Huntington, New York.

Ian Alan Patterson Burleuk was born on December 5, 1953 in Huntington, New York.

Virginia Courtney McLean Burleuk was born on August 15, 1950 in Huntington.

Lili Donan Burleuk was born on May 6, 1959 in Huntington.

Jason Roland Casperson was born on August 1, 1959 in New Mexico.

William Pickett lives in Richmond, Va.

Paul Pickett lives in Arlington, Va.

Dorothy Pickett lives in Durham, NC.

Donna Pickett lives in Alexandria, Va.

John Robertson Gresham lives in Ruther Glen, Va.

Walter Vernon Gresham, III lives in Kill Devil Hills, NC.

Wade Howard Osborne Kirby was born on September 23, 1957 in Norristown, New Jersey and he and his wife have triplet sons. They live in New York.

Annette Sutherland Kirby was born on January 7, 1962 in Norristown, lives in Roanoke, Virginia and has not married.

Roger Hillersdon Wigg Kirby was born on October 18, 1965 in Norristown. He is married and lives in Richmond, Virginia.

Keith David Kerpelman was born in Richmond, Virginia on July 17, 1951. He resides in Middleburg, Connecticut.

Generation
8   8
Children of Anne Proctor Powell and Richard Arnon Mathews

Gustave Xavier, III	Charles Powell	Julia Isles
m.	m.	m.
Judith Washer	Wendy Elaine Graham	Brian Charles Meneghin

8   8

Children of Lucrece Bilisoly Niemeyer and Franklin Edward Truax

Walter Davis	Lucrece Lee	Mary Cora
m.	m.	m.
I-Priscilla Thurow II-Linda Marie Steele	Paul Steven Bauer	Douglas Martin Opsahl

8   8

Children of Mary Camm Niemeyer and Lewis Leonard Pembroke Smith

Mary Pembroke	William Campbell	Linda Ware
m.	m.	m.
I- Donald Larson II-Jerry Juno	Susan Claire Cassidy	Darrell Elmer Sottesz

8   8

Children of William Campbell Niemeyer, Jr. and Joanne McCurry

William Campbell, III	Mary Chandler
m.	m.
Bonnie Leigh Pritchard Strange	I- Patrick Kevin Walsh II- Scot Lawrence Beach

8   8

Children of Gloria Marie Niemeyer and George C. Hudgins, Jr.

George C., III   Angela
m.   m.
Janet Herring   I-

II- Michael Stauder

8   8

Children of Oscar Vincent Niemeyer, Jr. and Gail O'Conner

Michael Scott   Brad Vincent   Kim Marie
m.   m.
Elise Ninesling   Frank Davis

8   8

Children of Antonio Bilisoly Niemeyer, Jr. and Alice
Virginia Berry

William Frederic   Frank Berry   John Stuart
m.   m.   m.
Carolyn Louise   Shannon Page   April Michelle
Holtzhauer   Eadie   Tripp

8   8

Children of Edwin Brooks Niemeyer and
I- Karina Aura Hagman   II-Hinda Rose

Barbara Elizabeth   Thomas Walter   Matthew (NMI)
m.   m.   m.
Michael Lynn Bolt   Ghada Ltief   Amy Castleberry

8   8

Child of Nancy Adele Niemeyer and Lewis Franklin Baxter, Jr.

Brian Donnan

8   8
Children of Elizabeth Nash Hudgins and Bryant Bonner Hamaker

Bryant Bonner, Jr.   Helen Monroe

8   8
Child of Henry Clay Hudgins, Jr. and Marie Bible

Elizabeth Mackenzie

8   8
Children of Julia Woodward McWhinney and Wilfred Magann

Chandler   Eugenia Hope

8   8
Children of Helen Nash McWhinney and Halley Moriyama

Caroline   Scott

8   8
Child of James Monroe McWhinney and Felicity Steffes

Ian

8   8
Child of Charles Monroe Nash and Donna White

Nicole Lynn

8   8

Child of James Nelms Nash and Cindy Ringer

Kate

8   8

Children Judy Chandler Nash and Dr. Finley Clarke Holmes

Finley Clarke, Jr.   John James   Chandler Harrison
m.
Jodie Lynn Taucher

8   8

Child of Mary Margaret Nash and William Thomas Reid

William Thomas, Jr.

8   8

Children of George Arthur Nash and Kathy Hughes

Judy Collyn   Jamie Susanne

8   8

Child of Nancy Elizabeth Nash and Andrew Scott Neely

Jennifer Chandler

8   8

Children of Kenneth McKinnon and Janet Marie Davis Brown

Matthew McKinnon Chapin   Jenifer Darden

8   8

Children opf Sarah Chandler Brown and George Merritt Stabler

        Benjamin Chandler   Elizabeth Dorette

8   8

    Children of Wade Howard Osborne and Linda Loretta Taylor
                                                            Kirby

        Taylor   Croft   Reade

Recap of Significant Data: Niemeyer

Generation 8

    Gustave Xavier Mathews, III was born on November 16, 1956. He married Judith Washer who was born on December 7, 1957. They married June 6, 1981 and had three children.

    Charles Powell Mathews was born on April 21, 1958. He married Wendy Elaine Graham on June 30, 1990. She was born on October 6, 1961 and had one child.

    Julia Isles Mathews was born January 16, 1961. She married Brian Charles Meneghin who was born on January 30, 1961. They married on September 12, 1987 and had one child.

    Walter Davis Truax was born in Minneapolis on October 18, 1946. He married first, Priscilla Thurow, in 1969 and they had one son. Secondly, he married on June 9, 1979 Linda Marie Steele who was born on October 7, 1952. They had one daughter. Walter is a neurosurgeon who practices in New Orleans.

    Lucrece Lee Truax was born in Minneapolis on May 30,

1948. She married Paul Steven Bauer on June 12, 1970 and had two children. He was born on April 8, 1947.

Mary Cora Truax was born in Minneapolis on May 27, 1951. She married Douglas Martin Opsahl on July 21, 1973 and had two children.

Mary Pembroke Smith was born in New London, Connecticut on September 20, 1951. She married twice. Her second husband was Jerry Juno who was born on May 12, 1951. The married on July 25, 1986 in Somerdale, New Jersey and had one child.

William Campbell Smith was born on January 24, 1953 in Portsmouth, VA. He married Susan Claire Cassidy on January 17, 1975 in Somerdale, New Jersey. She was born on June 29, 1954 and they have two children.

Linda Ware Smith was born in Portsmouth, Virginia on July 3, 1955. She married Darrell Elmer Soltesz on July 16, 1983 in Roebling, New Jersey. He was born on April 12, 1959 and they have two children.

William Campbell Niemeyer, III was born on January 17, 1955 and married Bonnie Leigh Pritchard Strange on March 31, 1990. Bonnie was born on July 10, 1965. They have two girls.

Mary Chandler Niemeyer was born on November 20, 1958. She married twice. On May 19, 1979 she married first Patrick Kevin Walsh who was born on December 5, 1957 and they were divorced before any children were born. Mary Chandler's first child was Christopher Regan Niemeyer who was born on June 21, 1984. Her second husband was Scot Lawrence Beach. They were married on June 29, 1992 and have three children. Scot was born on March 19, 1961.

George C. Hudgins, III was born in 1953 and married Janet Herring in 1988. They live in Lexington, Virginia and have one child.

Angela Hudgins married twice. Her second husband was

Michael Stauder. She was born in 1957 and married the second time in 1987. There were no children from the first marriage and two by the second.

Michael Scott Niemeyer was born on October 30, 1952 and married Elise Ninesling in 1972.

Brad Vincent Niemeyer was born on November 4, 1954.

Kim Marie Niemeyer was born on September 22, 1957.

William Frederic Niemeyer was born on April 5, 1967 in Portsmouth, Virginia. He married, on December 1, 1990, Carolyn Louise Holtzhauer who was born on April 19, 1968 in Washington, D. C. They have two children.

Frank Berry Niemeyer was born on November 20, 1968 in Portsmouth, Virginia. He married, on July 2, 1994, Shannon Page Eadie who was born on July 22, 1969. They have one child.

John Stuart Niemeyer was born on February 22, 1970 in Portsmouth. He married, on November 27, 1996, April Michelle Tripp from Norfolk who was born on December 19, 1960. April has a son from her first marriage and she and John have one son.

Barbara Elizabeth Niemeyer married Michael Lynn Bolt and they had one son. Barbara was born on November 17, 1962.

Thomas Walter Niemeyer was born on June 15, 1959 and married Ghada Ltief.

Matt Niemeyer was born on March 3, 1967 and married Amy Castleberry.

Brian Donnan Baxter was born on May 17, 1965. He served in the Army reaching the rank of Major but left to enter practice as an Emergency Room Doctor.

Finley Clarke Holmes, Jr. was born on January 12, 1968 in Memphis, TN.

John James Holmes was born on July 14, 1970 in Pensacola, FL. and married Jodi Lynn Taucher on May 26, 2001. She was born March 3, 1971.   He is employed at Shands Hospital in Gainesville, FL.

Chandler Harrison Holmes was born on December 12, 1973 in Pensacola, FL.

Bryant Bonner Hamaker, Jr. was born on July 2, 1968.

Helen Monroe Hamaker was born on February 16, 1970.

Elizabeth MacKensie Hudgins was born on May 11, 1974.

William Thomas Reid, Jr. was born on January 28, 1971 in Memphis, TN.

Judy Collyn Nash was born on August 9, 1982 in Madison, MS.

Jamie Susanne Nash was born on December 18, 1985.

Jennifer Chandler Neely was born on January 8, 1979 in Dallas, TX.

Matthew McKinnon Chapin Brown of Hollis, New hampshire was born on June 15, 1976 in Nashua, New Hampshire.

Jenifer Darden Brown was born on December 2, 1974 in Nashua.

Benjamin Chandler Stabler was born on December 31, 1979 in Nashua.

Elizabeth Dorette Stabler was born on December 1, 1981 in Nashua.

9   9

Children of Gustave Xavier Mathews, III and Judith Washer

    James Xavier   William Lanphear   Hillary Proctor

9   9

Child of Charles Powell Mathews and Wendy Elaine Graham

        Susanna Tilghman

9   9

Children of Julia Isles Mathews and Brian Charles Meneghin

       Elizabeth Powell   Charles Bellinger

9   9

       Children of Walter Davis Truax and
  I- Priscilla Thurow   II- Linda Marie Steele

        Allyn Edward   Chandler Marie

9   9

Children of Lucrece Lee Truax and Paul Steven Bauer

       Michael Paul   Jacob Lee

9   9

Children of Mary Cora Truax and Douglas Martin Opsahl

      Cora Marie   Daniel Martin

9   9

   Child of Mary Pembroke Smith and Jerry Juno

           Sarah Courtney

9   9

Children of William Campbell Smith and Susan Claire Cassidy

Christopher Campbell   Kevin Michael

9   9
Children of Linda Ware Smith and Darrell Elmer Soltesz

Zachery Darrell   Elicia Marie

9   9
Children of William Campbell Niemeyer, III and Bonnie
Pritchard Strange

Leigh Chandler   Brittany Campbell

9   9
Children of Mary Chandler Niemeyer and Scot Lawrence Beach

Christopher   Chad   Cody   Lydia
Niemeyer   Lawrence   James   Lucrece

9   9
Child of George C. Hudgins, III and Janet Herring

Melanie

9   9
Children of Angela Hudgins and Michael Stauder

Justin   Travis

289

9   9

Children of Michael Niemeyer and Elise Ninesling

Laura Daniele   Jessa Camille

9   9

Child of Kim Marie Niemeyer and Frank Davis

Crystal Marie

9   9

Children of William Frederic Niemeyer and Carolyn Louise
Holtzhauer

John Cameron   Kyle Antonio

9   9

Child of Frank Berry Niemeyer and Shannon Page Eadie

Jacob Douglas

9   9

Child of John Stuart Niemeyer and April Michelle Tripp

John Stuart, Jr.

9   9

Child of Barbara Elizabeth Niemeyer and Michael Lynn Bolt

Kaylin Michael Bolt

9   9

Child of Thomas Walter Niemeyer and Ghada Ltief

Recap of Significant Data: Niemeyer

Generation 9

    James Xavier Mathews was born on November 21, 1982.

    William Lamphear Mathews was born on February 10, 1987.

    Hillary Proctor Mathews was born on May 21, 1989.

    Susanna Tilghman Mathews was born on September 14, 1993.

    Charles Bellinger Meneghin was born on August 20, 1990.

    Elizabeth Powell Meneghin was born on May 10, 1994 and is called Eliza.

    Allen Edward Truax was born on September 8, 1973.

    Chandler Marie Truax was born on April 22, 1981.

    Michael Paul Bauer was born on September 23, 1973.

    Jacob Lee Bauer was born on July 19, 1981.

    Cora Marie Opsahl was born on July 25, 1980.

    Daniel Martin Opsahl was born on May 19, 1983.

    Sara Courtney Juno was born on March 19, 1987 in Stratford, NJ.

    Christopher Campbell Smith was born on November 15, 1976 in Stratford, NJ.

    Kevin Michael Smith was born on April 4, 1980 in Stratford, NJ.

    Zachery Darrell Soltesz was born on May 11, 1985 in Stratford, NJ.

    Elicia Marie Soltesz was born on July 31, 1989 in Stratford, NJ.

    Jessa Camille Niemeyer was born on February 11, 1981.

    Crystal Davis was born on April 9, 1980.

    Laura Daniele Niemeyer was born on February 7, 1985.

Leigh Chandler Niemeyer was born on September 3, 1992.

Brittany Campbell Niemeyer was born on November 12, 1996.

Christopher Niemeyer Beach was born on June 21, 1984.

Chad Lawrence Beach was born on January 10, 1992.

Cody Beach was born on January 14, 1993.

Lydia Lucrece Beach was born on April 8, 1996.

John Cameron Niemeyer was born on September 25, 1999 in Knoxville, TN and is called Cameron.

Kyle Antonio Niemeyer was born on September 28, 2001 in Knoxville, TN and is called Kyle.

Jacob Douglas Niemeyer was born on June 28, 1999 in Fairfax, VA and is called Jacob.

John Stuart Niemeyer, Jr. was born on March 22, 1996 in Chesapeake, VA and is called Stuart.

Kaylin Bolt is the son of Michael and Barbara Bolt. He was born on November 2, 1992.

The present Niemeyers are direct descendents of this Niemeyer line. In Tidewater Descendents the noted generation should be changed as follows.

4	4	Lt. Col. William Frederic Niemeyer, C. S. A. m. Sarah Campbell Smith
5	5	John Frederic Niemeyer m. Lucrece Bilisoly
6	6	Antonio Bilisoly Niemeyer m. Lutie Stuart Spotts
7	7	Antonio Bilisoly Niemeyer, Jr. m. Alice Virginia Berry

8	8	William Frederic Niemeyer	Frank Berry Niemeyer	John Stuart Niemeyer
		m.	m.	m.
		Carolyn Louise Holtzhauer	Shannon Page Eadie	April Michelle Tripp

9   9   John Cameron   Jacob Douglas   John Stuart
          Niemeyer   Niemeyer   Niemeyer, Jr.
          Kyle Antonio
          Niemeyer

"History of Norfolk County, Virginia, and Representative
Citizens, 1630-1900"
Compiled by Col. William H. Stewart
Published by Biographical Publishing Company

Page 150
Niemeyer-Shaw Camp, Confederate Veterans, Berkley, Virginia

The Niemeyer-Shaw Camp, Confederate Veterans, was organized in Pine Street Hall in Berkley, on May 2, 1892. There were present 17 veterans. Peleg Pritchard presided and E. E. Hathaway was chosen secretary. The purposes of the organization were the same as those of the Pickett-Buchanan Camp. It was named for Lieut. Col. William F. Niemeyer, who fell at Spottsyvania (sic), and Col. Henry M. Shaw, who was killed in the battle of Roanoke Island. The commanders of the camp since it was instituted have been Capt. John S. Whitworth, Dr. George W. Wallace, John A. Morgan and D. L. Cox.

Page 276

The Bench and Bar
Early Attorneys

The bench and bar of Norfolk County have always been a credit to the profession of law. In the Colonial period James Nimmo, William Spong, Walter Lyons, Thomas Clayborne, Thomas Nivison, Benjamin Crocker, Thomas Bourk, John Brickel, Miles Carey, Anthony Lawson and Thomas Emmerson were among practicing attorneys at the bar. William Robertson was the first attorney for the Commonwealth after the Declaration of Independence, having qualified on the 19th day of December 1776. Some of the distinguished members of the bar under the

Commonwealth were: William Wirt, Littleton Waller Tazewell, John S. Millson, John Murdaugh, John A. Chandler, Richard Gatewood, James Murdaugh, Tazewell Taylor, J. H. Langhorne, James G. Halloday, James W. Hinton, L. H. Chandler, John Neely, John H. Gayle, Charles B. Duffield, James Holt and Richard Walker.

Pages 325-326

Purchase of Lower Norfolk County Tract for Building of the Town of Norfolk. Land was purchased from Nicholas Wise for ten thousand pounds of tobacco and cash. "Feoffees in trust" for said County Capt. Wm. Robinson and Lt. Col. Anthony Lawson, of Lynnhaven Parish, in the county aforesaid. Gent.

Page 500-502

Lieut. Col. William Frederic Niemeyer
(Extracts)

... Letter written to His Grandmother Chandler on the death of her husband, John A. Chandler, when W. F. N. was not quite eight yeatrs old:

"My dear Grandma:

I am very sorry that grandpa died but the Lord will take care of you; do not weep, he is in the arms of the Lord Jesus Christ; he has got a crown of glory upon his head; he has an arm chair, and he is singing and is shouting in glory. We must try to be good, and when we die we may meet him there; he cannot come to us, but we can go to him if we are good.

Your loving grandson,
William F. Niemeyer

He received the rudiment of his education in the schools of Portsmouth and at the Norfolk Academy; and, upon the recommendation of Surgeon-General Lawson, United States Army, was appointed a cadet at-large at West Point by President James Buchanan … in 1857.

… His course at the Military Acacemy was marked with creditable distinction; but the tocsin of war having sounded, and although within a month of having graduated, he, (1861) with the heroic Gen. James Dearing, the dashing Gen. Thomas L. Rosser, and other noble spirits,, left the Academy to give their services to their native States.

…

Col. Niemeyer was engaged in the battles of Fredericksburg, Zoar Church, McCarty's Farm, Chancellorsville, Salem Church, Gettysburg, Hagerstown, Bristol Station, Mine Run, Wilderness, Shady Grove and Spottsylvania sic) Courthouse. He was severely woonded in the ankle at Bristol Station; and after having commanded his regiment in two brilliant and successful charges of the memorable 12th day of May, 1864, was killed by a sharpshooter in the shadow of that bloody day at Spottsylvania Court House. So fell a noble man, a brave soldier, a true citizen who loved his county better than his life, and who was loved by his soldiers with brotherly devotion. His remains were sent to Richmond and buried in Hollywood Cemetery, where they now rest.

He married, in Portsmouth, on the 2nd day of January 1862, Sarah Campbell Smith, who has, since the death of her husband, devoted her life to aiding the widows and orphans of Confederate soldiers, and in perpetuating memories of the Lost Cause, with ardor and devotion, unflagging and fearless, as a true daughter of the Confederacy.

Stonewall Camp, Confederate Veterans, Portsmouth, Virginia has on more than one occasion, tendered to her unanimous vote of thanks for her invaluable services in its behalf, and she shall have the thanks and esteem of every individual member as long as life lasts.

Colonel Niemeyer left on child - John Frederick Niemeyer."

Page 500

John Chandler Niemeyer

John Chandler Niemeyer, 1st lieutenant of Company I, 9th Regiment, Virginia Infantry, was killed in the famous charge of Pickett's Virginians at Gettysburg on the 2nd day of July 1863.

Returned After Twenty-four Years

(John Chandler Niemeyer Copied from an old scrap book compiled by Dr. Antonio Leon Bilisoly for the year April, 1884 to Sept. 1890)

On the 2nd of July, 1863, during the memorable battle of Gettysburg, John Chandler Niemeyer, of this city, a lieutenant of Company "I", Ninth Virginia Regiment, Armistead's Brigade, Pickett's Division, was killed while making the famous charge of Pickett's Division. Though he was seen to fall, pierced by a minnie ball, nothing further was known of him, and his body was never recovered, being buried with hundreds of others on the battlefield. At the time of his death he wore a gold pin, bearing the letters "O.D.G.", which was presented to him while a member of the Old Dominion Guard, of this city, by Captain James W. Brown, a dear friend. Several years after the war Captain Brown saw a gentleman from the north at Old Point, and on his coat he wore the pin which Captain Brown had presented to Lieutenant Niemeyer. Captain Brown spoke to the gentleman, whose name has been lost, asking him where he obtained it. The answer he received was; "I took it from a dead rebel lieutenant after the battle of Gettysburg."

Captain Brown begged for the pin, telling the man that he knew the parents of the dead soldier to whom it belonged, and wished to return it to them, but his pleas were in vain, as the man would not part with it. Nothing further was heard from it for some time, when Mr. Wm A. Niemeyer, father of Lieutenant Niemeyer, received from Philadelphia by mail one day, the pin which he still has in his possession.

At the re-union of Federals and Confederates held at Gettysburg on the 2nd of this month, a number of the veterans from Portsmouth who had known Lieutenant Niemeyer were present. While being shown over the battlefield by some of the Philadelphia Brigade, one of the Philadelphians asked: "Is there anyone here who wishes to know where Lieutenant Niemeyer fell?"

There were a number of responses, and the spot was pointed out. It was at this time that Mr. Charles H. Tizard of No. 1734 South Ninth Street, Philadelphia, a veteran of the war, said: "I have some papers which I took from the body of Lieutenant John C. Niemeyer" and held an envelop in his hand.

Major James F. Crocker and other gentlemen asked for the papers, but Mr. Tizard said he would send them to the family of the young man by mail. Several days ago Mr. Niemeyer received the following letter containing a number of papers belonging to his son:

Philadelphia, July 15, '87

William A. Niemeyer
Portsmouth, Virginia
Dear Sir:

Yours of the 13th to hand. In compliance I enclose you all the papers in my possession, taken from the body of

Lieutenant John C. Niemeyer, July 3, '63, at Gettysburg, Pa. I sent there (sic) papers north, but threw the pocketbook away after I was captured on the 22nd of June 1864, in front of Petersburg, Va. I did not find any diary or memorandum, except these I send you, which I do with great pleasure, as I have had them in my possession ever since, hoping that I would some day discover the friends or relatives of the deceased. It was through Major Crocker, of your town, that I first learned of the whereabouts of his family, and I promised to inform you when I met him at Gettysburg.

Very respectfully,
Chas. H. Tizard

It is strange that these papers should have been returned after a lapse of twenty-four years, and it shows clearly that the reunions of the "Blue and the Gray" will bind them closer together and cause many pleasing incidents that would not otherwise occur.

Portsmouth Enterprise

Married Fifty years

Volume I: From Dr. A. L. Bilisoly's scrap book; dated August 1, 1889. Newspaper clipping.

Yesterday our well-known townsman and his good lady celebrated the fiftieth anniversary of their marriage. On Wednesday, July 31, 1839, Mr. Niemeyer and Miss Sarah H. Chandler, both of this city, were married at Garysburg, North Carolina, and in the fifty years which have passed since then they have never had occasion to regret the step which bound them together. Eight* sons and three daughters, all grown were the fruit of the union and the venerable couple, still in vigorous health, have seen grow up around them a large family of children, grandchildren and great grandchildren.

Two sons, the oldest of the children, gave their lives to Virginia in her strength (?) for independence. One, Colonel Fred Niemeyer, of 61st Virginia, fell at Spottsylvania (sic), and the other, Lieutenant John C. Niemeyer of Company I, Ninth Virginia, fell in Pickett's charge at Gettysburg. The rest of the children are living and enjoy the respect and confidence of all who have come in contact with them.

We extend our congratulations to our venerable friends, and wish them many annual returns of their anniversary.
*Nine sons.

October 2, 1891   Early Morning Marriage
(From the Scrap Book of Dr. A. L. Bilisoly, Vol. II. P. 117)

There was a very pretty, though quiet (sic) early morning marriage at the residence of Mr. William A. Niemeyer, on Swimming Point, at 6:15 o'clock yesterday morning, when Dr. Robert R. Robertson, formerly of Petersburg, but now of Norfolk, led to the altar Miss Mary C., youngest daughter of Mr. & Mrs. W. A. Niemeyer. The ceremony was performed by the Rev. W. E. Edwards, D. D. pastor of Monumental M. E. Church. After a wedding breakfast the bride and groom left on the Chesapeake and Ohio Train for Richmond, Washington, Baltimore and Philadelphia.

Flag Presentation
(From Dr. Bilisoly's Scrap Book, Vol. II)
Sept. 13, 1892

The family of the late Colonel William Fred. Niemeyer of the Sixty-first Virginia Regiment, who was killed at Spottsylvania (sic) Courthouse, and for whom Niemeyer Shaw Camp, with headquarters in Berkley, is named, will, in appreciation of the honor conferred, present the camp with a handsome state flag.

The presentation will be made at the Town Hall, in Berkley tonight at 8 o'clock. Col. W. H. Stewart, who succeeded Col. Niemeyer as Lieutenant Colonel of the Sixty-first Regiment, will present the flag in behalf of the family, and it will be received by Captain John S. Whitworth, Commander of Niemeyer-Shaw Camp.

The flag is of blue silk, with the coat of arms of Virginia on both sides, is six by six and a half feet, and has a heavy gold fringe. On the front is the inscription, Niemeyer-Shaw Camp, V. V., Berkley, Virginia. On the reverse is, Niemeyer-Shaw Camp, C. V., organized May 9, 1892.

Stonewall Camp of this city, at its meeting last night, decided to be present at the presentation in a body, and also appointed a special committee of six to escort Mrs. Sarah C. Niemeyer, widow of Colonel Niemeyer, to Berkley.

BIOGRAPHICAL SKETCH

OF

Lieut.-Col. William Frederick Niemeyer,

OF THE

SIXTY-FIRST VIRGINIA INFANTRY.

BY

COL. WILLIAM H. STEWART,

PORTSMOUTH, VA.

BIOGRAPHICAL SKETCH OF LIEUTENANT-COLONEL WILLIAM FREDERICK NIEMEYER,

WILLIAM FREDERICK NIEMEYER was born in the county of Norfolk and State of Virginia, on the 12th day of May, 1840, and heroically met his death at the head of his regiment in the battle of Spotsylvania Court House, on the 12th day of May, 1864, his twenty-fourth birthday.

His great grandfather, Hans Heinrich Niemeyer, was born at Hoya, Germany, in 1734, and died in 1806.

His grandfather, John Christian Niemeyer, was born in 1776, at Verden, near Bremen, and came to America at the age of 18 years, and in 1813 he married Ann McLean, his second wife, the grandmother of the subject of this sketch, at Moyock, in Currituck county, North Carolina. His father, William Angus Niemeyer, died February 3d, 1900; was born April 28th, 1816, and married Sarah Howard Chandler (now living) on the 31st day of July, 1839. She is the daughter of John A. Chandler, who was one of the foremost citizens and most distinguished lawyers in Tidewater Virginia of his day.

Colonel Niemeyer was the eldest of twelve children, three sisters and nine brothers. His brother, John Chandler Niemeyer, First Lieutenant of Company "I," Ninth Virginia Infantry Regiment, was killed in the famous charge of Pickett's Virginians at Gettysburg on the 3d day of July, 1863.

William Frederick Niemeyer was a promising child with the noblest predilections. On the death of his grandfather Chandler, when not quite eight years old, he wrote the following tender and touching letter of condolence to his grandmother:

APRIL 16, 1848.

My Dear Grandma:

I am very sorry that grandpa died, but the Lord will take care of you ; do not weep, he is in the arms of the Lord Jesus Christ ; he has got a crown of glory upon his head ; he has an arm-chair, and he is singing and is shouting in glory. We must try to be good and when we die we may meet him there; he cannot come to us, but we can go to him if we are good.

Your loving grandson,

WILLIAM F. NIEMEYER.

He received the rudiments of his education in the schools of Portsmouth and at the Academy, in Norfolk; and upon the recommendation of Surgeon-General Lawson, United States Army, was appointed a cadet at large at West Point by President James Buchanan. His conditional appointment over the hand of Jefferson Davis, Secretary of War, was made on the 19th day of February, 1857, which directed that he should repair to West Point, in the State of New York, between the 1st and 20th of June, to be examined, and that under certain conditions in January next his warrant as a cadet, to be dated the 30th day of June, 1857, would be made. The conditions were fulfilled by creditable examinations and excellent deportment which secured the warrant as a cadet in the service of the United States, dated as promised over the hand of John B. Floyd, Secretary of War, January 22d, 1858. His course at the Academy was marked with creditable distinction; but the tocsin of war having sounded, and although within a month of graduation, he, with the heroic General James Dearing, the dashing General Thomas L. Rosser, and other noble spirits, left the Academy to give their services to their native States.

On May 1st, 1861, John Letcher, Governor of Virginia, commissioned W. F. Niemeyer Second Lieutenant in the Provisional Army of the State of Virginia, and on May 9th he was ordered by the Adjutant-General of Virginia to report to Major-General Walter Gwynn, commanding Virginia Forces at Norfolk; thereupon General Gwynn, on the 10th of May ordered him to report to Colonel R. E. Colston, under whom he served as drill master at the entrenched camp, near Norfolk. On the 19th day of July, 1861, the President appointed him Second Lieutenant Corps of Artillery, in the Army of the Confederate States over the hand of L. P. Walker, Secretary of War, C. S.; and his resignation as Second Lieutenant of Provisional Army of Virginia was accepted, to take effect on the 25th of July.

Samuel M. Wilson, a prominent citizen of Portsmouth, having been authorized by the Secretary of War to organize a battalion or regiment for the service of the Confederate States, called to his assistance the promising young lieutenant, whose military training was essential to Colonel Wilson's success.

"PORTSMOUTH, VA., May 5th, 1862.

Major Wm. F. Niemeyer:

Sir: I hereby certify that at election held for the office of Major of the Battalion or Regiment being raised by me for the service of the Confederate States, under authority of the War Department through letter of the Adjutant-General of the 6th of July, 1861, you have this day been duly elected Major of said Battalion or Regiment, and notice of your election has been sent to Major-General B. Huger, commanding Department of Norfolk, to whom you will report for duty.

I am very respectfully,

Your obedient servant,

SAMUEL M. WILSON."

HEADQUARTERS DEPARTMENT NORFOLK,
May 6th, 1862.

Report to General Blanchard for duty with Wilson's Battalion.
By order of General Huger.

S. S. ANDERSON,
Assistant Adjutant-General.

DEPARTMENT OF NORFOLK, HEADQUARTERS THIRD BRIGADE,
PORTSMOUTH, VA., May 6th, 1862.

SPECIAL ORDERS, No. 83.

I. Major Wm. F. Niemeyer, Wilson's Battalion, having reported for duty to Brigade Headquarters by order of Major-General Huger, is assigned to the command of the troops at Forrest Entrenchment.

By command of Brigadier-General Blanchard, Commanding Third Brigade.

W. T. RIDDICK,
Assistant Adjutant-General.

DEPARTMENT OF NORFOLK, HEADQUARTERS THIRD BRIGADE,
PORTSMOUTH, VA., May 7th, 1862.

SPECIAL ORDERS, No. 84.

II. Major Wm. F. Niemeyer, Wilson's Battalion, will proceed to Pig Point and superintend the election of company officers for Company "H," Ninth Virginia, Captain Neblett, and Sussex Defenders, Wilson's Battalion, Captain Mason, to be held to-morrow, 8th instant, in accordance with provision of Conscript Act.

Major Niemeyer will furnish each officer then elected with a certificate of election, and duplicates must be sent to Adjutant and Inspector General's office, Richmond, through Brigade Headquarters.

By command Brigadier-General Blanchard, Commanding Third Brigade.

W. L. RIDDICK,
Assistant Adjutant-General.

To Major W. F. Niemeyer, commanding Forrest Entrenchment.

Major Niemeyer, with his command, retreated from Forrest Entrenchment, near Hall's Corner, in Western Branch, Norfolk county, on the 10th of May, 1862, the day Norfolk and Portsmouth were evacuated, which he noted in his diary, "The saddest day of my life," and marched to Suffolk. On the 11th day of May he left for Petersburg via Weldon, where he arrived on the 13th, and assumed command of the city and the Department of Appomattox for a short while. On the 22d day of May, 1862, the officers of the line assembled at Jarrett's Hotel, in Petersburg, under supervision of Major George W. Grice, Assistant Quartermaster, and elected field officers of the Sixty-first Virginia Regiment Infantry, as follows:

Colonel—Samuel M. Wilson.

Lieutenant-Colonel—William F. Niemeyer.

Major—William H. Stewart.

And their commissions were issued on the 15th of July, 1862, by George W. Randolph, Secretary of War, to date from the 22d day of May, 1862.

HEADQUARTERS, PETERSBURG, VA.,
August 23d, 1862.

Pursuant to Special Order, Headquarters Petersburg, August 22d, the members of Board of Survey met this day at 12 M., and valued and mustered into Confederate service the following horses:

One roan mare belonging to Lieutenant-Colonel Wm. F. Niemeyer, valued at $175.

One bay horse belonging to Major William H. Stewart, valued at $225.

    (Signed) Lieutenant CHARLES D. MYERS, A. D. C.

          JOHN A. BAKER. " " "

          Lieutenant J. A. SHINGLEIN, " " "

Detachments of the Sixty-first Virginia Regiment were sent from

Petersburg to City Point, Port Walthall, and Point of Rocks, on the Appomattox river below the city of Petersburg.

On the 3d of September the Regiment was ordered to Richmond, and from thence to Brook Church, where it encamped until the 5th, when it was ordered to Rapidan Station to rebuild the railroad bridge. The Army of Northern Virginia was then in Maryland, and on its return to Virginia the Sixty-first Virginia Regiment was assigned to Mahone's Brigade by order of General Lee.

Lieutenant-Colonel Niemeyer was in active command of the Sixty-first Virginia Regiment from its organization until October, 1862, when its command devolved upon Colonel V. D. Groner, selected to succeed Colonel Wilson, who had resigned.

Colonel Niemeyer was engaged in the battles of Fredericksburg, Zoar Church, McCarty's Farm, Chancellorsville, Salem Church, Gettysburg, Hagerstown, Bristoe Station, Mine Run, Wilderness, Shady Grove, and Spotsylvania Court House. He was severely wounded in the ankle at Bristoe Station; and after having commanded his regiment in two brilliant and successful charges of the memorable 12th day of May, 1864, was killed by a sharpshooter in the shadow of that bloody day at Spotsylvania Court House. So fell a noble man, a brave soldier, a true citizen, who loved his country better than his life, and who was loved by his soldiers with brotherly devotion. His remains were sent to Richmond and buried in Hollywood Cemetery, where they now rest.

He married in Portsmouth on the 2d day of January, 1862, Sarah Campbell Smith, who has, since the death of her husband, devoted her life to aiding the widows and orphans of Confederate soldiers, and in perpetuating memories of the lost cause, with ardor and devotion, unflagging and fearless, as a true and faithful daughter of the Confederacy.

Stonewall Camp, Confederate Veterans, Portsmouth, Va., has on more than one occasion tendered to her unanimous vote of thanks in appreciation and gratitude for her invaluable services in its behalf, and she shall have the thanks and esteem of every individual member as long as life lasts.

Colonel Niemeyer left one child—John Frederick Niemeyer.

THE ARTHUR E. NIEMEYER FAMILY
ARTHUR, SARAH, ANGUS, JESSIE

Arthur Emerson Niemeyer was born January 19, 1852, the sixth son of
William Angus Niemeyer and Sarah Howard Chandler Niemeyer. The
Niemeyer home was on Swimming Point in Portsmouth, Virginia, however,
they moved to the Hewlett Farm, on the Old Deep Creek Road, about
five miles from Portsmouth in 1851 where Arthur Niemeyer was born.
After living in the country for a short time, they returned to the
Swimming Point home and built a new four storied pre-fabricated house
in 1854. It had large rooms with high ceilings and an ample front
porch where Grandmother Niemeyer often sat in her rocker on hot
summer days. The kitchen was a separate building in back detached
for fear of fire.

This frame and brick house was located on the Elizabeth River at
#1 Swimming Point next to the first home. The house had quite a
history in itself. In 1849 during the California gold rush, a half-
brother of William Angus Niemeyer, Henry Victor Niemeyer, together
with several business men started manufacture of the first prefabricated houses in America. The houses were shipped to California,
but due to the heavy earth tremors in that region, they were found to
be unsuitable. The houses were dismantled and reassembled as one
story dwellings giving birth to the bungalow. There were three of
these houses left in Portsmouth, and William Niemeyer purchased one
for his home.

Arthur Niemeyer lived a happy and rather uneventful life with his
parents, eight brothers, three sisters and his grandmother Chandler
until the outreak of the Civil War that followed the election of
Abraham Lincoln to the presidency. His grandmother was a lady of
great charm and told the children many interesting stories of her
youth which included memories of the War of 1812.

His three oldest brothers joined the Confederate Army. His oldest
brother, William Frederic, had graduated from West Point but returned
home and joined the Confederate Army. His next brother, John
Chandler, left Virginia Military Academy and enlisted, and Henry
Victor enlisted at sixteen as a private. John was killed in 1863 at
Gettysburg, and Frederic was killed in 1864 in the Battle of the
Wilderness, in Spottsylvania. Henry was taken prisoner but survived
the war, and later moved to St. Louis, Missouri, where he spent the
rest of his days with his wife and five children.

Arthur, a boy of twelve too young to join the army, worked as a
waterboy at the shipyard during the construction of the Civil War
ship Merrimac. Later, after it was completed and put into service,
he watched the famous battle of the Monitor and the Merrimac from a
hill near the shore line. At the actual time of the battle, the
Merrimac was named the S. S. Virginia and later changed to the
Merrimac. He was educated in private schools in Virginia and always
felt bitter that the war had deprived him of a college education.

In 1873 at twenty-one years of age he traveled to Memphis, Tennessee, where one of his brothers had a drug store. His brother left Memphis shortly thereafter, however, Arthur had found employment with A. J. White & Co., one of the oldest hardware stores in Memphis. The name of the firm was later changed to White, Langstaff & Co. When Mr. White retired from the business, the name was again changed to the Langstaff Hardware Co., and Arthur became its first Vice-president. The firm did an extensive wholesale business in the states tributary to Memphis, and he traveled these states as a young man starting with the company.

The downtown streets of Memphis were unpaved, and it was commonplace to see mule drawn wagons loaded with cotton driven down Main and Front Streets. Court Square between Main and Second Streets was a popular Memphis scene in the late 1800's with its roofed bandstand where band concerts were held. There was a beautiful hexagon shaped pond in the center of the square with exquisite iron work statues adorning the three tiered fountain and urns at intervals between the picket iron railing surrounding the pool.

Arthur was a handsome man exactly six feet tall, but his carriage was so erect that he looked much taller. He had redish brown hair, a full beard and mustache and lively blue eyes. He occasionally smoked a cigar which was more fashionable then than cigarettes, if indeed they were yet invented.

A bit later he met a girl, Sarah Hoyt Mahan, a petite young lady with brown hair and hazel eyes. She was an accomplished pianist and organist. Although she was a devout Presbyterian having joined Second Church in 1870, she was organist at a Baptist Church for many years. She was born July 3, 1858, and was the daughter of George Grundy Mahan and Sarah Poole Mahan. Originally from Muskatine, Iowa, where Sarah was born, George Mahan brought his wife, daughter, and two young sons, George and Frank, to Memphis just about the time Arthur migrated to Memphis. Their parents and many relatives remained in Muskatine. Unfortunately this was not long before the time of the yellow fever epidemics when many lives were lost to this dread disease. George Mahan was one of the fatalities and succumbed to the fever in February, 1875. Although only sixteen years old when her father died, Sarah taught piano and got a position as organist in a church to support her mother and brothers who had no other means. George was thirteen and little Frank was only eight.

Sarah and Arthur fell in love and did much corresponding as he was traveling for the hardware company at this time. Some of the letters are still in existance. His penmanship was beautiful, and for her birthday the year before they married, he inscribed a beautiful leather bound picture album for her. It is still in existance, also.

Arthur and Sarah were engaged and planned to be married in the spring, however, another outbreak of scarlet fever fatally affected her mother in February, 1878. Arthur and Sarah were married at her unconscious mother's deathbed while she held her mother's hand on February 7, 1878. They felt her mother would be happy that Sarah and her two young brothers had someone to look after them.

Their son, William Angus, named after his grandfather, was born Februray 27, 1879, almost on their first wedding anniversary. They called him Angus. Eleven years later, a daughter was born, Jessie Chandler, on July 20, 1890.

They purchased their first home April 4, 1884, from The First National Bank for $1,500, a little "shotgun" house on Pontotoc Street just east of Lauderdale Street and close to the Second Presbyterian Church where they became members for a lifetime. This was the house in which Jessie was born.

A "shotgun" house was the name given to a small frame house of that vintage built on a rather narrow lot, and the rooms were built in a row, one behind the other and usually three, however, this one was a bit larger. They were of open foundation construction, the house being set on brick pillows, two to three feet from the ground. Here one of the interesting, many times told family tales originated. Arthur was a gentle, soft spoken, mild mannered man and it took a good bit to make him angry. As the story goes, one night he awoke to find a burglar ransacking the house. He hopped out of bed in his nightshirt, as was the fashion for sleep in those days, and routed him from the house. All was quiet, and they had all dozed off again when he was awakened the second time to see that the burglar had returned for a second try. Well, sir, this made Arthur angry, and he hopped out of bed again and set out after the burglar, who, realizing he had pushed his luck, ran from the house and crawled under it attempting to hide. But Arthur had his dander up, and he crawled right under the house after him and pulled him out by the leg.

Jessie was a rather delicate child and almost succumbed to illness when she was three years old. However, with careful nursing she recovered although she had to learn to walk again. She also contracted diptheria the next year when she was four, but thankfully she survived that also.

Jessie was the joy of the family from the day she was born, adored by her parents and her loving big brother. She was a beautiful child with soft, golden, natural curls and lovely blue eyes. It has been said by all who tried to describe her eyes that they were a beautiful china blue, but words to describe the exact shade would elude them. She had a delicate milky complection and lips the color of a deep pink rosebud. Every spring her mother would buy her a little red straw bonnet for Easter. As she grew older, she became even more beautiful, vivacious and witty with a sweet and loving disposition. Everyone who knew her, loved her.

Angus was very handsome with finely chiseled features, dark brown hair and striking brown eyes that were almost black. He was always mischievous, and his parents decided to move to the country to give him plenty of room to wander and explore.

Sarah's brother, George was now 28 years old. He married Jessie Campbell Steele and remained in Memphis. However, Frank, 23 years, and his wife, Maude, moved to St. Louis where he had a position working with the Boy Scouts of America. He received recognition for his outstanding work with this fine pioneer organization. He and Maude had a son and two daughters and remained in St. Louis until his untimely death at the prime of his life.

On November 11, 1886, Arthur and Sarah bought a tract of land more particularly described as 2 and 19/100 acres on the north side of Central Avenue between Barksdale and McLean Streets for the sum of $1,500, from Harry A. Roynon payable in six notes of $100 each payable in installments until 33 months from date with interest and more specifically known as 1876 Central. They also bought an adjoining tract of land for $657.09 from Helen Roynon. The down payment was $57.09 with the remainder to be paid in six installments of $100.00 each for a term of 36 months with interest. This was a lovely wooded piece of land on a slight hill at the extreme edge of the eastern city limits and the end of the streetcar line. The streetcar was the main method of transportation.

This was a period of rapid advancement for Memphis as well as the entire country. Many inventions were taking place and implemented that the entire world would take for granted in the not too distant future.

Streetcar lines did much to influence development around Memphis. The first streetcar line ran along Main, Jefferson and Poplar in 1866, and by the 1880's horse drawn cars ran over 18 miles of track. Then rail building accelerated, and by 1895, over 70 miles of interurban track had been built.

One streetcar line went north to Raleigh Springs, where Memphians could enjoy a swim in the Wolf River that ran through Raleigh, drink mineral water and enjoy the band concerts held on the grounds of the Raleigh Hotel high up on the hill where the breezes were cool. In 1887 the East End Line was completed and people could ride the new steam engines to the race track at Montgomery Park (now the Fair Grounds) and the new East End Amusement Park on Madison Avenue at Cooper Street.

Electricity was first introduced to the city by the Brush Power and Light Company in 1882. However, the "electric age" did not become a reality in Memphis until 1887 when an enterprising group of citizens incorporated the Memphis, Light and Gas Company to supply electrical needs to the city. After much reorganization in the next decade and being in the hands of at least three succeeding companies, the electrical system became the Memphis Power and Light Company that is in existance today.

The first telephone lines were connected by General Carnes in 1880 who established a small company. This enterprise was small and of limited operation. It was taken over by the Cumberland Telephone Company in 1883 and expanded to meet growing needs.

In 1887 the first telephone demonstration was held at the home of Col. Mike Bourke on Shelby. A telephone line was strung from his residence to that of Mr. Montgomery's residence on Poplar four miles away. Mr. Bourke was superintendent of the Mississippi and Tennessee Railway and also had a line strung to the railway office.

The telephone was not made available to individual subscribers until 1893.

The Niemeyers lived on Pontotoc until September 27, 1900, when they sold the house to John R. Flippin for $2,950 and moved into a comfortable boarding house on Peabody Avenue for a short time while their home was being constructed on Central Avenue.

On this land they built a rambling country cottage of stained dark brown shingles with white trim and a wide front veranda, large living room with a beautiful mantle, large dining room and three bedrooms. All of the rooms had mantles for this was the method of heating the house. The kitchen was completely tiled, one of the first, and it was Sarah's domain. She loved to cook and was known throughout the sorrouning states for her culinary efforts which were admirable. Although she had volumes of recipe books, it was most difficult for others to duplicate her delicies because her recipes called for a pinch of this, and a dash of that, a bit of butter the size of a walnut, and a lump of shortening the size of an egg. Of course, the ingredients called for were fresh creamery butter, whipping cream and fresh eggs out of the henhouse. If unexpected company was coming for dinner, (which often happened), she would give Angus a quarter and say, "Run down to the grocers and get a porterhouse steak, and tell him to cut it extra thick."

The Seessel family had opened a market in 1858. By the early 1900's it had become a Memphis institution and was located at 1917 North Second Street where most Memphians shopped. However, there was a tiny grocery on Rembert Street between Higbee and Cowden just around the corner for daily shopping. It had changed owners and names several times and finally was just called by the neighborhood "The Little Store."

In later years Sarah was a bit on the plump side and was beginning to feel the discomfort of arthritis. When asked how she was feeling, she would say, "I'm feeling better, but you know, I'm under the influence of aspirin." That was as close as she ever came to being under the influence of anything. She kept a half pint of whiskey in the back corner of the huge wardrobe in the bedroom strictly for medicinal purposes; and sometimes for her deserts such as charlotte russe. It was alright to eat it just so long as you didn't drink it. She would sit on a chair at the large wooden table in the kitchen, and Cora, a large, angular black woman, would fetch her the ingredients she needed. Cora always wore a long gray dress, big white apron and a white kerchief knotted around her head.

Sarah was one of the first teachers and workers in the settlement
school at Second Presbyterian Church. She was always active in her
church and regularly attended bible study and other church events.
One such activity was evidenced by this newspaper clipping dated
March 4, 1891:

> "The Ladies of the Second Presbyterian Church opened to
> the public last evening their "Festival of Days" at
> 350 and 352 Main Street. Despite the stormy weather
> and the increasing cold their beautiful halls were
> thronged all the afternoon. The windows displayed
> a wealth of beautiful things wrought by deft fingers
> and placed there for sale by the ladies."

No doubt her culinery creations were most successfully and swiftly
sold.

And there was Grover Cleveland. Grover was slight of build but
strong as an ox and always with a ready flashing smile. He did all
the jobs around the place from tending the vegetable garden to
milking the cow and feeding the chickens, but his favorite task was
to play the part of butler. He loved to don the white jacket that
Sarah bought him and open the front door to guests with a flourish.
He liked especially to impress the young girls and boys that came to
call on Angus and young Jessie and there were many. They had a white
pedigreed terrier that won many ribbons and a cup or two. Grover and
the terrier were great friends and where you would see one, you would
usually see the other.

The children, Angus and Jessie, grew up in this happy environment.
Angus was seventeen and Jessie only six when they moved to Central
Avenue. They were educated in private schools. Jessie attended Miss
Higbee's School for girls and later attended Hollins College in
Virginia.

In 1900 the Langstaff Hardware Company liquidated, and Arthur
purchased the tile and mantle department and formed the
A. E. Niemeyer Tile and Mantle Company which was located on Madison
Avenue and later in the 600 block of Union Avenue. This department
was quite extensive at that time as Memphis was having a building
boom, and each house required from four to eight mantles for heating
with tile and grates. Then the furnace became popular and the use of
mantels was reduced to one and in some houses, not any. Tile became
a much larger volume of sales than the mantels had been. Arthur
installed the first tile swimming pool in Memphis at the Nineteenth
Century Club, a popular Women's Club.

I. Goldsmith & Bros. founded in 1870, began their dry goods store on
Beale between Front and Main Streets and around this time moved to
the corner of Main Street and McCall Avenue. A. Schwab opened his
dry goods store at 163 Beale between Main and Second. In 1995
Schwabs was still in the original location. The Schwabs were
neighbors of the Niemeyers living on the corner of Higbee and
Barksdale.

Each summer Arthur and Sarah would take the children to visit his
parents in Portsmouth. Travel was quite tedious, the main method of
travel for long distances being by train. Therefore when friends and
relatives came for a visit, they usually stayed several months,
sometimes as long as a year. A trip to visit the family home at
Portsmouth took several days. Arthur would return to work, and Sarah
and the children would stay for a two or three months in the large
four story home on the (beach.) Some of the family were still living
at home and many uncles, aunts and cousins lived close by. It was
wonderful for the family to be able to keep in touch.

Angus loved to go to Portsmouth, and he used to~fairly live in boats
when he was a boy. He'd row out to big ships in the harbor, both
American and foreign, and usually managed to be allowed on board,
where he had thrilling talks with sailors and men of the merchant
marine. He used to play the mouth harp well, could bring real music
out of one. One of his favorite spots in the big yard of the old
house on Swimming Point was the tool house, where many old things
other than tools were stored. Among them were stacks of Confederate
bills and of Continental money, bills used in the Revolutionary War.
The children played store with them, and unfortunately most of them
have disappeared. One time his grandfather gave him the big brass
key to the tool house for his own. It was six inches long, or more.

The outbuildings in the back were the kitchen, presided over by Rose
(black as ebony and beloved and feared by all of the children), the
tool house, the smokehouse, and a fourth building called, for want of
a better name, the shed, and the wood and coal sheds.

Rose was a little black slave of pure African origin who was
presented many years ago to Grandmother Chandler as a little
handmaiden. She remained firmly as part of the family all her life.
Someone once referred to the fact that she had once been a slave.
She turned on them, putting her fists on her hips, and said, "I ain't
no slave, never been a slave, I jest belongs to your grandma."

Rose was a tyrant to the children, but they all loved her because
they knew it was "all bark and no bite." As one by one the children
reached an age that Rose thought proper, she affixed to their names
the title of "Miss" or "Mister." When he had reached the age of
thirteen, Angus came for his regular summer visit; he had just
adopted long trousers. After greeting his grandparents he rushed out
to the kitchen to speak to Rose. "Hello, Rose!" he called out. To
which Rose replied politely, "How do, Mister Angus!" Angus was taken
aback at this response but started laughing and said, "You calling me
'Mister', Rose?" Rose flew into a rage and snatched up a broom.
Angus fled to the wood house. Rose followed, slammed the door and
locked it, and there he was! The younger children were terrified,
but Angus sent them into the house to get his father. His father
came out and inquired the reason for his imprisonment. When he heard
the story he said, "Son, I am sorry you were impolite to Rose. You
will have to stay there until she lets you out." An hour or so later
Rose opened the door with "You kin come out now, Mister Angus!"

314

George and Jessie Mahan moved to a large bungalow with twelve foot
ceilings and surrounded all around by a wide porch on Willett Street
across town. They had four boys, George, James, Frank, and Angus,
and one daughter, Jessie. The families were very close having Sunday
dinner together almost every Sunday at one house or the other. There
were many picnics held on their spacious lawns with family and
friends.

Next door to the east in a large two story brick house lived
Clarence W. Hussey and his lovely wife, Neva, and their six children,
C. W., Jr. called "Buh", Robert, Jones, Neva, King and Virginia.
Mr. Hussey was in the cotton business which was a very good business
in Memphis. Jessie was very fond of the Hussey children as were all
the Niemeyers. They were in and out of the Niemeyer home as if it
were their own. Jessie spent many hours swinging them in the
hammocks under the big, spreading trees and pulling them around in
their little red wagon.

As Jessie and Angus grew to maturity, Memphis was also growing at a
rapid rate. In 1888 in Leeds, England, Louis Aime' Augustin LePrince
photographed the first animated pictures ever made with a single lens
camera at 20 pictures per second. The first public motion picture
exhibit opened in New York in 1894, a kinetoscope parlor, with rows
of coin-operated viewing machines. In December of 1900, two men
appeared on Main Street with a motion picture camera, and to the
astonishment of the pedestrians, began to take motion pictures.
Thomas Nash and Henry Rehner of the Polyscope Company were filming
views of Memphis. A short time after this episode, Charles Dinstuhl,
who had a restaurant downtown, and a man named Wassman, who was a
clerk at Hammer-Ballard Drug Store, opened the first Theatorium next
door to the restaurant. The Dinstuhls later left the restaurant
business and started the leading confectioners store in Memphis for a
decade.

This was the start of the movie industry in Memphis. In 1906 a
nickelodeon opened on Main street and later changed its name to the
Ruby Theater. Nickelodeons were the rage in the United States. In
Memphis, the Palace Theater opened on North Main in 1907 showing
movies and Vaudeville Shows. Other Theaters were opened with
Vaudeville being a big attraction.

When Jessie became the age for boys to come to call, Sarah was in
heaven because she loved to entertain and had good reason to cook to
her heart's content. Jessie was so pretty and always smiling and the
life of every party. The Niemeyer home was a meeting place for the
young people, friends of both Jessie and Angus, and especially on
Sunday night. This was due mostly to Jessie's popularity, but her
mother's cooking and the fact that she always had six or so girls as
house guests was an added attraction. Sarah would put out a grand
feast every Sunday night for the young people, and they would eat and
dance and gather around the beautiful carved ebony piano on which
Jessie played the popular tunes by ear, their sweet young voices
merrily singing in harmony. The parents enjoyed having the young

315

people around. They called them Uncle Arthur and Miss Sallie.
On Sunday night Arthur would sit at the kitchen table and eat a bowl
of fresh clabber sprinkled with sugar and soda crackers while the
youngsters ate cake.

In 1908 Henry Ford invented the Model T, and in 1910 the powerful
politician, Edward H. Crump, became mayor of Memphis. He and Arthur
were friends, Mr. Crump lived just a few blocks away on the corner of
Peabody Avenue and Rembert. Mr. Crump hosted riverboat excursions
for his political friends and the Niemeyers were included in these
excursions.

The beautiful Peabody Hotel in 1910 was located on North Main Street
and in 1925 relocated on Union Avenue between Second and Third. It
has for almost a century enjoyed its reputation as "the South's Grand
Hotel." The elegant Orpheum Theatre was a few blocks south on the
corner of Main and Beale and also has regained it elegance for over a
century. Angus particularly enjoyed dining with his friends in the
Peabody's excellent dining room.

Angus and his close friends were members of the "Tennessee Club", a
fine establishment for gentlemen. He spent many happy hours there
with his friends, lunching, dining, playing games and attending
elaborate evening balls. The club was situated on the northwest
corner of Court and Second across from Court Square. It was a four
storied house of coral brick with a circular turret with pointed roof
to one side of the wide, steep stairsteps that ascended to the second
floor entrance.

To Angus delight, his father decided to buy one of the newly invented
Buick automobiles. It was a big, black box like vehicle with four
doors and open all round with a roof on top. Angus thought it was a
thing of beauty and would hop in it and take off every chance he
got. He had many friends and always a crowd with him. Jessie
learned to drive but was hard put to get to it before him. Sarah
wanted to learn to drive but due to her arthritis, Arthur thought it
was most unwise. One Sunday on the way to church Sarah said,
"Arthur, when you die, the very first thing I am going to do is to
learn to drive. Arthur had a very dry wit, and he replied, "Yes,
Sadie, and first thing you know I'll look up and say, 'Hello, Sadie,
when did you get here.'" Sometimes Jessie would drive down to the
store on Union Avenue to drive her father home in the evening.

There was always an abundance of food at the Niemeyer house, potato
salad, glazed ham, fried chicken, and ice cream straight from the old
crank handle freezer. The table would be set with every vegetable in
season, fresh from the garden, biscuits, homemade bread, applesauce,
jellies, jams and pickles. There were usually one or two extra
places set at the table. Grover Cleveland in his white jacket would
serve and Cora in the kitchen would keep the food coming--and then
there was Christmas.

Holidays were especially fun times. Sarah for years talked about the
Christmas she made twenty-two different cakes, and she could name
every one. The Portsmouth relatives sent tins of oysters, shrimp,
herring, and the unforgetable Smithfield ham. Jessie would stay up
all night Christmas Eve, her room a mass of paper and ribbon,
wrapping presents for the Hussey children who would arise before
daylight and troup over the snow crusted ground to have Christmas at
the Niemeyer's before they had Christmas at home. Then later on
Sarah's brother, George, would come for Christmas dinner with his
wife and five children, and what a feast they would have. Roast
turkey and dressing, Smithfield ham, sweet potato casserole, corn
pudding, suet pudding, charlotte russe, charlotte polainaise cake,
ambrosia and coconut cake. Then by late afternoon callers would
start coming so you can understand why Sarah made twenty-two cakes.

Actually summer was probably the happiest time of all. People used
to stay outside as much as possible then in search of a cool breeze,
and porches and hammocks were most popular. The large front porch
was well filled with comfortable, cushioned wicker furniture and
there was a very large hammock between two giant trees in front that
would hold Jessie and the five little Hussey children at one time.
The cows roamed around at will and every now and then one of the
children would decide to ride one of them. They were most gentle,
and were probably used to it. When a beau would come calling, it was
a great thing to catch the streetcar and go downtown to Pantezes Drug
Store for a soda. Sodas cost a dime and street car fare was three
cents. Jessie enjoyed the Hussey children so, she usually would take
one of them with her. Childlike talk would never embarass her. She
would throw back her head and laugh, and it was so infectious that
everyone would soon be laughing with her. One of her favorite songs
she would play, and how she would laugh until she had all the boys
and girls around her laughing, too. It went like this:

> "I went down town a-feelin' sorta shaky
> Sat down beside a big, fat lady,
> Went to scratch my leg
> And it ain't no joke
> I thought I'd had a paraletic stroke.
> The lady said "Conductor, stop this car,
> This familiarity's gone too far,
> Put off this man or my pardon you'll beg,
> For the last ten minutes he's been
> Scratching my leg."

Jessie had many girl friends who would come out and stay for days and
were always welcome, Mary Hays, Martha McDonald, Anne VanDyke. Of
course, that meant the boys were there, too. Angus had many friends
also, Dover Barrett, Curtis Dewey and Tom Watkins were a few. Anne
and Ramsey Potts became engaged on the wide, cushioned wicker swing.
They were married and had six children, three boys and three girls,
and had a wonderfully happy life. Also Fanny and Frank Graham met at
the Niemeyers and did their courting there. They also had a long and
happy marriage and two sons and two daughters.

Angus was a very loving brother. He had a job traveling and he took his young sister for her first trip to New York. She was about sixteen or seventeen, and it was the thrill of her life. The train trip in itself was an experience. There was no airconditioning and one slept in pullman compartments. It gave him a thrill, also, to see her so happy. He would tell of the restaurants and shops they visited and the plays and museums they saw, and how he went to her hotel room one morning and she was sitting in bed eating a bunch of grapes. He said those grapes cost him $6.00, but she was the prettiest sight he ever saw.

Memphis continued to prosper and grow. The Baptist Memorial Hospital opened its doors in 1912 as the last word in hospitals. In 1916 the first self-service grocery store in the country was opened at 79 Jefferson by an enterprising young man named Clarence Saunders. Bread cost 5 cents a loaf. Overton Park and the zoo were 10 years old, and many animals including monkeys were added. An entrepreneur, Mrs. Samuel Hamilton Brooks, had donated $100,000 to build Memphis' first Art Gallery as a memorial to her late husband, a wealthy wholesale grocer who moved to Memphis before the Civil War. Mrs. Brooks dedicated a classical white marble building of intricate design on May 26, 1916, that houses one of the finest collections of art in the south. The Harahan Bridge was built, the second bridge across the Mississippi River, and Hardy, Arkansas, was a popular summer resort. Many Memphians had cabins on Whapeton Hill by the Spring River near the rapids. Children from Memphis went camping at the Boy Scout Camp KiaKima and Camp Miramichee for girls.

When Jessie was older, she went to Portsmouth quite often for the summer. There were not only many aunts and uncles but cousins by the score. There were Louise, Dixie, Sarah, Helen, and Margaret who were Uncle Herman's daughters, all beauties, living in Portsmouth and many more. She also had many friends who would invite her to be their house guest. One particular friend was Virginia Jett who she once visited for three months.

One place that was popular with the young people was Virginia Beach. It was a good little drive from Portsmouth, but that didn't matter. There they would meet the other groups from Norfolk. They had such good times with clambakes, singing around a fire on the beach at night, and swimming and boating by day. It was here that Jessie met a handsome man from Norfolk named Lester Rose Graves.

He and a group of his men friends had a beach house that they turned into a club house and called it the Pocahuntas Club. It was a place to meet and have lemonade on a hot day. There was a porch with wide steps, a perfect place to have pictures taken of the crowd, the girls in their middie blouses and the boys in their caps.

Lester Graves was born November 10, 1888, and was the son of William Armistead Graves, Jr. and Clara Rose Graves. He had fine features with dark hair and dark brown eyes under heavy eyebrows. His father owned a shipyard, and he had lived on the water all his life and was

318

an excellent sailor. They lived in a large brick home on Duke Street on the Elizabeth River. In fact, his father had been born in the house before him. His parents had Jessie as their house guest often as they were very fond of her. Lester's sister, Marion, was Jessie's age and they became close friends. Marion often visited Jessie in Memphis. Of course, Jessie spent more and more time in Portsmouth, and several years later they were married.

She was such a devoted daughter that it was very difficult for her to make up her mind to marry a man whose life was so far away even though she loved him very much. Fate has a way of making up ones mind, and World War I was declared with Germany. Lester was in training at St. Petersburg, Virginia, where he was inducted into the Unites States 314th Field Artillery as a Captain. He called her and told her that he was to be shipped out to France and asked her to meet him in St. Louis and marry him. She accepted his proposal at once, and told her parents that she would never love anyone but him so they arranged to be married before he left for France. Jessie hurriedly assembled her trousseau and went to St. Louis with her parents and brother where they were married on April 20, 1918, in St. Louis Cathedral by the Rev. John P. Spencer. Lester was shipped out one week later after, as Jessie put it, a heavenly time together that she would never forget. It sustained her for the year that he was gone to war.

She returned to Memphis with her parents and nine months later on January 22, 1919, their daughter was born. Jessie named her Sarah Hoyt after her mother. Lester returned home from the war in April of that year when the baby was three months old.

Jessie was estatic to have him safely home from the war as were the parents. The only sadness was when she and the baby left for his home in Virginia which was now to be hers, however, they all understood that he wanted to be with his family.

Angus was working in Texas and with Jessie and the baby gone, Arthur and Sarah decided there was no need to keep up such a large place. They sold the house on Central and moved around the corner to 1977 Higbee Avenue, a large, two story, frame house but on a much smaller lot. There was a "L" shaped porch on the front and side with a big, wooden swing and the house had large rooms, big entrance hall, living room, dining room with a beautiful mantle (it always seemed strange that the mantle was in the dining room rather than the living room). The kitchen was big and square with a latticed back porch where the ice box was kept. There were three bedrooms upstairs and a narrow back porch that ran the length of the house. In back was a garage, a small servants house, a grape arbor and five fig trees.

Fate again took a hand and Jessie became pregnant with their second child and was so homesick for her family that Lester had to bring her home and seek employment in Memphis. The house had already been sold, and it was a very sad occasion when father and daughter walked down the drive and looked back at their home for the last time. They realized they were leaving the scene of many happy and unforgetable memories.

319

Jessie and Lester moved into the house on Higbee with the family, and
Lester found a position that required him to do some traveling. In
February of 1920, when Jessie was eight months pregnant, a severe
influenza epidemic broke out in Memphis and she became ill and died
with the baby boy she was carrying on February 22, 1920.

Her family and friends were devastated. It was Sunday morning, but
she was so loved, that the owner of Memphis finest ladies shop,
Summerfields, opened his store in order that her friends could select
her burial robes. They selected a pale pink chiffon robe that made
her indeed look like an angel.

After the funeral they had to turn all her pictures to the wall
because little Sarah ran around the house pointing to them and crying
"Mama." Lester took his little girl to his parents in Virginia in
order that Jessie's grieving parents could recover as well as
possible.

Lester's mother took the year old baby to her heart, as did all the
family. Clara Graves had two sisters that lived in Westminister,
Maryland, who had never married, Theresa and Irene. Theresa, the
elder, moved to the Graves home in Norfolk to help care for little
Sarah. Lester decided to change the baby's name to "Jessie Chandler"
after her mother and this was done.

Little Jessie lived in Norfolk in the Graves home until she was two
years old, when Lester came and got her and returned her to Memphis
to be raised by her maternal grandparents. They had recovered
somewhat, but would never be fully recovered in their grief. Arthur
and Sarah Niemeyer were then sixty-nine and sixty-five years old.
How brave they were to take that two year old child to raise. She
was raised in a loving family that always spoke of her mother as your
"Precious Mother" and that is what Jessie called her. When she was
four years old and strong enough to walk to the trolly, her
grandfather took her to the cemetery every Sunday afternoon to her
mother's grave.

Due to arthritis her grandmother could not walk well enough to make
the trip. Little Jessie and her grandfather would stroll all around
the beautiful historic Elmwood Cemetery, and he would tell her tales
about the marble statues of people buried there. The pink granite
spire of the Thomas family, the mausoleum of Robert Church, the first
black millionaire in Memphis, and the monument to Patrick Henry's
daughter, Dorothea. There are also 17 generals, a daughter of a
signer of the Declaration of Independence, many yellow fever victims
and Civil War veterans and Kit Dalton, a member of Jesse James' gang,
buried in Elmwood Cemetery.

When Lester returned to Memphis after his wife died, he rented a room
at the home of the Gibsons. It was a large, stone house with stone
columns around a wide porch on the corner of Monroe Avenue and
McNeil. Every night right after dinner, he would drive over to see
little Jessie. On warm summer nights, she would wait for him sitting

on the curb at the corner by the fireplug. Sometimes he would take her for a drive in his convertible down the Parkway. He would let her stand clutching the dashboard with the wind in her face and hair blowing wildly as they sped along. Sometimes they would just sit on the porch with her grandparents and swing in the big swing.

When Jessie was five years old, Lester met his second wife, Julie LePrince. She was a French teacher at Miss Marsh's School, and lived with her parents, Cuban grandmother, three sisters and a brother on Pasadena Street in an old part of town. She had a younger sister, Aimee, who was about eighteen months older than Jessie, and Lester would take Jessie with him when he went to see Julie to play with Aimee. Julie was the granddaughter of Louis Aime' Augustin LePrince who invented the first motion picture machine.

After a five year courtship, Lester and Julie were married at an early mass at 5:00 a.m. in Sacred Heart Catholic Church on April 21, 1929. They moved into a new brick and stone house at 989 Stonewall with ten year old Jessie.

Arthur and Sarah were well in their seventies. Arthur had developed heart trouble after his beloved daughter died, it actually broke his heart, and Sarah had become severely crippled with arthritis. This health problem necessitated his selling his tile and mantle business. When Lester remarried, they had their large home turned into a duplex, and rented out the lower floor. Their nephew, George Mahan, Jr., was the leading architect in Memphis, and they turned the project over to him and spent that time in Florida while it was being converted. He added a large bedroom and bathroom behind the dining room downstairs and converted the upstairs back porch into a kitchen, eating area, and a little porch area. The great market crash of 1929 had affected them as well as the rest of the people in the nation, and they needed the extra income. It was truly the great depression, everyone had to pinch their pennies if they had any pennies.

Jessie was devoted to her grandparents and spent summers and week-ends during the school term with them. They enjoyed having her and her young friends bring some happiness into their quiet lives. When she graduated from high school, she went to live with them to keep house and do the cooking. Her grandmother would sit in a chair between the sink and range and grandfather would hand her whatever she needed to cook. With Jessie doing the cooking, she could sit in the bedroom in her rocking chair and tell her how to prepare the food. It worked out very well.

Jessie was only seventeen years old at the time, but as soon as she turned eighteen on January 22, her grandfather introduced her to the personnel manager of The First National Bank and said, "Mr. Maxwell, this is my granddaughter. I would like for you to give her a job." -- and he did. She worked in the Bookkeeping Department with dear Mrs. Brady, the Niemeyer's next door neighbor of many years. This is where Jessie met her future husband, George William Nash.

Sarah could walk only with great difficulty having to rest every little distance. Arthur continued his daily walks for his health, and often he and Jessie would walk together as he had with her mother. His pet name for her was "Girl." When she was little, he would call her "Big Girl" and the "Girl" stuck. He would tell her stories about the people who lived in the fine houses on Central Avenue near the house where she was born. They would walk to the bakery several blocks away and buy cheap broken cookies to take to Sarah. She did love her sweets.

Sarah's health continued to deteriorate, and she died on July 1, 1938, at the age of 80 years. She and Arthur had celebrated their 60th wedding anniversary in February.

In October Of 1938, Arthur made the decision to sell the house and take up residence at the King's Daughters Home. It was in the middle of the depression, and that large, lovely home sold for only $3,000. This arrangement greatly upset Jessie, but he knew it was for the best. He lived there six years, and Jessie went to see him every possible day. He was well cared for until his death and very comfortable and content. Jessie made it possible for him to make his periodic trips to Elmwood. It meant so much to him. He remained a student, a philosopher and a wit until the end. He read widely and jotted down notes on geography and natural history--his favorite subjects--and retained an avid interest in world news.

Arthur lived to see Jessie married the following May and later to know and enjoy his great-granddaughter, Judy Chandler, who was born a year before he died. Subsequently Jessie and George had three more children, Mary Margaret (Peggy), George Arthur, Nancy Elizabeth and seven grandchildren.

Arthur Niemeyer died quietly of a heart attack with Jessie at his bedside on April 2, 1944, at the age of 92 years.

Angus Niemeyer never married. After the home on Higbee was sold, he moved to Forest City, Arkansas, where he managed a small country hotel until his death. He remained very close to Jessie and her family always coming to join them for the Easter holidays and Christmas. He loved the children and spoiled them shamelessly. Several times a year Jessie and the four children would pile in the old Chevrolet or sometimes catch a train for the fifty mile trip to Forest City for a week-end visit. It was a great excursion. They all had their hair done, went to a movie and ate at the old Morris Restaurant on Main Street.

Angus Niemeyer died in the hotel at Forest City, Arkansas, of a heart attack on September 12, 1958. He was 79 years old.

Henry Niemeyer's Idea Grows Up . . . .

Prefabricated Houses Complete
Portsmouth-California Circle

First Were Built Here and Sent West, And Now It's the Other Way Round

By Milton Friedman

THE PREFABRICATED housing bird, which flew around Cape Horn and to our West Coast, has come home to Portsmouth to roost.

It's by a strange twist of fate that these ready-made houses are being sown in double thickness in Portsmouth, for it was here that they had their inception.

It's an ironic twist of fate. For a Portsmouth concern introduced prefabricated dwellings for shipment to California when the fabulous 1849 gold rush created a housing shortage there. And now, almost a century later, California contractors, Barrett and Hilp, are in Portsmouth throwing up demountables in the largest, fastest building project in history—and they're using sidings of California redwood!

Typical Portsmouth Architecture

With a penchant for planning and an aptitude for innovations, Henry V. Niemeyer, a leading nineteenth century citizen of Portsmouth, devised a four-story, prefabricated house in 1849. It could be shipped knocked down, with its parts bundled, labeled, and ready for quick assembly. And it brought quite a fancy price in the bonanza gold fields of California.

Mr. Niemeyer and his company of backers sent a Portsmouth institution to the West in the form of the "ready-made" dwellings. They were all the English basement type of structure, typical of architecture in nineteenth century Portsmouth.

Constructed with the finest seasoned timbers obtainable, the units were as sound as houses could be. As testimony to this fact, one of the houses, which was not shipped but set up here, is still standing on the northeast corner of Glasgow and Court streets.

Until a few years ago two others could be seen in Portsmouth. One, at Swimming Point, originally belonging to William A. Niemeyer, brother of the manufacturer, was discovered to be almost as sturdy as new when taken down just five years ago. The other house was situated on High street, between Court and Dinwiddie.

After the first few shipments to California, Niemeyer's houses proved impractical. Transportation necessitated a nine-month sailing around South America's Horn. Because of their seismic topography, Californians feared being trapped in the tall, four-storied affairs, preferring bungalows which are safer in earthquake country. And after the gold mania subsided, continued shipment of the houses proved economically unsound because the "forty-niners" took to building their own homes—and shacks—in preference to the expensive "Portsmouth Palaces."

New Models—a Far Cry Indeed

In contrast to this pioneering Portsmouth experiment, prefabricated houses now have come into their own. In Portsmouth 5,000 are being erected in an emergency program for Navy Yard workers. Near the junction of the Old and New Suffolk Highways 4,250 units are springing up for white workers. In Truxtun 750 more are under way for Negroes.

All the prefabricating for Barrett and Hilp's 1,000-acre project is being performed in their Money Point shops. More than 2,000 men are employed in all phases of the work—truly the greatest, fastest-building housing project in all history. In addition to other attendant outstanding features, Barrett and Hilp's houses can be constructed in as little as 78 minutes!

The new prefabricated units are, indeed, a far cry from Mr. Niemeyer's houses. Today's structures are small, bungalow type, 24 feet three inches by 28 feet. They feature 12 distinct floor plans. With both exterior and interior insulation, the houses are comfortably compact. Inside the California redwood siding walls on the prewaxed, oaken floors stand kitchen cabinets, electric refrigerators and cooking ranges, and there are six convenient closets.

The Homosote Company, of Trenton, N. J., negotiated the Government contract for the Portsmouth project and placed it in the hands of Barrett and Hilp, who previously were affiliated with Homosote on similar but lesser jobs.

Yes, fate has decreed that Portsmouth's prefabricated housing bird come home to roost.

Prefabricated house, 1849 style (left)

323

One Still Stands in City Today

Prefabricated Houses Were Built in Portsmouth for 49'ers

There's a Ghost-Tale Concerning One of Them, Too

By Rosa Brown Garrett

PORTSMOUTH—If we are not mistaken the phrase, "There is no new thing under the sun" may be found in the Old Testament, in Ecclesiastes. This being true, the "Do It Yourself" movement which has swept into every cranny of our country, like an English fog, is nothing new, particularly to Portsmouth.

Following the Gold Rush fever back in 1849, people from all over the world found their way to California, without thought of anything but returning home rich beyond their wildest dreams. Housing conditions never entered their heads. Consequently, many of them were forced to live in hastily put up leantos, or just living under the wide blue sky.

However, when word reached Portsmouth, a group of progressive business men, headed by Henry Victor Niemeyer, held a meeting and came up with the idea of pre-fabricated housing for the gold-hungry individuals breaking their backs out California way.

A site was found, carpenters hired, wood bought and the saws hummed, while the fine white wood dust piled up, as the four-story houses, all from the same pattern, were cut, marked and crated.

These huge crates were loaded into vessels for their long voyage down the coast of South America, around Cape Horn and up to California. Fortunately for these enterprising gentlemen, all the vessels reached their destination in fact.

Sold Easily

The houses sold like balloons at a circus and were bought up and proudly built in order by the brave women who had made the long trek with their husbands to find their fortunes.

All went well until the earth in that section of the country decided to take a deep breath, causing tremors of some magnitude. It was only then, that the four story pre-fabricated Portsmouth houses, began to creak and separate at the seams. And, finding them unsuitable for that country, many of them were dismantled and the wood used to build one story houses, thereby giving birth to the California bungalow.

As the death knell sounded for the Portsmouth firm, it was found that there were only three of the houses left. However, it was not difficult to dispose of them. One was bought and erected on High street somewhere between Court and Washington streets. It's loca-

William Angus Niemeyer, and father of Miss Louise Niemeyer Fontaine, a well known and much loved lady of Portsmouth. The house was erected on Swimming Point in 1854, just over the wooden foot bridge which for many years spanned the water separating the point from the north end of Dinwiddie street. It was known as No. 1 Swimming Point. And up until the building of the Harborview Apartments, when it was razed, that home stood midst its boxwoods and roses.

During the summer after the death of grandfather, the family with the exception of father, spent a month at the springs. As was the custom, it was during one of these absence of his family that father invited a young relative to spend some time with him. One morning at breakfast the young relative asked:

"Uncle, what were you walking up and down the stairs for all night?" And Uncle replied "Don't

The home of the late Dr. R. R. Robertson who married Miss Mary Niemeyer, still stands at the corner of Court and Glasgow streets. It has been changed by the addition of porches and bay windows.

talk so foolishly," and thinking he had frightened his young relative, he changed the subject. But the following morning the young relative asked the same question. He was told this happened frequently.

But Uncle, gasped the young man, Grandpa died so long ago.

That's true, answered Uncle, but it's loved this place.

It was said that the spirit of the old gentleman William Angus Niemeyer, never really left the home, for down through the years it was heard walking about the house up and down the stairs at night.

John Christian Niemeyer, a well known gentleman of Portsmouth and his family were the last occupants of No. 1 Swimming Point. After the death of his wife, he moved with his daughter and son to a home on North street.

Planned to Close

He asked a good friend to see to the closing of the old home, as he intended to sell it. During the process of making it ready for the real estate agent, according to legend, the good friend began at the attic to close the windows and shutters, locking each one securely. Then he went to the floor below and

though he had locked them shortly before.

No doubt, closing that the old place became monotonous, but finally, it was secured and as he walked down the boxwood bordered lane to the street he turned back only to see every window shutter and door wide open. He tipped his hat and said, "Have it your way, Grandfather, you win."

Still Standing

The third house was put up on the corner of Court and Glasgow streets, where Dr. R. R. Robertson who married Miss Mary Niemeyer, lived with his family. This house is now in the family of Jerome Weiss, who added porches and a bay window on one side.

Mr. Weiss told us that when the place was being converted into apartments, the contractor showed him the heavy, hard timbers used in its construction. It is no doubt, said the contractor, but this house was built by skillful

The house bought and erected by William Angus Neimeyer in 1854 and erected just over the old wooden bridge which spanned the water between Swimming Point and Dinwiddie streets. It was left exactly according to the plans.

stairs the good friend was aghast at what he saw, for every window and shutter was wide open. He went through the same closing process again, and as he finished he realized things were amiss on the floor below, and when he descended he found those windows

And what is the story of the effect of the California Gold Rush of 1849 on Our Town? The house at the corner of Court and Glasgow streets is all that remains of the ingenuity of the progressive gentlemen who had their part in that famous era.

MEMORANDUM

TO: Mrs. Katharine Fontaine Heath and Calvert Chair Cousins

FROM: Lewis Kirby

DATE: January 10, 1991

SUBJECT: Niemeyer Bible

Dear Katharine,

YOU HAVE DONE IT AGAIN! The Niemeyer Family Bible, printed in 1832, has reached me
safely. Attached is a copy of the pages that are relevant from our office copy
machine, for your interest and reference.

We will have a slipcase made for the Bible! Do you feel that we should keep it
in our Archives here at "Claremont Manor", or eventually present it to the Virginia
Historical Society, or the Sargeant Room of the Norfolk Public Library, or a member
of the family, by the name of Niemeyer? The only thing wrong with the last—is that
Bill Niemeyer, today, might be very interested, but who would say what would happen
in the future?

In the meantime, it has arrived safely. I am most grateful to you for sending it.
All of the information in it will be in "Tidewater Ancestors", in facsimile copy
fashion, I hope. That book is progressing rapidly, but we cannot keep delaying
the 'blue line' for inclusions that keep developing!

Warm regards,

Lewis

JLK:lw

PS. I have tried to call you several times on the phone to thank you, but you

     ain't never home!

Dear Lewis,

This is the bible that I ask
you to evaluate and use or dispose
of according to your judgment.

I'm still enjoying the Claremont
History books — Congratulations.

Best wishes for 1991

Katharine

December 28, 1990

My Brother —

Where art thou laid — on what untrodden shore,
Where nought is heard, save ocean's sullen roar,
Dost thou in lowly state,
At last repose firm all the storms of fate?
Methinks I see thee struggling with the wave,
Without one aiding hand stretched out to save,
See thee convulsed, thy looks to heaven bend,
And send thy parting sigh unto thy friends;
I see thee, the stormy struggle o'er
Think on thy native land — and rise no more!
Would thou couldst see me at this moment here,
Embalm thy memory with a pious tear —
But thou art gone, and I am left below,
To struggle through this world of care and wo.

S. M. Copied from — Henry Kirke White's Poem on
Niemeyer   "Childhood — Part 2d — Pages 217 & 222.

Henry K. White Poetical Works

Henry K. White was born at Nottingham, England
March 21, 1785 — Died October 19, 1806 — Aged 21 yrs.

God of the just — Thou gavest the bitter cup
I bow to thy behest, and drink it up.
                                          Sonnet — page 152,
                                          Henry Kirke White.

By S. Martha Niemeyer

Died on the 9 June 1863

Died in Portsmouth Va Jan 29th 1883.
Mary Ann Niemeyer, wife of Charles
F. Niemeyer aged 81 yrs. buried on
her birth day, my darling Mother

BLE

Mary Ann Neimeyer

THE
OLD TESTAMENT

ILLUSTRATED WITH ENGRAVINGS
BY
WRIGHT & SMITH
FROM THE DESIGNS OF
Richard Westall Esq.
R.A.

HOLY BIBLE,

OLD AND NEW TESTAMENTS

THE APOCRYPHA:

TRANSLATED OUT OF THE ORIGINAL TONGUES

THE FORMER TRANSLATIONS DILIGENTLY COMPARED AND REVISED

CANNE'S MARGINAL NOTES AND REFERENCES.

AN INDEX

all ir
lence
This is
us. Th
plead ig
But in t

NEW YORK:
PUBLISHED AND SOLD BY DANIEL D. SMITH.
FRANKLIN JUVENILE BOOK AND STATIONARY STORE, N. 190 GREENWICH STREET.
ALSO BY THE PRINCIPAL BOOKSELLERS IN THE UNITED STATES.

Arrangement of the Names in the Following
Family Record to Show Relationship

A. John Christian Niemeyer, born at Verden, near Bremen,
in Germany (1776); (emigrated to Virginia); married
(March 27, 1800) Catharine Adams Keys, born
on Staten Island, New York. John Christian
Niemeyer died October 20, 1820, and his wife,
Catharine Adams Keys Niemeyer, died Sept. 20, 1812.
Their children were:

I. Charles Frederic Niemeyer, born April 11, 1801; died
Sept. 21, 1834; married, Dec. 23, 1823,
Mary Ann Reed, b. 1802, d. 1883.
Their children were:

II. Ann Matilda Niemeyer
1803 — 1831

    1. Catharine Adams. b. Jan. 23, 1825;
       d. March 22, 1825

III. Washington Augustus
Niemeyer, 1805 — 1824

    2. Charles Henry, b. Mar. 18, 1826,
       d. July 21, 1826.

    3. Virginia Adams, b. 1827

IV. Henry Victor Niemeyer,
1808 — 1883; m.
(1) Jane Frances Benthall
(2) Martha Caroline
Vaughn. No children
of either marriage)

    4. Susan Matilda, 1830 — 1875

    5. Henry Wardin, b. May 30, 1833;
      m. Alivina C. Wilson, Apr. 28,
      1859; entered the Confederate
      Service and was killed at
      Island No. 10, April, 1862.
      His wife and infant son
      died in December, 1862, of
      scarlet fever.

A. (John Christian Niemeyer was married a second
time to Anne McLean d. of Duncan McLean, of Scotland.
Their children were:)
I. Eliza Ann, 1814-1846;   II. William Angus,   (III. Virginia
                        b. April 28, 1816,   Margretha,
                        m. Sarah Howard   1818 — 1820)
                        chandler.

FAMILY RECORD.

BIRTHS.	BIRTHS.
John C. Niemeyer born at Verden near Bremen in Germany	Of Charles F. Niemeyer's family. —
wife of John C. N. Catharine ~~Adams~~ Keys. born on Staten Island New York.	Catharine Adams *born* on the 23ᵈ January 1825. *Died in March following.*
Charles F. Niemeyer April 11ᵗʰ 1801. *Sabbath night* died Sept 21ˢᵗ 1834 *10 o'clock*	Charles Henry born 18 March 1826 — Died 21 of July of the same year.
Anna Matilda Niemeyer born December 28. 1803.	Virginia Adams, August 7 1827. 7 ... Aug. 7, 1827.
	Susan Matilda Niemeyer Dec'br 15. 1830.
	Henry Woodis Niemeyer May 30ᵗʰ 1833
Henry Victor Niemeyer born December 3ᵈ 1848. in Norfolk Virginia. Dec. 3ᵈ	William Augus Niemeyer born April 28. 1816
1871 1848	Washington Augustus Niemeyer born March 27. 1805

FAMILY RECORD.

DEATHS.	DEATHS.
John C. Niemeyer, died on the 20th October 1820 aged 44 years.	Charles Frederic Niemeyer son of Henry Woodis & Alexina Constantina Niemeyer: died of scarlet fever at Camposella, Norfolk County on Saturday morning at 8½ o'clock December 13. 1863.
Catharine his wife died 27 Sept 1812 aged 29 yrs. or 30 yrs.	Alexina Constantina Niemeyer (wife of Henry Woodis Niemeyer) died at her Father's residence "Camposella", Norfolk County, Virginia, 20 minutes past 7 o'clock Wednesday morning December 17. 1862.
Washington Augustus son of Jno. C & Catharine Niemeyer died 1824.	
Charles Frederic Niemeyer, died September 21. 1834 on Sabbath night at 10 o'clock.	Henry Woodis Niemeyer Son of Charles F. Niemeyer and Mary A. Niemeyer died April 1862 at Island No 10. on the Mississippi River.
Catharine Adams daughter of Chas. Fred & Mary Ann Niemeyer died March 22. 1825.	
Charles Henry, son of Chas. Fred & Mary A. Niemeyer died July 21. 1826.	
Anna Matilda Niemeyer, daughter of John Christian & Catharine Niemeyer) died Octor 15. 1831; having been on a visit to her relatives in Germany, died a few days after her arrival, in Norfolk Va, at the residence of her Aunt Mrs Ann Woodis.	Susan Matilda Niemeyer daughter of Charles F. and Mary A. Niemeyer died August 2 1875
Mrs Ann Woodis died December 1831. in Norfolk Virginia.	Mary A. Niemeyer wife of Charles F. Niemeyer died January 31st 1883 aged 81 years, died Wedn. at night,

FAMILY RECORD.

MARRIAGES.	MARRIAGES.

John C. Niemeyer, Feb. to
Miss Catharine Keys.
1800.

Charles F. Niemeyer to
miss Mary Ann Peed of Virginia
Princess Ann Co. Dec. 25.
1823. By Rev. Charles Moseley.

Henry Woodis Niemeyer, son of
Chas. F. & Mary A. Niemeyer
married to Miss Alexina C.
Wilson, daughter of Frederic
& Ellen Wilson, of Norfolk County,
on Thursday, April 28. 1859.
at "Campostella", Norfolk County,
by Rev. Robert A. Taylor of
Portsmouth. Va

Henry W Niemeyer
Son of Wm C and
Catharine Niemeyer
married to Miss Jane
Francis Berkhall
May 11th 1837

Wm A. Niemeyer married
to miss Sarah H.
Chandler July 31 1840
by the
Jany 31. 1839

337

FAMILY RECORD.

Of Charles Frederic and Mary Ann

Mary Ann Peed wife of Chas. Fred. Niemeyer born in Princess Ann County, Virginia.

January 31. 1802.

Charles Frederic Niemeyer born April 11. 1801. in Norfolk, Virginia.

Catharine Adams, (daughter of Chas. F. & Mary A. Niemeyer,) born January 23. 1825 in Portsmouth, Va.

Chas. Henry, (son of Chas. Fred. & Mary A. Niemeyer,) born March 18. 1826 in Portsmouth, Va.

Virginia Adams, (daughter of Chas. F. & Mary A. Niemeyer,) born August 7. 1827 in Portsmouth, Va.

Susan Matilda, (daughter of Chas. F. & Mary A. Niemeyer,) born December. 15. 1830. in Portsmouth, Va.

Henry Woodis, (son of Chas. Fred. & Mary A. Niemeyer,) born May 30. 1833. in Portsmouth, Va.

Charles Frederic Niemeyer (son of Henry Woodis & Alexina Constantina Niemeyer,) born January 12. 1860 in Portsmouth Virginia.

338

March 16, 1989

Dear Bill:

The enclosed I copied from a "history" ? which
mother has had for years. I suppose Granny had it. I have
no idea who wrote it. Anyway what I have, started with page 6
and ended with page 11. The paper is yellow and brittle and
the typing almost faded to the point of being unreadable
however, I could make it out.

The part about Sr. Martina is quite familar. She was
married to Mr. Gray and after he died she joined the Sisters.
I remember her as I am sure the Hills do. I think Mr.
Gray is buried in our cemetery - probably in Aunt Belle's
lot. John and Bill probably know the answer to that.

The line that states Alonza married Madge Lamb says
they had no children. I think they had a daughter - Margaret.
They lived in the big house on the corner of Court and Waverly
Blvd. The house is probably gone. Anyway Margaret was
quite a bit older than I and I remember she died maybe while
she was in her late teens or early twenties. I remember
thinking how strange it was for somebody so young to die. I
guess she was the first person that I knew to do so I'm not
sure Bill and John would know anything about her.

In the same box with this history there is another
set of papers which start with Yeardley or Yardley then
follow Thorowgood, Offley, Hewitt - Osborne, Lawson, Sayer
(sometimes spelled Sayre), Mason. There are 11 pages in this
set and one of the last things recorded is "The Will of
Anthony Lawson'. It is single spaced typing and I will try to
get it done for you sometime soon. The last sentence is "In
witness Whereof I hereunto set my Hand and Seal this fourth Day
of February in the year of our Lord one thousand seven hundred
and eighty five. Signed Sealed Published and Declared, In the
presence of Anthony Lawson, William White) Lucretia Gordon) William
Russell).

It is rather hot here today but the weather man says it
might get cloudy and finally that we might have some rain
which we need badly.

Louise received a letter from Lucrece in which she
said she would probably not get down here until the last
of April or the first of May. Lucrece, Buck and Rosemary
are in New Orleans at Walt's.

I can't believe Easter is so near. I'm glad, maybe some
of these visitors will go back North.

Enjoy your dinner - I'm having supper - sour stew and rolls!
Love to each of you - and a pat for Charlie -

Personal Recollections

by Henry V. Niemeyer

I was born on Swimming Point, Portsmouth, Virginia, February 24, 1845, in the house north of the Niemeyer mansion where most of the children were born. My father built this house, in which my sister Sallie, and brother, George, were born. He afterwards built the large house in which he lived until his death.

When the War between the States began in April, 1861, I was sixteen years and two months old. Every boy in town was anxious to fly to arms, and become a hero before the war would end, which was set down at six months maximum. Many companies were being organized and drilled. In the town there was no lack of volunteers. I never knew of a conscription in Portsmouth. My brother Fred came on from West Point, where he had just completed his four-year course. He was appointed a lieutenant in the regular army, and put to drilling troops. My brother John came from the Virginia Military Institute, at Lexington, and was made a sergeant in the Old Dominion Guards, and also helped in training the soldiers.

At first young men under the age of eighteen were refused enlistment, but not to be outdone, they raised what was known as "a boy company", young fellows from fourteen to eighteen years of age. It was the custom at that time to adopt high-sounding names for the companies. The word "Light" was considered necessary to impress their admirers. "Blues" was also a favorite name at that time. So we called ourselves "The Blanchard Light Infantry Blues", named for General Blanchard, in command of Portsmouth troops.

"Light" was probably intended to denote something "quick" and strategical, that would enable us to land quickly on the flanks of the enemy and get away before they could recover from their surprise. The name "Blues" has never been made very clear to me, but I have no doubt it

was intended for something very terrifying. Then there was a company called the "Dismal Swamp Rangers" from the Deep Creek section of the county.

Our boy company elected my brother John, from the Old Dominion Guards, as one of our lieutenants. The Blanchard Light Infantry Blues were never mustered into service, as the boys could brook no delay, and begged the captains of the other companies to accept them. Capt. Kearns, of the Old Dominion Guards, afterwards Company K, 9th Virginia Infantry was kind enough to consent to my joining him. We were quartered at Pinner's Point, in charge of the fort at that place for the protection of the Elizabeth River.

Another company, known as the Craney Island Artillery Blues, was also quartered there. This Blues company was never to enjoy the firing off of their artillery. They were merged into the 9th Regiment, along with the Old Dominion Guards, and called Company I, given a musket instead of a cannon, and did valiant service as infantry until the end of the war. My brother John, first sergeant of Company K, was elected lieutenant of this company, and was with them in the charge of Pickett's Division at Gettysburg, where he was killed July 3, 1863. He was not twenty-one years old, and had seen two years of service. His body was never recovered. We remained around our home until May 10, 1862.

General McClellan, with 120,000 Union soldiers, was within 10 miles of Richmond, attacking our army of half its numbers, under General Joseph E. Johnston. Reinforcements were necessary, and the ten thousand men in defense of Norfolk and Portsmouth were compelled to abandon these two cities and hurry to Richmond.

Our mothers had packed our knapsacks with clothes enough to last a long time. We were soon in the swamps at Seven Pines, fighting, sometimes in water knee deep. Our knapsacks, with clothes, bibles, and many precious articles, began to feel so heavy on the tired men, that we took them off and laid them under a tree, expecting to return and get

them. But we were doomed to disappointment, and there was seldom a time after that when I could boast of an extra pair of socks or shirt. I have often stopped long enough to wash my thin cotton shirt in a ditch, wring it out as dry as I could, put it on, and let it dry the best way possible.

General Johnston was severely wounded at Seven Pines, and President Davis rode out from Richmond, with General Lee, near where we were, and placed him in command of the army. There was to be no more retreating from that time.

General "Stonewall" Jackson was called from the valley with his troops, and with Longstreet's men, and the cavalry of General J. E. B. Stuart, the offensive against McClellan began. McClellan was forced back to Malvern Hill, on the James River, under the protection of his gunboats. He was on his way to Harrison's Landing on the north side, in order to place his army on the transports to go up the Potomac River. General Lee did not intend to fight a battle at Malvern Hill, but one of his subordinates, a Major General, brought on the battle on his own responsibility. McClellan had 120 cannon and most of his army ready to defend this position. Captain Carey Grimes, of Portsmouth, climbed a steep hill with his battery of artillery, and opened fire on the Union army. The Federal cannon soon began to feel him out, and getting the range, swept his men and guns from the field. Our brigade, Armistead's, was lying on the ground behind him in support. I can remember Grimes as he looked, in his shirtsleeves, mounted on his horse, showing no concern as to the danger. At the battle of Sharpsburg, he showed the same reckless spirit, was wounded, and placed on a litter. While in that position, he received his second wound, which proved fatal. After our artillery was silenced at Malvern Hill, the infantry was ordered forward. A Louisiana brigade was sent in, Mahone's and Armistead's brigades, Wright's Georgiana, and possibly others that I cannot remember.

It was up hill and down dale with us. We would run to the top of a hill, and down the next, re-form, climb the next hill and fight with our mus-

These heretofore unpublished recollections of Henry Victor Niemeyer, CSA were dictated to his daughter and later typed by his granddaughter June G. Benson (Mrs. Gerald W.) of the Pisgah Chapter #2375, Brevard, North Carolina.

kets, then forward again to the next protection. In this way we were soon close up under the Union guns. The twilight was falling, and with the smoke of the black powder of that time, we could scarcely see the enemy, except when the flame from their guns brightened the field. The fighting against these artillery and infantry was terrific. In addition, the gunboats in the James River would fire their large shells over the bluff and onto us. I remember a great shell burst within a foot of me, but scattered without striking me. The concussion was so great that it seemed to loosen my ear drums. A grapeshot came plowing through the ground, rose above the surface, struck me a glancing blow, as if someone had struck me with a brick, and went on its way. I can remember that I felt that our next rush would bring us into a hand-to-hand encounter. I did not relish having a fellow punching at me with a bayonet, so I stopped firing, and with a bullet and three buckshot in my gun, felt that this would give me some advantage before a bayonet could strike.

Just then I saw banks of infantry coming from behind their guns to receive the final charge. Everything stopped, and all firing ceased. That night we remained on the field, shivering in the summer night and drizzling rain, and sleeping the best way we could. Seeing a little fire down in the ravine made from a few twigs, Arthur Harvey of Company G and I went down to investigate. We noticed four men standing around, and we tried to crowd in and join them. The smallest of them was a little man weighing about 100 pounds. Then there was a big man and two medium-sized men. The little fellow said to Arthur, "Come up here and get warm, and then go up on the hill, and tell all the boys to come down to the fire, and then we will have a damned fine line of battle up there." The little fellow who was trying to be funny was General Mahone; the big one was General Wright. The others were General Armistead, and another that I cannot recall. They were holding a council of war.

The next morning, much to my delight, we discovered that the Union army had fallen back on their march to Harrison's Landing, and left us in possession of the field. I walked over the ground that morning, and saw great numbers of dead and wounded from both armies. I saw Captain Den-

nis Vermillion of our company, lying dead from a bullet wound. Melzer Fiske, a boy of 16, was dead. John Bennet, of our company, was mortally wounded with a bullet through his thigh. I found two men carrying a litter, and we placed John upon it and took him to the rear. He was sent to the hospital where he died a few days later.

We remained around Richmond for several weeks and were then started off to oppose General Pope, who had been given another army sent out from Washington. Our regiment was engaged in the battle of Warrenton Springs, and we could see the hotel, which had been set on fire, burning. One of our pickets had been left in a dangerous position, and it was difficult to withdraw them from the field. We had captured a woman in man's clothes, who proved to be Dr. Mary Walker. Colonel White of Portsmouth put a piece of cloth on a stick as a flag of truce, and took his prisoner to the Union lines. The pickets took advantage of this and escaped.

We marched all night, and the next day appeared on the battlefield of Second Manassas or Bull Run. When we were going forward we met our friend Mahone lying on a litter, wounded and being brought to the rear by four men. We told the men to let one of them take the general under his arm, and go get the surgeon, and the others must go back where they came from. Pope was defeated in this battle, and driven back across the Potomac river.

1862—We went into camp at Winchester; and in September, my father came from Portsmouth through the Union lines, and asked for my discharge from the army, as I was under eighteen. In a short time, orders came from the Secretary of War ordering my discharge. I went to Richmond by railroad and after remaining out of service a short time, reenlisted in the Signal Service before I had reached the eighteen year limit.

I was sent to a signal station on the lower James river to get information, and passed it by flag signal to Petersburg. I was more than a year doing service around the Chickahominy River, where it empties into the James. We were many times shelled out by gunboats, and our line temporarily broken. But we would get back to work as soon as the boats would go away. Finally the Union fleet with warships and transports bearing

"The Army of the James", under General Butler, came along, and we made our escape to the south side at night, in a rowboat, with a piece of blanket tied around the oars to muffle the sound.

Our squad of six men was put on watch for troops that might be landed from transports. While there I was captured by two companies of Indiana cavalry, who had come down from City Point, and were running a telegraph wire to connect with Fortress Monroe. A boat was signaled, and I was put on board and sent to the prison at Point Lookout, Maryland. There were fourteen thousand of us divided into fourteen divisions and crowded into tents. Our rations were very scarce, a half loaf of bread, a tin cup full of bean soup, and a pie of salt meat each day. We were never given any vegetables, and as a consequence, scurvy prevailed to a great extent. I know that the doctors would at times write in a prescription a diet of potatoes or onions or vinegar.

In reconstructing the sewers, I at one time saw hundreds of rats killed by the prisoners which were cooked and eaten. My hunger never led me to this extreme, but I have been offered a piece of this kind of food.

The northern people were incensed at what they called "starvation rations" to their men in southern prisons. I believe they did not know that the Confederate army was subsisting on corn meal and strong bacon, mainly. With our ports closed and our crops destroyed, we were doing the best we could by the prisoners and our own men. The southerners were constantly pleading for a general exchange of prisoners, but the northern generals concluded that it was better judgment to let their men stay in prison and suffer than to send back a large army, and prolong the war. This may have been a wise conclusion, but it was what General Sherman said it was.

I was in prison from June, 1864, to March, 1865. No exchange of prisoners would be permitted, but in order to get some of their sick from the southern prisons, the Union people would agree to parole a boatload of Confederates, for a like number of their own men. The complaints from their own people compelled some action. This at last relieved us of the care of many thousand prisoners, and at the same time released our own men from northern prisons. In

(continued next page)

March 1865, I was included in a boatload of men, and sent up the James River under a flag of truce. When we landed at Rocketts, we were enthusiastically received by a dilapidated brass band, and orators chosen for the occasion. We were called "Patriots" and praised to the utmost degree. We marched up Main street, the ladies waving to us from the windows, and a joyous welcome was given. We were told that a substantial banquet had been arranged, and were escorted to a tobacco warehouse where planks had been placed for tables. There were no seats, but we stood up, and soon the waiters appeared with large sheets of iron pans with a big slab of cornbread. The waiters told us it was good and hot, and they passed us a canteen of sorghum molasses, and invited us to take as much as we wanted. Things had been sagging down gradually in the food line, and those good friends of ours thought everything was just right. It was easy to see that the Confederacy was on its last legs. We were given passes to our homes if we could get there, but mine being in the enemy lines, I spent my furlough in Richmond. In about two weeks things began to happen. Sunday afternoon, April 2, 1865, I walked through Capitol Square, and much to my surprise, I saw men bringing bank notes, arms full, and piling them on a fire. There must have been a carload and more coming. This was money that our printing presses had been pounding out for four years, all duly signed in pen and ink by an army of women and bearing such names as "Susan Smith" for Treasurer, and "Mary Jones" for Registrar. One of the men informed me that General Lee was evacuating Richmond, and everything of that kind that could not be carried away was being destroyed. Truly, I have seen "money to burn" in my time.

It was with intense sadness that we gave up Richmond. We had been fighting four long years to keep out the enemy, and at last it had to be surrendered. I recalled the death of my brother John, who had been killed, and my brother William Frederic, lieutenant colonel of the 61st Virginia, who was killed at Spotsylvania, May 12, 1864, on his 24th birthday.

I left Richmond at about three o'clock in the morning and ran over the bridge to Manchester, which had been set on fire to cover our retreat. Then commenced the march of the Confederate army in the direction of Appomattox Courthouse. In the seven days from Richmond to Appomattox, I did not draw a ration. We were constantly burning our wagons to escape capture. Sometimes we would find an ear of corn that was intended for a mule. We would roast the grains in the hot ashes, or else eat it raw. The men had begun to struggle and look out for themselves, and when they were hard pressed by the calvary, would band together of their own accord and fight off pursuers. Every man had become a general in experience and knew just what to do.

Several times I saw General Lee entirely alone, riding on his horse, Traveler. If he had any worries he did not betray it. I remember his calm, handsome face to this day. We finally reached Appomattox Courthouse. It was the intention to march until we could form a junction with General Joseph E. Johnston, who was coming through North Carolina to meet us. Our ammunition was exhausted, and food, too, and with our twelve thousand men we accepted General Grant's liberal terms. General Grant and General Lee had met at the home of Mr. McLean in the village to discuss terms. We were to be disbanded and permitted to return to our homes. This was Sunday, the ninth of April, 1865.

The men did not wait for the promised rations. Those living in distant states would get their bearings and start to walk in the general direction of their homes. I wended my way over many a mile of mud and rain until I arrived at City Point. I had not drawn any food since leaving Richmond, but the Union soldiers were good to us and would give us coffee and hard tack. At City Point I found many new recruits who had not been uniformed or armed, and called "One Hundred Day Men". They had enlisted for that length of time. Somehow the impression prevailed among them that General Lee had surrendered to General Grant under an apple tree, and that some of the Confederates had pieces of that tree for souvenirs. They were anxious to possess such a valuable relic, and were willing to trade a generous supply of hard tack for a piece. The old "Rebs" were quite quick to catch on, and they invaded the orchards of City Point and were ready to supply the demand for a piece of honest-to-goodness apple tree.

I got aboard a steamboat and went down the James river to Norfolk. I found my father waiting to see if I was among the men. With him were my three brothers, George, Arthur, and Crawford. We crossed over on the ferry, and arrived home after dark, where I met my mother after three years of absence. She could not keep back her tears for her two other boys who did not return.

It was thought that many of our soldier friends might return with me and a bountiful supper had been provided. But I came home alone, and I remember the piles of hot biscuits, sure enough coffee with sugar, a great bowl of stewed oysters, and a Virginia ham. I have thought since that I must have been at the point of starvation without being aware of it. I certainly would have consumed all of the ham, along with the other food, if my father had not stopped me. They were afraid that I would gorge myself to death. It was the first time in three years that I had had enough to eat. I was twenty years old and weighed 120 pounds, and so inured to hardship that my system seemed proof to anything. I went to my room and got into a real bed, but I could not sleep; so I lay down on the floor and soon dropped off to sleep, feeling so well and strong in the morning when I awoke.

(NOTE: On the site of the Old Point Lookout prison, where Henry was imprisoned during the war, with 14,000 other Confederate prisoners, the United States Government has, within recent years, erected a magnificent monument to the Confederate soldiers who died there during the war. This demonstrates that we are again one country—no North, no South, East or West, but all for the common good. S. W. N.)

Genealogical Chart

YEARDLY FOLDER
- Thoroughgood
- Yeardley
- Sheers
- Marston
- DeSalle
- Appleyard
- Skinner
- Payne
- Flowerdew
- Byrkes
- Stanley
- Scott
- Marsham
- Chevall
- DeEardle

THOROUGHGOOD FOLDER
- Thoroughgood
- Edwards
- Mason
- Mardaunt
- Sayre
- Seawell

NIEMEYER FOLDER
- Niemeyer 1
- Niemeyer 2
- Maclean
- Woodward

CALVERT FOLDER
- Calvert
- Bennett/Snayle/Saunders

OSBORNE FOLDER
- Osborne
- Bodley
- Bradbury
- Broughton
- Fyldene
- Hewitt
- Leech
- Leveson Folder
  - Leveson
  - deRushal
  - Prestwood
  - Clement

OFFLEY FOLDER
- Offley
- Rogerson

LAWSON FOLDER
- Lawson
- Keeling
- Chandler Folder
  - Chandler
  - Burr
  - Hancock
  - Matlack

LOOKING BACKWARD
From August 6, 1865 to August 6, 1943
By
Mamie Niemeyer Robertson
(Mary Chandler Niemeyer Robertson)

I was born in our old home on Swimming Point, which was then in Norfolk County, but later in Portsmouth, Virginia. I was the youngest of twelve children, nine boys and three girls. *Two of my brothers were killed in the War Between the States. The oldest educated at West Point and the second at Virginia Military Institute. They left college and were made officers in the Confederate Army and later killed by the Yankees. The **third brother joined the Army at the age of sixteen and after being in many battles, he was taken prisoner and kept in prison for fifteen months. All this was before I was born.

*William Frederic and John Chandler   **Henry Victor

Our home on Swimming Point, on the Elizabeth River, was a great meeting place for young people to gather. I remember the tub races the boys would have. They would sit in large wooden tubs, hang their feet out in the water, and paddle until one would win the race. So many boys would come over to swim; some of the boys would tie the clothes together. The Police would sometimes come over and run the boys off for being naked. Then the boys would have a time trying to untie their clothes, and we would hear them sing "Beef so tough, we can't get enough; General Jackson chaw beef."

We were all small children when we learned to swim and if we were to fall overboard, no one would pay any attention to us. One of my brothers had a very nice small rowboat for me and I could row over the river. Some of the boys had battaus that they had made to paddle all over the river. Often we would go crabbing and bring them to be cooked by our Rose. Rose was my nurse when I was a baby. She lived with our family for over fifty years, and was devoted to us all. She lived with us until she was too old to work but we saw that she was well taken care of as long as she lived.

There used to be a long bridge, one end of which was at Swimming Point and it went all the way to Court Street. Where the boulevard is now used to be the river. It is all made land. Also Dinwiddie Street. I used to row my boat through the rushes all the way back to the old Dinwiddie Street Methodist Church. Now Monumental Church is build there. My father was a steward in the church and contributed a large amount when the church was built. At that time we had to go over the long bridge to Court, then walk to London until we got to Dinwiddie where the church was.

Swimming Point was a great place for colored people to come to be baptized. Sometimes they would have to break the ice to go in. The preacher would duck them way down in the water and they would come up shivering but happy. On one occasion, the bridge was so crowded with sightseers. Brother Henry was on the bridge with Fred who was my nephew, and myself. All of a sudden the bridge broke down and we all went in the river, with my brother' arm around Fred and me. There was a colored church on North Street and still is a prosperous church. The A.M.E. church. When they had a revival we could hear them shouting all the way from our home. When one was converted, they would all go over town shouting "My soul is free" and shake hands with everybody, white or colored.

John, our janitor, is the old fashioned kind. Says you had better not shout in church, people would look at you, some will frown and some will snicker. He says it is not like the good old times.

We had a bathhouse on the river, which my father had made for us all. Often the young people from town would come over and ask to go bathing. One of the boys living on the Point came and asked my father for the bathhouse key, saying he was hot as hell. My father told him if he was as hot as that he might set the bathhouse on fire, so would not let him have the key.

Portsmouth, like most places had its ghosts. When the LeMosey house was pulled down to build the beautiful house which Judge Bain's father had built, in digging the foundation of the new house, working men dug up nine skulls. Before the LeMoseys lived there, a family who had moved afterwards to Washington lived there. One day they came to see my mother and told about seeing three sailors sitting on the bottom steps, but when they would go down the stairs the sailors would vanish. The beautiful house Mr. Bain had built with all the inside work of solid walnut, doors and all furnishings. On the third floor a large billard (sic) room with a fine billard table. Getting back to the ghosts, after my father died we would hear footsteps coming up from the basement. One night Sam was getting ready for bed, he called me and asked me if I had opened his door. I was upstairs and told him no. He said someone had opened it. So many of our family heard the footsteps coming up from the basement.

After the old home was sold, there were some very nice people there, I asked the lady who lived there if they ever heard footsteps from the basement. She said often, and one night they put the baby, their grandchild, to sleep in the basement and they all heard someone coming up the steps, so the baby's grandfather went to see if there was anyone there. No one was ever seen. One of our town ghosts was seen in a window where Dr. Bilisoly lived on the corner of High and Dinwiddie Streets. Almost everyone in town would go there to look at the picture of a mother with a child in her arms. I myself saw it too. I remember when all the churches let out one Sunday. Almost everyone crowded across Dinwiddie Street to see the picture. Some people thought perhaps that the lightning had made the impression, but they never knew. The pane of glass was sent away, but did not show except in the Bilisoly house.

Another ghost story was when a house on Middle Street near County drew such crowds. Dishes, knives and all kinds of things were flying out of the windows. The house had a small porch and narrow stairway. With such a crowd the porch gave way and I remember two prominent men had broken legs. That ghost proved to be woman who lived there and who was doing the throwing.

I was married in the old home. The time was six o'clock in the morning, a beautiful October morning. Two of my little nieces dressed in white organdy were the only attendants. My mother had a wonderful wedding breakfast and everyone thoroughly enjoyed it. My daughter was born in the old home, where we lived several years with my parents. My son was born in the Dinwiddie Street house which Dr. Robertson had built.

It seems to me that almost every invention had come in my lifetime. In our old home we did not then have running water, or furnaces to heat the house. Brother Henry said he and some of his brothers would get up very early in the morning and chop wood to make fires to keep the house warm. We used to have cold winters and the river would freeze over.

I learned to skate by taking a chair out on the ice and holding on to the back of the chair I would slide along. My mother used to tell us about the big freeze when the river was frozen over for two weeks. I think that was in 1855, ten years before I was born. My grandmother was then in Norfolk and my Mother's mother walked over to see her brother. The river was frozen so solid that horses and carts would go over hauling wood. There was a bar-room built out on the ice and a big fight started.

My children grew up and my daughter went to Guam where her husband was stationed. I had quite a hard time getting transportation there when my first grandchild was born, but my brother, Sam, was a friend of Senator Martin and Senator Swanson, and I had their consent to go. I had to take a liner, the Matsonia, to Honolulu, where I spent five days waiting for a transport to Guam, where I stayed two months. At that time we did not have airplanes and only once a month the transport landed at Guam, so we had to wait a long time to get letter from home.

When I was in Guam we felt earthquakes seven times. We would feel the house violently shaken, but the houses were built with very thick walls, so did not fall down. A large Catholic church with just the walls standing from an earthquake was there. I spent two months in Guam, then started for home. I went from Guam to the transport, Thomas, to Manila where one of the marine officer's wife and baby traveled with me and we had a beautiful room in the Manila Hotel looking out over the water. We were there two weeks simply waiting for a transport home. We went around sightseeing and visited Bilibit prison where the Japs had so many prisoners during World War Two.

After we left Manila, the transport took us to Nagasaki, where we stayed a night and a day on the transport, but we went ashore and I got in a rickshaw with a native trotting along in between the shafts. I found it very comfortable going and returning. It took me three months to make the trip. Coming back we reached Honolulu and I felt I was almost home. Looking back I think I have traveled on almost everything except a submarine.

First when I lived at the old home, I would be on row boats, sail boats, ferry boats, tug boats, bay boats and liners. In Guam I rode in a sidecar of a motorcycle, then in the rickshaw. Coming back before we had automobiles I visited in Orange County, New York, and we went everywhere in Sleighs drawn by horses. I think I liked the horse and buggy times much better than the crowded roads in an automobile. But I like, I think, most of the airplane. In my old age I have made three trips, the last one four weeks ago. My grandson always with me and takes such good care of me that I have never felt the slightest fear and enjoyed every minute of the trip from Washington to Portsmouth. On one occasion when we had daylight in Norfolk and Portsmouth, and in Washington standard time, we left Norfolk airport at one o'clock and got to Washington at five minutes to one. Can you beat that? I have been blessed with my two children, daughter and son, who have taken such good care of me. Also my fine four grandchildren and two little great grandgirls who call me GG.

I lived in the Harbor View Apt for nearly eighteen years and call the people living there my Harbor View family. They were all so good to me and I was very fond of them all, and I think they were of me.

If there is anything good in me I owe it to such a fine father and mother who brought me up so I can look back to them with the greatest love and respect. Brother Henry lived to be ninety-six. His mind was wonderfully clear to the last. I heard him say that he would wake at four in the morning and everything that happened in his life would come before him. I think that is they way most of us who have grown old feel. I would live my life very differently if I could over it. I have left undone the things I should have done and done the things I should not have done. I am very fond of all my nieces and nephews and they are nice to me.

Last Easter one of my nieces from California and two from St. Louis and Norfolk and Portsmouth all got together and sent me such a beautiful remembrance with flowers. I was very proud of them thinking of me.

Before Virginia Beach became a famous resort, and only a small hotel and pavilion, my father decided to take us there, so he hired two negroes with a large boat to row us all to Norfolk. In the boat was all the family with Rose and a very large market basket packed with good things for us to eat at the beach. After we landed in Norfolk, we got on a tugboat which took us across Broadcreek then on a train to Virginia Beach. The ocean that day was wonderful and we were soon in our bathing suits swimming.

I think by bathing suit would be much laughed at but I still like it better than the modern small strips of material. My bathing suit was a dark blue suit with white braid, the skirt down to my knees and black stocking. I suppose now the bathers would say they could not swim in anything like that, but I doubt if they could swim much better now than we did then. I would dash in the surf, watch for a big wave, swim over it, then a breaker could catch us and roll us up on the shore. Three of my Niemeyer brothers, Arthur, Crawford and Herman, two Le Mosey boys, Mr. Jim Brown, who lived on Court St. and Nat White, who lived in the house on Court Street, now occupied by William Pezas and his sister. Nat was the coxswain. The raceboats were shell and our rowers were fine. They won all the races except one which an Irish crew from Gosport won.

My brothers taught me how to row as they did. When I looked out on the river at my Harbor View home, I never saw a boy who was a good rower. We were taught to take long strokes, then feather the oar back. I felt like going up and showing them how to row as they should. Since my young days, it seems as if everything has been invented. When I look back to my childhood, we did not have electricity. The lamplighters would come around with a small ladder and light the lamps. We did not have city water, but we had a cistern and well. In town people who did not have cisterns would have to go to they street pumps with buckets to get water.

I remember a large pump in the middle of Court Street near London. The first cars were drawn by two horses and later by the electric cars. It was sometime before we had telephones, then automobiles. My husband was the fifth man in town to buy an automobile. It was a long time before we had radios. When the first plane flew over Portsmouth, we all ran out to see it. Now it is an everyday occurrence and the nicest way to travel.

If I were younger, I think if Harry were with me I would be willing to fly over the Atlantic. I am interested now what will be seen with the new telescope which has taken twenty years to build. I am like Brother Henry.

He said if he were to wake up in the morning and find we had connected with Mars he would no be surprised. He would not be surprised at anything. I am just wondering what next myself.

Before I was married, I would do the family marketing. I would get a good dinner for a large family for fifty cents. Then, large spots were selling for ten cents a dozen, sturgeon for six cents a dozen, a large trout for fifteen cents, corn a dozen for eight cents, tomatoes, two quarts for five cents, butterbeans and black eye peas for eight cents a quart. At the meat stand, a fine sausage for twelve and a half cents, pork chops for eight cents, backbone for ten cents a pound. Then too, you could buy the finest Smithfield hams for twelve and a half cents a pound. Strawberries after the fields were turned over to the pickers, two cents a quart. Crabmeat sold for twenty cents a quart. My brothers would row over to Roanoke dock in Norfolk where the sloops would bring in a load of watermelons. They would buy a boat full of splendid melons, paying five cents each. Nice cantaloupes were two cents each. At that time, if a man earned Sixty Dollars a month he was able to get married. One of the best houses to rent he would pay Twenty-five Dollars a month. Others were twelve and a Half a month, smaller ones for as little as Ten Dollars a month.

We did not have any movies or much entertainment at that time, but we all liked to sit around and read which we were fond of. We had morning prayers and often we had visiting Methodist ministers when the conference was in session. One of my mother's sisters, married Dr. Rodger, highly educated. He wrote a book in Greek language. He would preach revival sermons, which were so real about the devil that they could hear his chains clanking and coming near.

People would get so wrought up that sometimes someone would faint, which would please the preacher. I suppose in this day he would be called a great actor. My father for years was bookkeeper for the Bank of Portsmouth. Afterwards, he was in the firm of Niemeyer, Etheridge and Brooks, a commission house. It was a three story building which the bus company now has. The building was stored with many bales of cotton and on the top floor quantities of peanuts were stored in large bags. Just before Christmas my father would send a bag of peanuts to the baker to be roasted. We would sit around the fire with a paper on our laps filled with peanuts. Often some of the neighbors would join us and all enjoyed it.

My son came out of college and was one of our first Portsmouth boys to volunteer for World War One. Over in France it was not long before he was in the thick of the fight, in so many of the worst battles. In that besides my son, six of my nephews. Frederick Niemeyer was so badly wounded that the doctors feared he would lose an arm but after the treatment he had for a long time, his arm was saved.

My grandson, Henry Pickett, went in a second class private (in World War II) and when he returned after the war. He had his captains bars. He was flying over the Pacific and had some narrow escapes. Two of my great nephews were killed in that war. Duncan Jungbeck, son of Virginia Wigg Jungbeck, also Charlie Nash, Helen and Monroe Nash's son. Also Henry Hudgins, Monroe and Helen Nash's son-in-law.

GARNER-BIGGS BULLETIN No. 18
Volume No. 1

1 December 1978

We recently completed the tracing of our Haggoman ancestors, and, before we get
too far away from them, it might be appropriate for us to move to another Eastern Shore family which is a part of our ancestry. This is the Yeardley or
Yardley family, which became a part of our Family Tree with the marriage of
Sarah Yardley to John Powell, a son of Walter Powell, of Somerset County,
Maryland. One of their daughters, Sarah Powell, married John Haggoman (3)-72
(see page A-62).

As with many other early families, we have found many variations in the spelling of the name: Yeardley, Yardley, Yardlie, Yardele, Yerdly, Yerdeley, Yardely,
and Yardly. In general, however, our ancestors appear to have used either
Yeardley or Yardley. The earliest of these ancestors which we have found was a
man called Raph (or Ralph) Yardley who was born in the sixteenth century and
died early in the seventeenth century. Much research appears to have been done
by persons other than ourselves in an effort to trace the ancestors of Raph
Yardley, but to no avail. We will therefore begin the Yardley line with this
man.

Raph Yardley (1)-2352 (he appears to have used this spelling for his name), was
a citizen and merchant tailor of London, and at the time of his death was
residing in the Parish of St. Saviours in Southwark. His will was written 25
August 1603, and was probated 27 February 1603/4. He appears to have had two
marriages. A condensed version of his will is as follows:

> After my debts paid and my funerals discharged I will that
> all and singular my goods, chattels and debts shall be parted
> and divided into three equal portions according to the laudable
> use and custom of the City of London. One full third part
> thereof I give and bequeath to Rhoda my well beloved wife, to
> her own use, in full satisfaction of such part or portion of my
> goods, chattels and debts as she may claim to have by the custom
> of the same city. One other full third part thereof I give and
> bequeath amongst my children, Raphe, George, John, Thomas and
> Anne Yardley and to such other child or children as yet unborn
> as I shall happen to have at the time of my decease, to be
> equally parted, shared and divided between them, and to be satis-
> fied and paid to my said sons at the accomplishment of their
> several ages of one and twenty years, and to my said daughter at
> the accomplishment of her age of one and twenty years or marriage,
> which shall happen first, etc., etc. And the other third part
> thereof I reserve to myself therewith to perform and pay these my
> legacies hereafter mentioned, that is to say, I give and bequeath
> to the poor of the Parish of St. Saviours in Southwark where I now
> dwell, twenty shillings to be divided amongst them by the discretion
> of the overseers of the poor there for the time being, and to such
> of the batchelors and sixteen men of the company of merchant tailors,
> London, as shall accompany my body to burial, twenty shillings for a
> recreation to be made unto them, and to the Vestrymen of the said
> parish, twenty shillings more for a recreation to be made unto them.
> I give and bequeath unto my sister Palmer a ring of gold to the
> value of six shillings eight pence, and to my cousin, John Palmer,
> her husband, a like ring of like value, and to my daughter, Earbye,

355

my first wife's wedding ring, and to my son Earbye, her husband, my best cloak, and to my cousin Richard Yearwood, my black cloth gown of Turkish fashion. The rest and residue of all and singular of my goods, etc., etc., I wholly give unto my said children, etc., etc. Item - I give and bequeath to my brother Yardley, a ring of gold of the value of six shillings eight pence. And I ordain and make the said Raph Yardley, my son, to be the executor, etc., etc., and the said Richard Yearwood and my son Edward Earbye, overseers. As to my freehold lands and hereditiments, I will, devise, give and bequeath my messuage, lands, etc. in Southwark or elsewhere with my said children.

The son-in-law, Edward Earbye (or Irbie) died in 1616/17, and the wife, Catherine, who survived him, was probably "my daughter Earbye" to whom Raph Yardley referred in his will. Edward Irbie's will was written 27 February 1616/17 and was proved 24 March 1616/17 by Catherine Irbie, relict and executrix.

Son, Ralph Yardley, a citizen and apothecary of London, dwelling in the Parish of St. Alban, Wood Street, probably died in December 1655/56. His will was dated 5 June 1654 and was proved 4 January 1655/56, by John Yardley, his son and executor.

Our next Yardley ancestor was George Yardley (2)-1176, the son of Raph Yardley. During his lifetime, George appears to have used the family name as Yeardley. We do not know exactly when George Yeardley was born, but he appears to have been baptized 28 July 1588, and probably was born earlier in the same year. When his father wrote his will in August 1603, he indicated that George was under twenty-one years of age at that time. If our surmise as to his year of birth is correct, he was, in fact, just fifteen years of age. We also have not been able to determine whether George was a son by the first wife, or by Rhoda, the surviving wife of Raph Yardley. *(By Rhoda Marston)*

At some point after the death of his father, George appears to have embarked upon a military career and to have spent some years of service in the Low Countries before coming to Virginia in the "Deliverance" in the year 1609.

The Virginia Magazine of History and Biography, Volume 1, pages 85/86, says this of George Yeardley:

> "George Yeardley, Gent. after serving some time in the Low Countries, came to Virginia in 1609. A contemporary says of him that he was 'a soldier truly bred in the University of War in the Low Countries.' He was a member of the Virginia Company in 1609; Deputy Governor of Virginia in the absence of Dale 1616-1617; went to England in 1618, and in the latter part of that year was appointed Governor of Virginia and Knighted. A contemporary letter (in English State Paper Office) dated 28 November 1618, states that the King had that week knighted Yeardley at Newmarket, and that since, he had 'flaunted it up and down the streets with extraordinary bravery, with fourteen or fifteen fair liveries after him.'

> "He had acquired considerable estate during his residence in Virginia and seems now to have spent it freely. Pory, writing in 1619, says 'The Governor here, who at his first coming, besides a great deal

356

of worth in his person, brought only his sword with him; was at his last being in London together with his lady, out of his mere gettings here, able to disburse very near three thousand pounds to furnish him with the voyage.' Soon after Sir George returned to Virginia in 1619, he summoned at Jamestown the first legislative assembly ever convened in America. His commission as Governor expired in November 1621, but he continued as a member of the Council. In the massacre of 1622, twenty-two of his people were killed at Weyanoke, his plantation on James River. On 18 September 1625 he was appointed Deputy Governor, in the absence of Sir Francis Wyatt, and on 19 April 1626 appointed Governor. He held the office until his death in November 1627, and was buried on the 13th of that month. His will is dated 12 October 1627, proved 14 February 1628 (Ridley, 9). The cultivation of tobacco was commenced and negroes were introduced during his government, two things destined to effect most deeply through centuries, the Colony and State of Virginia and all the American continent. He was frequently engaged in conflict with the Indians. In 1616 he defeated the Chickahominies and in 1622, with 300 men, devastated the country of the Nansemonds. Yeardly was an amiable and upright man, and anxious to advance the prosperity of the colonists, among whom he was much respected, and his administration was popular. He married Temperance Flowerdew."

Sir George and his wife, Temperance, had three children. We find a record of them in a muster of persons living in Virginia in 1624/25. The Muster Roll List shows:

> Sir George Yeardley, Knt., came in the "Deliverance" in 1609.
> Temperance Lady Yeardley, came in the "Falcon" in 1608.
> Elizabeth Yeardley   age 6 years
> Argall Yeardley   age 4 years
> Francis Yeardley   age 1 year
>   "Children born heare"

As to the children of George and Temperance Yeardley, no trace of the eldest child, Elizabeth, can be found, and what became of her is not known. *

The second child, Argall, (later known as Argoll) is our ancestor and we will devote time to him later.

The third, and youngest child, Francis, about 1645 married Sarah Offley as her third husband. Sarah had previously been the widow of Captain Adam Thoroughgood and Captain John Gookin. Francis Yeardley died without heirs, in Norfolk County, Virginia, in 1655.

During his residence in Virginia, Sir George became possessed of large tracts of land. After his return from England in 1619, he visited Virginia's Eastern Shore, and made friends with Debedeavon, "The Laughing King," the Emperor of the Eastern Shore and King of the Great Nuswattocks of Nandua Creek. About 1620 Sir George was granted a large tract of land by Debedeavon, and this was later confirmed when Sir George was granted patents for 3700 acres of land at Hungars, by order of the Court in 1625. Sir George never lived on this land.

Sir George's home plantation was called "Weyanoke" and it contained about 2200 acres. Regarding this plantation, the following article which appeared in Tyler's Quarterly, Volume 16, pages 85/88, inc., may prove of interest to you:

* an Elizabeth YARDLEY married a Richard ALEXANDER 7 Nov. 1637 Saint Andrew by the Wardrobe, London. This could be Sir George's daughter, Elizabeth, who would have been age 17 at time of marriage.

"When the settlers arrived at Jamestown in 1607, The Weyanoke
Indians held the country on the north side of James River,
between the Chickahominy River and Queen's Creek in Charles
City County, which they called Little Weyanoke, and on the
south side of the James River, from Upper Chippokes Creek to
Powell's Creek, which they called Greater Weyanoke. A land
grant issued in 1650 located Weyanoke Old Town at the head of
Powell's Creek, on the southside of the river."

"It was in the Weyanoke Region on the north side of the James
River that in 1617 one of the earliest Junior companies, formed
with consent of the Virginia Company of London for the culture
of tobacco, obtained a grant of 10,000 acres. The organization
was a strong one, owning many ships and sending many emigrants
to its own account, and it owned an interest in Hog Island as
well. The Company was first known as Smith's Hundred Company,
but when Sir Edwin Sandys succeeded Sir Thomas Smith as Treasurer
of the London Company, Smith sold his shares, and in 1619 the
name was changed to Southampton Hundred, in honor of Henry
Wriothesley, Earl of Southampton, who was a leading member.
Sir George Yeardley, Governor of Virginia, was for many years
Commander of the Hundred, and in 1617 he received from the
Indian King a grant of 2200 acres of land on Queen's Creek,
which was confirmed to him by the London Company. This land
lay upon the Weyanoke bend of the river, between Queen's
Creek and Mapsico Creek back to the headwaters thereof."

"Besides owning 2200 acres on the north side of the James
River, Sir George Yeardley owned 1000 acres on the south side,
in Greater Weyanoke. He called this place after his wife's
family, Flowerdew Hundred, and here on a point nearly opposite,
called Tobacco Point on recent maps, he erected in 1621, a
windmill - the first mill of any kind in the United States.
About three years before his death, which occurred in November 1627, he deeded the land on both sides of the creek to
the cape merchant of the Colony, the rich Abraham Peirsey.
In 1624 there were on Peirsey's land, which then included
Windmill Point, twelve dwellings, three storehouses, four
tobacco houses and one windmill."

"Peirsey, who married Frances West, widow of Nathaniel West
and daughter of Sir Thomas Hinton, died in March 1628. After
his death his widow married thirdly, Col. Samuel Mathews, and
his daughter, Elizabeth Peirsey, married first, Capt. Richard
Stephens, and after his death, Governor Sir John Harvey;
and his daughter, Mary Peirsey, married first, Capt. Thomas
Hill, and second, Capt. Thomas Bushrod, of Essex Lodge, York
County. After Peirsey's purchase Flowerdew Hundred was
called Peirsey's Hundred, but in 1635, Mrs. Elizabeth
Stephens patented it as Flowerdew Hundred.'

Sir George Yeardley died in November 1627, and was buried at Jamestown on
the 13th day of that month. An article in "Virginia Magazine of History
and Biography" says:

"The 'Knights Tomb' discovered by excavation of the original chancel of Jamestown Church, is believed to be that of Yeardley, though the brass inscription plate was destroyed when the Church burned in 1676."

Sir George Yeardley wrote his will 12 October 1627, and it was proved 14 February 1628 by Temperance Yeardley, relict and executrix. A condensed version of his will is as follows:

To wife Temperance all and every part and parcell of all such household stuff, plate, linen, woollen or any other goods, moveable or immoveable, of what nature or quality soever, as to me are belonging, and which now at the time of the date hereof are being and remaining within this house in James City wherein I now dwell. Item, as touching and concerning all the rest of my whole estate consisting of goods, debts, servants, "negars," cattle, or any other thing or things, commodities or profits whatsoever to me belonging or appertaining, either here in this country of Virginia, in England or elsewhere, together with my plantation of 1000 acres of land at Stanley in Warwicke River, my will and desire is that the same be, all and every part and parcell thereof, sold to the best advantage for tobacco, and the same to be transported as soon as may be either this year or the next, as my wife shall find occasion, into England, and there to be sold and turned into money, etc., and etc. The money resulting from this (with sundry additions) to be divided into three parts, of which one part to go to said wife, one part to eldest son Argoll Yeardley, and the other part to son Francis and to Elizabeth Yeardley equally.

Sir George Yeardley

Witnesses:
Abraham Peirsey
Susanna Hall
William Clayborne

There was a codicil to the will, dated 29 October 1627, witnessed by the same persons shown above, but we have no record of the contents of the codicil.

* * * * * * * * * * * * * * * * * *

This concludes Bulletin No. 18. Our next issue will deal with the Flowerdew family, after which we will continue with our Yeardley or Yardley ancestors.

GARNER/BIGGS Bulletin #18 Up-date:

Over the past couple of years, while not intensely researching, additional details have come to light which add to Souil's original bulletins. This information is being passed along on individual pages which can be inserted directly behind the respective bulletin which deals with the various families. As further information comes to light, it will be passed along in this manner.

✓Bulletin #18 - YEARDLEY

Please refer to Page A-86a (revised):

From the book, George Yeardley - Governor of Virginia and Organizer of the General Assembly in 1619, by Nora Miller Turman, M.A., published by Garrett and Massie, Inc., Richmond, Va., MCMLIX, it can be determined, fairly accurately, that the marriage of Sir George Yeardley and Temperance Flowerdew took place in November 1617 and that their first child, Argoll, was born 31 August 1618, in London, England. Therefore, Argoll was 6 years of age when the muster of persons living in Virginia was taken in 1624/25. On Page 100 of the book, Miss Turman states that, ". . . the last week in February, 1619, Sir George, Lady Yeardley and little Argoll sailed for Virginia . . ."

The second paragraph on Page A-86a begins:

"In 1609, George Yeardley . . ."

It should read:

"In 1610, George Yeardley . . ."

From the book, Before the Mayflower, by J. H. R. Yardley, published by The Windmill Press, Kingswood, Surrey, England, 1931, we find on Page 104 that Rhoda was a daughter of James Marston, of the City of London, and his wife, Catherine Chevall. Catherine was the daughter of Henry Chevall, "another worthy citizen of London." When Rhoda's father died, her mother remarried. Her second husband was Thomas Saris, also a London merchant, whom she survived to marry again for the third time, her last choice being John Hyde, a member of the Merchant Taylors' Guild. By Thomas Saris, Catherine (Chevall) Marston Saris had a son, John, a half-brother to Rhoda Marston and, therefore, uncle to young George Yeardley. This John Saris became a famous navigator and traveller, and enriched posterity by writing a book on his voyages to India, China, and the Far East.

So, from the book, Before the Mayflower, we have learned the names of Sir George Yeardley's grandparents, James Marston and Catherine Chevall, and his great-grandfather, Henry Chevall.

Using the International Genealogical Index, a worldwide birth/baptism and marriage index compiled by the Church of Latter-Day Saints (Mormons), we found the marriage of a Henricus Chevell to Alicia Robinson, 16 June 1560, St. Martins-in-the-Field, Westminster, London, but at this moment cannot find any children of this couple to determine if Catherine Chevall was their daughter. More work to be done on that!

Original issue date 1 February 1979
Revised and reissued as of 1 June 1981

Since the time when we originally issued this bulletin, it has been our
pleasure, privilege and good fortune, to have made the acquaintance of some
present-day members of the Flowerdew family, Mr. and Mrs. Alan Flowerdew,
of Glengarry Estate, Thyolo, Malawi. Both Alan and Ruth are of the Flowerdew
family, they being first cousins and grandchildren of Arthur John Blomfield
Flowerdew, formerly of Billingford Hall, Norfolk County, England.

For some years, Ruth has been interested in the history of the Flowerdew
family, and in recent years she began a project to try to trace her branch
of the family back to the family which lived at Hethersett, Norfolk County,
in the sixteenth century. While Ruth has done a vast amount of research
on the Flowerdew lines, particularly on the Hethersett line, she has not
yet found the link which ties her branch to the Hethersett branch of the
Flowerdew family, so her research goes on.

In March 1979, Ruth began to issue a newsletter which she calls "Flowerdew
News - Ancient and Modern." Copies of this newsletter are mailed to
Flowerdews and Flowerdew connections in Kenya, Australia, Great Britain
and the United States. It was this publication which led to our contact
with Ruth. Our sister-in-law, Gwen Garner, saw mention of the "Flowerdew
News" in a list of publications, and wrote to the editor and publisher,
asking if she might be placed on the mailing list to receive future issues,
since her husband, Wilbur C. Garner, had Flowerdew ancestors running back
from Temperance Flowerdew. Not only did Ruth, most graciously, agree to
place her name on the mailing list, but she also sent a chart of the
Flowerdew family which she had prepared from her own research, showing
the Flowerdew line running back from Temperance Flowerdew to one, William
Flowerdew, who was living in the early 1500s. The receipt of this chart
had the immediate effect of rendering obsolete our Bulletin No. 19 as
originally issued. We have, therefore, decided to rewrite the entire
bulletin. The revised version follows herewith.

* *

The Flowerdew name has been used over the years as Flourday, Flowerdieu,
Flourdew, Flowerdewe and Flowerdew.

Ruth Flowerdew's chart moves our ancestral line back one more generation
than we had previously discovered, and identifies several of the Flowerdew
wives, who were not known to us earlier. Therefore, at the time of this
writing, our earliest known Flowerdew ancestor is William Flowerdew (1)-
18,832, who lived in Wymondham, Norfolk County, England. On present-day
maps, Wymondham appears as lying about nine miles southwest of the City of
Norwich. William Flowerdew married Katherine Payne, a daughter of William
Payne, also of Wymondham. We only know of one child by this marriage, a
son, John Flowerdew. William Flowerdew (1)-18,832, died in the year 1536.

John Flowerdew (2)-9,416, the son of William, is our next Flowerdew
ancestor. He purchased Cromwell's Manor and settled at Hethersett, Norfolk
County, England. On present-day maps, Hethersett lies in the same direction

from Norwich as does Wymondham, but is only about six miles distant. John married Catheran Sheers, a daughter of William Sheers, of Ashwell Thorp, and they raised a large family. Their children were:

1 - William, our ancestor.
2 - Thomas, died in 1564.
3 - Martin (or Mark), married Margaret Hawes, of Ipswich.
4 - Edward, who became 4th Baron of the Exchequer and Lord of Stanfield Hall. He died 31 March 1586.
5 - Edmund, Gent., of Hethersett. His will was proved 1606 (PCC).
6 - Frances, who married Thomas Amyas.
7 - Margaret, who married William Southals, of Suffolk.
8 - Amy, who married Michael Heath at Little Massingham, 1586.
9 - Elizabeth, who married William Hollis, son and heir of Sir Thomas Hollis, of Flitcham, Norfolk County.
10 - Alice, who married John Kemp.
11 - John, who married Elizabeth Slegg, of Comberton, Lincolnshire. He died in 1588.
12 - Christopher, who married Cecilia Billingford, of Blackford Hall. He was still living in 1606.

John Flowerdew (2)-9,416, was a very prominent landowner. He died in 1565, for his will was proved in September of that year. He was buried at Hethersett Church, as also were his wife, Catherine, and his son, Thomas.

The most well known of these children was the son, Edward Flowerdew. We quote the following from the Dictionary of National Biography, Vol. VII, Finch/Gloucester, page 342:

> "Flowerdew, Edward (d. 1586) judge, 4th son of John Flowerdew of Hethersett, Norfolk, a large landed proprietor, was educated at Cambridge, but took no degree.

> "In the winter of 1585-1586 he went circuit in South Wales, and in March held the assizes at Exeter. Here gaol fever broke out, and, seizing upon him, carried him off between 14 March and 4 April. He was buried at Hethersett Church. He was a man of grasping temper, but apparently not of fine feelings. In 1564 he purchased Stanfield Hall and its furniture of John Appleyard in order to live there, and he also married Elizabeth, daughter of William Foster of Wymondham, who had long been Appleyard's mistress. His lands were dispersed at his death and he left no heirs."

Edward Flowerdew wrote his will 15 June 1583, and it was proved 5 May 1586 (PCC 23 Windsor). It is a long will, most of which does not concern us. However, he mentions the will of his father, John Flowerdew, and he also bequeaths to the daughters of his nephew, Anthony, 10 pounds each to be paid to them on their wedding days.

At an Inquisition post mortem, taken at Harlston, Norfolk County, 12 October 1586, it was stated that ". . . Edward Flowerdew died on the 31st March, last past, and Elizabeth, his wife, survives him. Anthony

Flowerdew is his next heir, being the son and heir of William Flowerdew, brother and heir of the aforesaid Edward. The said Anthony is aged twenty-nine. . ." (PRO Chancery Inquisition post mortem, Series II, Vol. 210, No. 132).

Our next Flowerdew ancestor is William Flowerdew (3)-4708, son of John Flowerdew and brother of Edward Flowerdew. William married Frances Appleyard, a daughter of Roger Appleyard of Stanfield Hall, and his wife, Elizabeth Scott. William and Frances Flowerdew were the parents of:

     1 - Anthony, our ancestor.
     2 - Marie, who married _____ Lilmore.
     3 - Elizabeth, who married _____ Bradshaw.

William Flowerdew died before 1565.

Anthony Flowerdew (4)-2354, son of William, is our next ancestor. At the Inquisition post mortem held after the death of his uncle, Edward Flowerdew, it was stated that Anthony's age was then twenty-nine years. This would place his year of birth at about 1557. Anthony married Martha Stanley, daughter of John Stanley of Scottow, Norfolk County, and his wife, Mary Marsham. Anthony and Martha were the parents of:

     1 - A daughter, who married Thomas, a son of Sir Robert
         Shilton, Knight.
     2 - Stanley, who died without heirs in 1620.
     3 - Mary (or Marie), who married Dyonis Rossingham, Gent.,
         who was Usher to James I. He was buried at
         Westminster Abbey, 1617.
     4 - Temperance, who married twice; first, Sir George
         Yeardley and second, Francis West.

In our earlier bulletin we did some guessing as to when Temperance may have been born, and arrived at the year 1586. We based our reasoning on the assumption that Temperance was the youngest daughter of Anthony and Martha. This assumption may not have been correct. In a recent letter received from Ruth Flowerdew, she advises of the discovery of a baptism, on 9 May 1591, of an Elizabeth, daughter of Anthony Flowerdew, at St. Ann's Church, Blackfriars, London. If this girl was a daughter of "our" Anthony Flowerdew, then it would appear that she was the youngest daughter, and probably was the one who married Thomas, the son of Sir Robert Shilton. It follows then, that Mary (or Marie) and Temperance must have been the older daughters, and the daughters of Anthony that Edward Flowerdew had in mind when he wrote his will 15 June 1583. Temperance, therefore, may have been four or five years older than we had previously thought.

After the death of Anthony Flowerdew (and we do not know when that occurred), his widow, Martha, married Captain Godfrey Garrett. In the will of Martha Garrett of Scottow, Norfolk County, dated 3 February 1625/1626, proved 4 December 1626 (PCC 149 Hele), she bequeaths ". . . unto my daughter Temperance Yardle alias Flowerdew, my seal ring of gold. . ." She also named ". . . my grandson, Edmund Rossingham. . ." as executor of her will.

Our last ancestor of the Flowerdew name is Temperance Flowerdew (5)-1177, the daughter of Anthony Flowerdew (4)-2354. A muster of persons living in

Virginia in 1624/25 indicates that Temperance came to Virginia in the "Falcon" in 1608. After that year, we have not found further record of Temperance until her marriage in 1618.

In 1608, the Virginia Colony was barely one year old, the first settlers having landed on Jamestown Island on 13 May 1607. Food shortages, disease, and the ever-present threat of Indian attacks, made life in the Colony one of hardship and peril. We cannot help but wonder what the circumstances were that caused Temperance to leave the relative comforts of England for the hardships and perils of life in the Colony. We wonder also, who it was that accompanied her on her trip to Virginia. It is highly unlikely that she travelled to the New World without escort. Finally, we wonder where she spent the next ten years of her life. Did she remain in Virginia during this entire time or did she return to England after a short stay in Virginia? Frankly, we have not found any answers to these questions. It is certain, however, that she was back in England in 1618.

In 1609, George Yeardley, the man who would later marry Temperance, arrived in Virginia. He was a son of Ralph Yardley, of London, and his second wife, Rhoda Marston. He commenced his career as a soldier, and by the time he was sixteen years old had already seen active service, having fought in the battle of Oudewater in the Low Countries. Returning from this campaign, he linked his fortunes with those of his old Commander, Sir Thomas Gates, and assisted him in planning his expedition for the relief of the settlers in Virginia. He sailed with the expedition in the little ship "Sea Adventure," one of the nine vessels which set out on the long voyage on 15 May 1609.

By ill fortune, the flotilla ran into a terrible storm, which continued for two days, and their condition became desperate. All, however, eventually reached their haven, excepting one of the fleet, Captain Yeardley's ship, "Sea Adventure." She was blown out of her course and, battered and leaking badly, was on the point of sinking when the look-out providentially sighted an unknown island, which we now know as Bermuda, and they were just able to reach its coast. Their vessel went to pieces on its rocks but the ship's company were all saved. Working for months with the poor means at their disposal, they managed to build two small boats, and in these they succeeded in making their way to Jamestown, Virginia, and rejoined the rest of the company. We assume that one of these small boats was the one called the "Deliverance" in which George Yeardley is said to have arrived.

Following his arrival in Virginia, George Yeardley served with credit in a military capacity for several years thereafter. From the departure of Sir Thomas Dale in April 1616, he was acting governor until 15 May 1617. He ~~returned to~~ was in England in 1618, and in September of that year, probably at Newmarket, he married Temperance Flowerdew. Later in that year, on the 18th* of November, he was commissioned governor of Virginia. King James added to his rank the distinction of knighthood, and Sir George sailed for Virginia the following January.

We now believe the marriage took place in November 1617.

Sir George Yeardley and his wife, Temperance, were the parents of three children, Elizabeth, Argall, and Francis (see pg. A-81). As previously reported, Sir George died in James City, Virginia, in November 1627, and he named his wife as Executrix of his will.

* another record has date of 24 November

About 31 March 1628, Temperance Yeardley, widow of Sir George, married Col. Francis West, brother of Lord Delaware, and at the time, deputy governor of Virginia. This marriage was of short duration as Temperance died intestate within the year following her second marriage. After her death, the brother of Sir George, Ralph Yardley, an Apothecary, of London, was granted administration on the estate of Sir George, and much litigation ensued. All of the children of Sir George and Temperance Yeardley would have been under-age at the time of their mother's death, but we have not found a record as to whom assumed their care and custody. It may be that they were sent to England and placed in the care of their uncle, Ralph Yardley, the brother of Sir George and the administrator of his estate.

Soon after the death of Temperance, her husband, Francis West, returned to England and entered suit against the estate of Sir George. The following is an abstract of a Bill of Complaint in Chancery Proceedings, Charles I, W. 63, No. 42:

Bill dated 1 February 1629/30
Francis West of the City of Winchester, County Southants, esquire, complainant vs. Ralph Yardley of London, Apothecary of London, defendant.

The complainant shows that about the last day of March, 3 Charles I, he married Dame Temperance Yeardley, late wife of Sir George Yeardley, Knight, and by means thereof and of the last will of the said Sir George was to have had a full third part of all the estate of the said Sir George in Virginia and elsewhere, over and above all household stuff in Sir George's house in James City at the time of his death, which third part so belonging to the complainant amounted to at least 3,000 pounds, the said Sir George's estate, of which he bequeathed a full third part to his wife, Dame Temperance, being worth 10,000 pounds at least. The said Dame Temperance proved the will, of which she was executrix, and within one year after her marriage to the complainant she died in Virginia without having made any will, by means whereof her said third part of right belonged to the complainant. The said third part mainly consisted of tobacco growing in Virginia or transported into England, as also servants, negroes, etc., and of a plantation of 1,000 acres of land with tobacco at Stanley on Warwick River in Virginia, and being all appointed by Sir George's will to be sold for tobacco money or other commodities of that country and to be transported into England and sold there, a third part thereof was to be delivered to the said Dame Temperance for her own use. This was done partly in Dame Temperance's life time and partly since her death. But Ralph Yardley, the defendant, having knowledge of this and of Dame Temperance's death, and knowing by Sir George's will that a third part belonged to his said wife, and by her death to the complainant, and the other two parts to Sir George's three children (the complainant being then in Virginia where Dame Temperance died) the said Ralph obtained letters of administration of the goods of the said Sir George and by colour thereof possessed himself of all the personal estate of the said Sir George. About last Easter the complainant arrived in England, and hearing that the said Ralph had possessed himself not only of Sir George's estate, but also of the complainant's third part thereof, he repaired to the said Ralph Yardley and asked him to tell him what the said estate amounted to, and to pay him a full third part of the same. All of which the said Ralph Yardley utterly refused to do.

The demurrer of Ralph Yardley, defendant, to the Bill of Francis West, complainant, was as follows:

The defendant says that by the complainant's own showing letters of administration of the goods of Sir George Yeardley, Knight, have been granted to this defendant. It does not appear by anything set forth in the bill that the complainant has any purparty in the personal estate of Sir George. This defendant is advised by his counsel that neither in law or in quity is he bound to give the complainant any account of the said estate as is required by his bill.

We do not know how this suit was ultimately settled, but as to Francis West, he married again to Jane, a daughter of Sir Henry Davys, and lived only a few years longer. His Will was written 5 December 1629 and was proved 28 April 1634 by Jane West, his relict and executrix.

This concludes Bulletin No. 19 (Revised). We will return to our Yeardley or Yardley family in our next bulletin.

* * * * * * * * * * * * * * * * * * *

It is with sorrow and regret that we report and record the death of Miss Lydia Irene Garner on 19 November 1978, at her home in Village, Northumberland County, Virginia. Miss Irene was born in Northumberland County, 6 June 1882, a daughter of Albert White Garner and his wife, Geneva Burgess. She was laid to rest in the family plot in the churchyard of Bethany Baptist Church, Callao, Virginia, 22 November 1978.

* * * * * * * * * * * * * * * * * * *

Instructions

Please remove from your file the original pages Nos. A-84, A-85 and A-86, and destroy them.

Please place in your file in their place, the enclosed pages Nos. A-84, A-85, A-86, A-86a, A-86b, and A-86c, all of which are marked "Revised."

<u>I April 1979</u>

* As mentioned in our previous bulletin, we have not been able to discover who had the care and custody of the children of Sir George and Temperance Yeardley after the deaths of their father and mother. All three were under age, but their whereabouts for the next several years is not known. As a matter of fact, no further record of Elizabeth Yeardley has been found, and what became of her no one knows.

Record of the two boys, Argoll and Francis, is found on Virginia's Eastern Shore. In 1638, a patent was granted to our ancestor, Argoll Yeardley (3)-588, for 3700 acres of land. This was the same land which the Indian King Debedeavon gave to Argoll's father in 1620 and which was confirmed to Sir George in 1625 by order of the Court. Argoll Yeardley established himself on this land, and became a man of prominence in the affairs of the Eastern Shore community.

In 1640, orders came from James City for all land patents and bounds of land to be sent to the seat of government, and in the same year, Argoll Yeardley employed Edmund Scarburgh to survey his father's land at Mattawoman Creek.

J. C. Wise, in his history of Virginia's Eastern Shore, says:

> "The houses on the Eastern Shore with a few exceptions such as Arlington and Bowman's Folly, have never been as spacious and as pretentious as those in other parts of the state. The smallness of some of the houses inhabited by the wealthiest citizens is amazing. For instance, the house of Southey Littleton of Accomac contained a parlor, a porch chamber, a hall chamber, a hall, two garrets, a little room over the kitchen, the kitchen, the dairy room; making in all but a small house. The residence of Argoll Yeardley, of Northampton, was equally small, containing a hall, a hall chamber, a parlor, two small chambers next to the parlor, a kitchen and a dairy, both of the latter probably detached."

It appears likely that Francis Yeardley, for a time at least, resided with his brother Argoll. In 1642, Francis Yeardley received his Commission as the first regularly appointed Captain of the militia on the Eastern Shore. We are told that the assemblies or musters of the militia in Northampton were regularly held at Argoll Yeardley's plantation on Mattawoman Creek.

The territory of Virginia's Eastern Shore was early known as Accomack County, but in March of 1642, the name of the county was changed to Northampton. Still later, the area was divided into two parts, the northern part being designated Accomack County and the lower part being designated Northampton County, which it remains today. The first court after the 1642 name change was held 18 July 1642 and the Justices present were: Argoll Yeardley, Esq., Commander, Col. Obedience Robins, Capt. William Roper, John Wilkins, William Andrews, Philip Taylor, Edward Douglas.

Argoll Yeardley imported the first horse to the Eastern Shore, this being one conveyed to Col. Argoll Yeardley by George Ludlow of the Western Shore, by Bill of Sale dated 30 January 1642. By 1669, so many horses had been brought in and the natural increase been so great, that horses had become a burden by reason of their unrestrained depredations, in consequence of which, further importation was prohibited.

* p.17 - "The Eastern Shore of Virginia 1603-1964 by Nora Miller Turman "Ralph Yeardley became guardian of the children." (Ralph was Sir George's brother)

✓ On the 25 March 1651, Argoll Yeardley was one of 116 people of Northampton who signed a pledge "...to bee true and faithfull to the Commonwealth of England as it is nowe established without Kinge or House of Lords."

Col. Argoll Yeardley married twice. The identity of his first wife appears to be lost forever in the dim reaches of the past.* However, she was the mother of his three children, Argoll, Rose and Frances. Col. Yeardley, as with most planters of those days, raised tobacco as his main crop, and as his father before him had done, shipped much of his tobacco to Rotterdam, Holland, in his own vessels. After the death of his first wife, and on a trip to Rotterdam, he married Ann Custis, whom he brought back to Virginia with him. She was a daughter of John and Joane Custis. By Ann, Yeardley had two sons, Edmund and Henry.

. John Custis, father of Ann, was born in Gloucester County, England, but moved to Rotterdam, where he was a famous host, keeping the tavern which the English made their headquarters.

✓ In 1650, an incident occurred which, as reported by Jennings Cropper Wise, is as follows:

> "About the fifteenth day of September, 1649, the 'Virginia Merchant,' Captain John Locker, a ship of three hundred tons burden, sailed for Jamestown with many passengers. Among those who engaged passage were Colonel Norwood, a relative of Governor Berkeley; Major Francis Morison, a sympathizer with the King, and Major Stevens, who had served under Waller in the Parliamentary Army when it besieged Exeter, then held by Sir John Berkely, the Governor's brother. Driven by a storm, the ship found itself on the 12th of January, 1650, among the islands of Assateague Bay, on the Atlantic coast of Maryland. Upon one of these, Col. Norwood, Major Morison, Stevens, Francis Cary and others landed, and after several days, crossed over to the main land and were hospitably treated by the Indians. A white fur trader, Jenkin Price, arrived, and under his guidance, they began their journey to Nathaniel Littleton's plantation, the nearest in Accomac.

> "Toward night of the first day, they reached a point opposite Chincoteague Island, and at the close of the second day, after twenty-five miles of travel, they came to Price's post on the Littleton Plantation. From thence they proceeded to the Plantation of Stephen Charlton, who gave them fresh clothing. Lower down in Accomac, now Northampton County, they visited Argoll Yeardley, the son of the former Governor, who was born at Jamestown in 1621, and had recently married."

✓ Norwood, in his narrative, writes:

> "It fell out very luckily for my better welcome, that he had not long before brought over a wife, from Rotterdam, that I had known almost from a child. Her father, Custis by name, kept a victualling house in that town, lived in good repute, and was the general host of our nation there. The Esquire knowing I had the honour to be the Governor's kinsman, and his wife knowing my conversation in Holland,

* She was Frances KNIGHT of the parish of St. Giles-in-the-Field, London. They were married 9 March 1635/6 in the church of St. Stephen Coleman, London.

I was received, caressed more like a domestick, and near relation, than a man in misery, and a stranger. I stayed there for a passage over the Bay, about ten days welcomed and feasted not only by the Esquire and his wife, but by many neighbors that were not too remote."

Col. Argoll Yeardley died intestate in Northampton County sometime before 29 October 1655, for on that date an appraisal of his estate was returned. His widow, Ann, married John Wilcox, and after he died about 1662, she probably married John Luke.

Rose Yeardley married 1st Thomas Ryding (4 January 1662 in Hungars Parish) and 2nd Robert Peale.

Frances Yeardley married Lt. Col. Adam Thoroughgood of Lynhaven.

We have no information on Edmund and Henry Yeardley, the sons of Ann.

Our next ancestor was Argoll Yardley (4)-294, born about 1644, the son and heir-at-law of Col. Argoll Yeardley (3)-588. He succeeded to the estate of his father and became known as Capt. Argoll Yardley. Like his father, he, too, became a man of prominence in the affairs of Virginia's Eastern Shore.

He appears to have become enamored of a young lady by the name of Sarah, the eldest daughter of John Michael, Senior. In January 1671, he entered into a marriage agreement with Sarah, in which he made Sarah an outright gift of 1000 acres of his land, wherever she might choose to take it.

Captain Argoll Yardley (4)-294 died in Northampton County, Virginia, in 1683. He was survived by his widow, Sarah, and five children, John, Argoll, Frances, Elizabeth and Sarah Yardley. The text of his will (Northampton Co., Wills, Order Book No. XIII, 1679-1683, page 287) is as follows:

> "In the name of God Amen I Argoll Yardley of the County of North-
> ampton in Virginia, Gent. beinge in effect sound health and memory
> praised bee the Allmighty. But knowinge the uncertainty of life in
> this world and that wee are all bound to dye for the better settlinge
> of those worldly goods hee hath blessed mee - herewith I make and
> ordaine this my last will and Testament in manner and form followinge.
> Imprimis I bequeath my Soule to God who gave it and my body to
> returne unto the Earth from whence it came to bee buried in such
> Devout and christian way of buriall as my Executors hereafter named
> shall thinke fitt hopeinge and beinge well assured that through the
> meritts and passion of my Saviour Christ Jesus I shall arise againe
> att the last day and receive that Glory promised to his Elect to
> whome bee praise for evermore Amen.
> Item I give bequeath and devise unto my lovinge sonne Jno. Yardley
> six hundred acres of land more or less included within the bounds
> followinge, viz. - Beginninge att the Old Town Branch runninge by
> the house where William Tipshur now dwelleth extendinge alongst the
> said Branch and soe runninge untill it include one half of the place
> now knowne and called by the name of the Woodyard and thence extendinge
> to the Northernmost bounds of Simon Michaels land for the Southerne
> and Easterne bounds, Westernly on a Branch of Mattewoames Creeke,
> Southerly on the said Maine Creeke includinge within the bounds the
> whole place called the old Towne to him the said John Yardley and the
> heires lawfully begotten by his body. And for want of such issue to
> descend to the next heire at Common Law.

www.ingramcontent.com/pod-product-compliance
Lightning Source LLC
Chambersburg PA
CBHW081143270326
41930CB00014B/3023